JAMES IVORY IN CONVERSATION

HOW MERCHANT IVORY MAKES ITS MOVIES

ROBERT EMMET LONG

FOREWORD BY JANET MASLIN

UNIVERSITY OF CALIFORNIA PRESS   BERKELEY LOS ANGELES LONDON

For Carl and Inge Sonn

University of California Press
Berkeley and Los Angeles, California

University of California Press, Ltd.
London, England

© 2005 by The Regents of the University of California

Library of Congress Cataloging-in-Publication Data

Ivory, James.
    James Ivory in conversation : how Merchant Ivory makes
its movies / Robert Emmet Long ; with a foreword by Janet
Maslin.
        p.   cm.
Includes index.
ISBN 0-520-23415-4 (alk. paper)
1. Ivory, James—Interviews.   2. Merchant Ivory
Productions.   I. Long, Robert Emmet.   II. Title.
PN1998.3.I89A3   2005
791.4302'33'092—dc22   2004022679

Manufactured in the United States of America

14   13   12   11   10   09   08   07   06   05
10   9   8   7   6   5   4   3   2   1

The paper used in this publication meets the minimum
requirements of ANSI/NISO Z39.48-1992 (R 1997)
(*Permanence of Paper*).

Who is James Ivory beneath all that composure?

—ANDREW SARRIS SPEAKING TO ROBERT EMMET LONG

CONTENTS

FOREWORD

JANET MASLIN

There is a perfect Merchant Ivory moment midway through *Quartet,* their ménage-à-trois story set in Paris in the 1920s. Beautiful, hapless Marya Zelli has wandered into the orbit of a powerful and urbane English couple. While H. J. Heidler (Alan Bates) prepares to make the inevitable move on his house-guest (after all, she is played in alluring if desolate fashion by Isabelle Adjani), his wife Lois (Maggie Smith) maintains brittle sangfroid and a gimlet eye.

Now it's the morning after. We don't know exactly what went on between Marya and H.J., and we never will. But within the Merchant Ivory universe, this much is dependable: this is not a time to behave badly. It's not a time to be excitable. It's a time for knowingly raised eyebrows, impeccable manners, and the civilized cup of breakfast tea.

What makes this scene so representative? First, it shows the kind of cast-ing clout that this team consistently wields. Whether drawn in by Ismail Mer-chant's business panache, Ruth Prawer Jhabvala's fine-tuned dialogue, or the sheer civilized pleasure of being directed by a filmmaker with James Ivory's body of work, smart actors wind up looking even smarter for stepping into the Merchant Ivory universe.

Second, there's the ingenuity. *Quartet* isn't a lavish film, but it conjures a whole city and era with artful, minimal flashes of style. Third, there is the lit-erary pedigree. *Quartet* is an autobiographical novel by Jean Rhys, featuring a thinly veiled version of Ford Madox Ford as a man who preyed upon her weak-nesses. On screen, in Merchant Ivory incarnations, such characters tend to become more broodingly elegant than they were on the page.

As Mr. Ivory explains in the course of this book-length conversation, he hates to be called genteel. "Decorous," "languorous," and "stately" are critics' code words for similarly unappetizing qualities, and "literary" can be given a similar spin. But his body of work really is literary, and not just because he has tackled such a remarkably diverse group of book adaptations: from Tama Janowitz to E. M. Forster, from Diane Johnson to Henry James. His films are literate in their own right, united by a style that overrides the source material, no matter how august that material may be. Merchant Ivory films have their own clear voice, their own stamp of distinction.

For ceremonial reasons best known to Mr. Merchant, they always inaugurate the shooting process with a *mahurrat:* the celebration to mark the start of an Indian film. "We can always find a coconut, but the marigold garland is harder to come up with," says Mr. Ivory, with the attractive nonchalance that runs throughout his comments here. As he provides an overview of the long and unpredictable path that his work has followed, he reveals a trademark combination of intellectual curiosity, seen-it-all business experience, and cool, practiced grasp of human nature.

He sounds clear, sophisticated, and utterly unflappable. There is the sense that even when he made the mistake of using the word "dull" to describe the way Raquel Welch played a love scene in *The Wild Party* ("That's it, boys," she said, and walked off the set), he may have been more amused than sorry. She left; they sued; the film might have been permanently derailed. But in retrospect, Mr. Ivory seems to have been more curious about the actress's misdirected psychic energy than her tantrum. Either that, or discretion is one more essential part of his nature.

This interview, like the career it describes, has a broad span. It follows Mr. Ivory from his early days making documentaries to *The Householder,* the feature film made in 1963 for $125,000, in both English and Hindi. And the discussion here is sure to surprise any but the best-versed students of his work, since there is so much variety to his undertakings. At seventy-six, with nearly five decades' worth of filmmaking behind him, he remains open to new authors, projects, and possibilities in ways that any aspiring young filmmaker should envy.

The team's E. M. Forster decade—which ran from the mid-1980s to the mid-1990s and actually included adaptations of work by Henry James (*The Bostonians*) and Evan Connell (*Mr. and Mrs. Bridge*) too—is inevitably treated as a creative zenith. Certainly there's some justice to that: films like *Howards End, Maurice, A Room with a View,* and *The Remains of the Day* achieved a perfect fusion of style and subject. These superb films display a rare assurance, an absolute clarity of vision, that beautifully reflects the books on which their stories are based. But they also have a virtually automatic prestige and define conventional wisdom about the Merchant Ivory canon. Their adventurousness is obscured by their refinement and—yes—their stately, decorous manner.

The reader will want to revisit them in light of Mr. Ivory's running commentary here. But this book also offers an occasion to reassess some of the so-called misfires. As an artist whose work is the very antithesis of thumbs-up/thumbs-down thinking, Mr. Ivory has never been well served by snap judgments. Though he himself expresses reservations about some of the team's chancier undertakings, they can now be seen in a more generous light. Yes, he cast Nick Nolte as Thomas Jefferson. But yes, it's also remarkable for him to have filmed the story of Jefferson in Paris in any way, shape, or form.

After all these years, all these classics, all these artists (*Surviving Picasso* was another gutsy move, despite the director's own doubts), Mr. Ivory has more than proven his consummate skill. He has more than earned the status of a hidebound classicist. But by refusing to rest on those laurels and sustaining the free spirit that this book displays, he's accomplished much, much more.

SETTING THE SCENE

Robert Emmet Long: Merchant Ivory is known to be *the* independent film production team of the last few decades, achieving its success on its own, outside the Hollywood studio system—or maybe in defiance of it. But, in fact, what has your experience with Hollywood been like? What sort of dealings have you had with the studios?

James Ivory: There has been this idea—people have often spoken or written in this way—that Merchant Ivory shuns Hollywood or feels that it is too good for it. Something of that kind. But people would be surprised at the number of our films that had a big studio connection, and also when that connection first took place—at the very beginning of our career. Our first feature was *The Householder,* which we made in India and then sold to Columbia (now Sony). You might say that it had even been partially financed with Hollywood money. One of our Indian investors on that film was a theater owner in Bombay who made a fortune off *The Guns of Navarone,* a Columbia hit. He put some of that in *The Householder,* so we might claim in a way that Columbia Pictures itself invested in it.

Long: So Columbia was your first backer?

Ivory: Yes, but only in the sense that they bought the film, as I say, and gave us what's called a "minimum guarantee." The way Columbia paid us for *The Householder* (they bought the world rights) was with four hundred thousand of their blocked, or "frozen," rupees—earnings from their films in India that they could not, by law, repatriate. All the American studios had fortunes in rupees sitting in Indian banks. Right away Ismail saw the advantages for us in such a situation. The studios—MGM, Fox, Warner Brothers, and so on—were free to spend that "frozen" money on productions in India. It was all quite regulated, you can be sure, and prying it loose was a bureaucratic nightmare; but all of our Indian features were shot, more or less, in this manner. Fox spent a million dollars on our third film, *The Guru*—the rupee equivalent, that is—which was a lot of money to us but nothing to them.

Long: What about films you have made in the West?

Ivory: When we began making films outside India, there was again some studio involvement. *Quartet* was made that way; Fox put money into it. *The Wild Party* was financed by the Hollywood-based American International Pictures, a sort of Miramax-like "little studio" setup, with a Harvey Weinstein–like boss named Samuel Arkoff, who, like Weinstein, loved dismembering his pictures.

Long: Later, with the great success of *A Room with a View*, the studios came knocking at your door.

Ivory: After *A Room with a View*, Hollywood welcomed us. They thought we had some secret; we could parlay three and a half million dollars into seventy million, and get terrific reviews and Academy Awards. There were several three-picture deals made with the studios then, which sounds exciting, but these usually fizzled out after the first picture (as in the case of TriStar and *Slaves of New York*). But there were films like *The Remains of the Day* and *Surviving Picasso*, which were studio films from the beginning, films that were made from properties they'd acquired. We were hired to make these for the studios.

Long: How much creative freedom did you have once you were in a contractual arrangement with the studios?

Ivory: Some studios were absolutely princely, like Disney. Others were the opposite, penny-pinching and suspicious. But not one—no, wait, there *was*, or *is* one—gave us any real trouble over so-called creative matters. I always have had the final cut. I won't do a film if I don't get that, and up to now—with the exception of *The Wild Party*—I've always been given it. No film but that one has ever been recut (at least in the United States; outside the United States you don't know what's going to happen to your movie).

Long: How do these studios treat you as independent filmmakers? And do you feel that you have anything in common with Hollywood?

Ivory: The studio people are genuinely respectful; if there was a disagreement over some point, it was usually expressed in a diffident tone, almost murmured, apologetic. Well, you have to take that seriously; it would be very bad manners to go stomping about saying, "I'm the director!" We've made many friends in Hollywood. I'd hate to think of what our careers would have been like without them. And then both Ismail and I cut our teeth on Hollywood movies; in our tastes we precede the great days of international filmmaking, the French New Wave and all the other national "waves," except, I suppose, the Italian. Hollywood set the standard for us when we were most receptive and the studios most creative. Strange, when you think how unlike a big studio picture any Merchant Ivory film is!

Long: A number of independent filmmaking companies exist today. How is your company different from these others, the indies, as they are called?

Ivory: Our company is different in that the three of us—Ismail, Ruth, and myself—are permanent. She writes, I direct, and Ismail produces what we write and direct. We're all lucky in that way. Most producers who have a project they want to do have to search for a writer and then a director; or a director has to look for a writer and producer when he finds something he's keen on doing. It's worst of all for the writer in that respect. There's a constant delay and changing of minds in most producing partnerships, but not in ours.

Long: What special problems do you have as an independent filmmaking company?

Ivory: The problem, of course, is in finding the money to make our films. And then, once they're made, making sure the distributor brings them out in the right way.

Long: I saw you and Ismail one night on *60 Minutes,* and got the impression that the two of you often speak heatedly and may have many differences of opinion. How do you work together so well when you are both so independently minded? What happens when you have a disagreement and there is no one else to referee or arbitrate?

Ivory: I've always said that Merchant Ivory is a bit like the U.S. government; I'm the president, Ismail is the Congress, and Ruth is the Supreme Court. Though Ismail and I disagree sometimes, Ruth acts as a referee, or she and I

James Ivory (left) and Ismail Merchant at Lake of the Woods in southern Oregon, 1963. Merchant is reading *Vertical and Horizontal,* the novel by Lillian Ross about psychoanalysis that Merchant and Ivory hoped to film.

may gang up on him, or vice versa. The main thing is, no one ever truly interferes in the area of work of the other. At a certain point respect compels us to back off.

Long: What is there about Ismail that sets him apart from anyone else you know?

Ivory: He's never uninteresting, never dull. He's remained vital and youthful and enthusiastic about what he does and we do together and of course is prodigiously energetic. He has a lot of ideas—certainly far more than Ruth and I, who are pretty much going along in our grooves. Some of his ideas seem crazy when we first hear about them, but they tend to turn out successfully.

Long: Does Ismail still haunt auction houses? What sort of things does he bid on?

Ivory: Portable things, suiting his nomadic lifestyle: Kashmir shawls, rugs, silver, now and then a miniature. He buys china sometimes. But not big heavy things on the whole. However, it can't be said that Ismail "haunts" auction houses. Because of all our moving around, it takes some arranging to actually bid.

Long: On a train bound for New York I fell into conversation with an Indian youth from Calcutta. We talked about India and eventually about Merchant Ivory, and it seemed as if one of the most important questions he could ask was about Ismail's cooking. Had I ever eaten one of Ismail's meals? How do you feel about Ismail's, in this case, almost overshadowing celebrity as a chef?

Ivory: Overshadowing what? His legendary prowess as a producer and filmmaker? I think he'd be very sorry to feel that his cooking has eclipsed his life's work in any way.

Long: When he began to direct films as well as produce them, did he call on you for advice and assistance?

Ivory: He never asked me directly to assist him in any way beyond reading his scripts. But of course I feel I would be letting him down, letting the company down, letting everybody down if I didn't speak up when I think he's about to make some mistake. During shooting I go for a while to wherever Ismail is making his film—Trinidad most recently, South India before that—and hang around in case I'm needed. Sometimes I am; once in a while I rewrite a scene or make up a new one entirely for him if I think it's useful. Once, in Bhopal, during *In Custody,* Ismail said one morning, "Oh, I'm tired today, you shoot it," and I was happy to let him lie down for a bit.

Long: As you know, Ismail has a sense of humor. One day at the Merchant Ivory office, I asked him if he felt overshadowed by you as a director, and he replied with some aplomb that he had given you a head start.

Ivory: I really think he's happiest of all directing; he loves the process and wades right into anything, as a director must. *But* he won't relinquish his producer's role, so instead of worrying about getting a tricky scene exactly right sometimes, he's berating the production manager over some air tickets. He's happy doing that too. That's actually a moment, if I see it happening, when I can be useful, and I yell at him and drag him away to his set.

Long: Rightly or wrongly, I have the feeling that you were influential on his New York/Paris-based film, *The Proprietor,* a very cosmopolitan picture (with Jeanne Moreau, no less). When I see a film directed by Ismail, however different it may be from one of yours, I have the feeling that it has come out of the same school of filmmaking as your own. Both your films and his have a rich look, shared production values, even the use of some of the same actors, and of course there is Dick Robbins's music.

Ivory: Well, it would be surprising if there weren't similarities of style, tone, look. We have used the same actors and cameramen and editor, and on *The Proprietor* even the same scriptwriter, George Trow. Sometimes the music Dick Robbins writes for Ismail's films makes me a bit jealous, I have to say. It's the content of our films, however, that's mainly different. Except for *The Proprietor,* which was about rich, worldly people in Paris and New York, Ismail's films are almost always about poor, struggling people, often living on the edge. This has been true since he directed his first film, *Mahatma and the Mad Boy,* which was about a beggar. His films might right a balance at Merchant Ivory and offset mine, which are almost all exclusively about well-off people from the upper middle class. When lazy critics try to lump Ismail's films with mine, as they sometimes do, calling them "genteel," their favorite pejorative word, I wonder whether they have ever seen them. Ismail has made films about mad people, prostitutes and pimps, drunken poets who fall down in their own vomit. Perhaps the high surface gloss of his films is what makes these careless reviewers think there's a real similarity.

Long: Now that Ismail is directing as well as producing, he is working at a prodigious rate. What is it that drives him?

Ivory: He does get run-down, it's true, and that's very worrying to us. But he has a rare ability to put all his worries aside, drop straight off to sleep, and above all enjoy himself outside the office. He is fueled by an extraordinary optimism and by a young Indian's desire to "make name and fame" that he has never lost, and about which we tease him.

Long: Ismail must have one of the biggest address books of anyone in New York. Is there anyone he doesn't know?

Ivory: Or remember? That's the point.

Long: Is there a colony of Indians who are prominent in the arts in New York that Ismail is in close touch with?

Ivory: Not really. There are a few people we see constantly. Madhur Jaffrey is one. We know Ved Mehta very well, and Ismail and I are both friendly with Zubin Mehta. When the dancer Indrani was alive we saw her, and now we see her children, who are also in the arts. Anita Desai, of course, but she's not a New Yorker.

Long: Because you and Ismail have been such close partners for such a record number of years, do you ever feel as if you were half of a person?

Ivory: Not at all. I feel sometimes that we are the *same* person.

Long: Simon Callow told a reporter that Ismail was so many different people that he couldn't imagine what he would be like when he was alone. How many different people does he contain?

Ivory: He may seem very complicated to people who know nothing of India and the Indian character. To those who do, Ismail's behavior is more understandable, easier to place. As I stayed on in India year after year, Ismail himself came into sharper focus for me. And now, when we're mostly in Europe and America, and seldom in India together, he sometimes appears in even sharper focus—as in relief, against backgrounds that play up the difference between him and the "natives," you might say: Americans, Englishmen, Frenchmen, Italians . . .

Long: People tend to think of the two of you as being total opposites: he's flamboyant, and you're discreet. But I wonder if there isn't some kind of symbiosis here, the notion of two opposites who are often together and share qualities. Do you have any of Ismail's qualities?

Ivory: Well, his optimism perhaps, but untinged by his fatalism, which is perhaps a Muslim or even a general Indian quality. I think I share in his energy; I may possess my own or be energized by his. At any rate I watch people half my age drop with exhaustion (particularly during shooting), and I'm always the last person in the house to go to bed.

Long: In his recent book, *My Passage from India,* Ismail describes himself as a film director in the following way: "I cut scenes if I felt they weren't working, or suddenly adapted scenes to take advantage of an unusual location, a striking face, a new idea. Although I have been observing Jim at work for thirty years and have learned a lot from him, I have my own way of working that is different from his. Instead of being thrown by the unexpected elements that can occur during the filming, I actively welcome them. I like the sense of spontaneity and surprise." Would you care to comment on the differences between Ismail and yourself as film directors?

Ivory: Well, Ismail certainly has far less patience than I have on the set; as in everything in life, he hates delays. I saw him once, an expression of exasperation on his face, during the filming of *In Custody,* as he listened to a long-winded scene being read aloud by the Urdu co-scriptwriter. Ismail took the pages away from him, went inside where he couldn't be seen, crumpled them up, and rewrote the scene himself on the spot with Shashi Kapoor. On the other hand, I don't think I'm that much "thrown" by the unexpected during my own shooting. But I might want a little more time to decide how best to deal with it—which might also mean how best to exploit it for the good of the film.

Long: I wasn't aware that Ismail spoke Urdu.

Ivory: He would have to be fluent in Urdu in order to make a film like *In Custody,* which is all about an Urdu poet. Ismail's Urdu, in which he delights, is very fluent; he speaks it beautifully, in a slightly old-fashioned way. It's always full of jokes and puns that make people laugh.

Long: I tend to think of Satyajit Ray as a figure you met and admired tremendously at the beginning of your career rather than someone with whom you have had an ongoing relationship; but Ismail speaks of Ray's seeing *A Room with a View* and of their meeting at Ray's hotel suite at that time. How close were you and Ismail with Ray during those intervening years between *The Householder* and *A Room with a View?*

Ivory: We were always close, corresponding during those years when I didn't go very often to India, and almost always managing to meet him when we did. Sometimes we saw Ray in the West, in Paris—Ismail writes about that in his book on France—or in New York. Here's a funny story: Satyajit came to New York for some reason—this must have been before his heart attack—and was staying at one of the hotels on Central Park South. I went up to his room to see him, and while I was there a delivery man arrived bearing a luxu-

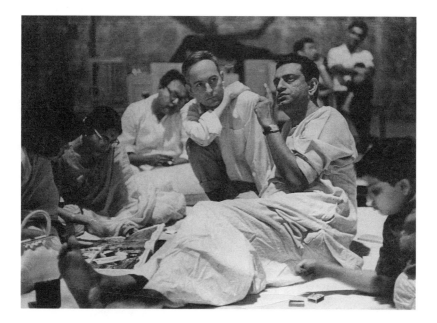

Satyajit Ray with James Ivory in Calcutta during the music recording session of *Shake-speare Wallah* (1965).

rious chocolate cake. It had been sent by Richard Avedon. Ray explained that Avedon wanted him to pose, but Ray said, "I'm not going to be photographed by Richard Avedon. He makes you look like a corpse, or in the last stages of senility." He was referring to the series of portraits Avedon made of famous directors, which certainly did make them look as if they had one foot in the grave, especially the one of Jean Renoir, a hero of his. Then he offered me some of the cake, which he proceeded to slice, and we ate it. It was excellent.

Another time when Ray was in New York he stayed with us. In those days it was virtually impossible for Indians to get any foreign exchange in order to travel abroad, not even the greatest artist in the land. Anyway, while he was with us, we gave a little party for him. He wanted to meet Pauline Kael, who loved his movies and wrote wonderfully about them. But when she came they ended up having an argument over the Russian director Eisenstein, another of Satyajit's heroes. Kael said Eisenstein was an overrated director and really lousy. Ray couldn't believe his ears. Being very, very polite, he changed the subject, but she wouldn't let it drop. When she was safely out of the door, he exploded: "She's crazy! She's out of her mind!"

Long: In addition to being Ismail's collaborator, you are often Ruth Jhabvala's screenwriting collaborator. Do you and she have the same tastes, the same methods of working?

Ivory: When we collaborate on a screenplay these days, we follow a certain pattern that seems to work for us both. It goes like this: I write the first draft; she takes that and rewrites it and gives it back to me. I then modify my original ideas, reject some of hers, and finally we sit down together and go through it line by line. Of course we do argue sometimes. Then I give in, or she does, or we compromise. Our biases are different, certainly, but I think in most things our tastes are pretty similar. We differ on the subject of humor. Sometimes I like things she thinks are too broad, even stupid. For instance, the famous "birds and bees" sequences in *The Remains of the Day* . . .

Long: I loved that business . . .

Ivory: Or the episode in *A Soldier's Daughter* when the Marcella character throws sand in the eyes of the teacher tormenting her young son. Ruth wanted to cut that. I refused. Ruth most likely didn't feel so strongly about these two sequences. If it had been a case of "over my dead body," I suppose I would have felt duty-bound to cut them. There have been such cases, scenes in which from her point of view everything has gone wrong: bad acting, bad writing, bad directing—just plain bad. Scenes, maybe, where I'd liked the photography or some extraneous element. At such times she can be very withering. Like a Supreme Court justice's acid dissent.

Long: In working with Ruth, have your ideas for a film ever diverged so much that you have just reached an impasse?

Ivory: Yes. We started out together in the mideighties on an original screenplay of *Three Continents,* which then, after we disagreed on it, Ruth turned into a novel, having got interested in the theme and characters. I wanted the first two sections of the story to be seen through the eyes of the homosexual brother, Michael, and the last section only to be seen through the eyes of his sister, Har-

Ruth Jhabvala in Central Park in 1966, during her first visit to New York.

riet. Ruth didn't go for that idea, and as I felt Harriet was too passive a figure to sustain interest as the main protagonist throughout the whole story, I dropped out. I think that's the only time this has ever happened. Perhaps I could have pushed it more, have convinced Ruth, but I was already at work on the two Forster films back-to-back, *A Room with a View* and *Maurice*, which kept me busy for more than three years.

Long: Ruth has a formidable reputation as a novelist and short-story writer. Does she prize her screenplays as highly as her other work, or do they take second place to her fiction?

Ivory: Second place, definitely. Fiction writing is her first love, and doing films with us is more for the fun of it than anything else. If she doesn't think some project will be fun for her, she ducks it.

Long: What is it chiefly that Ruth brings to your films?

Ivory: A secure, a profound, grasp of character and story. As an original fiction writer she is well placed to do that. That is how she is so different from, and better than, so many professional screenwriters who lack these gifts.

Long: Has there been a particular collaboration with her that has given you the most pleasure and satisfaction?

Ivory: I think I most enjoyed our early films, the ones set in India. We worked very closely on all those, from *Shakespeare Wallah* up through *Heat and Dust*, which, in small ways, came out of an earlier collaboration, *Autobiography of a Princess*. When it came to doing the big novels—*The Bostonians, Howards End, The Golden Bowl*—Ruth worked far more on her own, struggled on her own. How to compress all that mass of writing was a task far beyond me. The same was true of the Bridge novels, which were far closer to me than Ruth in terms of subject matter and were about people, times, places that I had firsthand knowledge of, but which she lacked. Still, she had to struggle on her own with those books, too.

Long: Not everyone realizes, I think, that you write as well as direct. This isn't true of most directors, is it?

Ivory: It has been said, and I think it's mostly true, that directors are better off when their writers are not themselves. Yet in some cases a director can spin out his own story, too—as, for example, Woody Allen can—and then he is truly blessed. If I'm an effective scriptwriter, it's mostly because I have Ruth at my side.

Long: The other member of your inner circle of collaborators is the composer Richard Robbins. How did he come to join you?

Ivory: Dick was on the faculty of the Mannes School of Music in Manhattan, where Ruth's youngest daughter, Firoza, was his piano student. He became a friend and then gradually offered advice on things musical in our films. This was in the midseventies, and we had no longtime composer then as we had an ongoing cameraman, say, like Walter Lassally or like Subrata Mitra in India. Then, in 1978, during *The Europeans*, Dick provided his first score. It was mostly source music, such as early piano works and hymns, but there were some original compositions as well. He's been with us ever since, with the exception of *The Five Forty-eight*.

Long: Has your working method changed much over the years? Robbins has done sixteen scores for you, as well as scores for other Merchant Ivory films not directed by you, such as Ismail's films, and for the films of directors completely apart from Merchant Ivory, such as Nicole Garcia's *Place Vendôme.*

Ivory: And in all of them he's shown the most refined craftsmanship—I should say, instead, musicianship—and an originality of approach that makes him different from anyone else that I know of these days. It's now hard for me to imagine a film of mine without his music.

Long: I know that Ismail is musical, but about yourself I am not quite so clear. Judging by some of your references, I gather that you had some sort of training or at least some sort of background in classical music. Is this so?

Ivory: No. Not really. I was never musical in the sense that I could play—or even want to play—any instrument. I began to listen to 78 records of classical music about the time I was a senior in high school, and my tastes were very primitive. When the first long-playing records appeared around 1950, I'd somehow trained my ear (I don't know how) and become an addict of Bach and Handel, buying every cantata that came out by the former and every oratorio or opera by the latter.

Long: Ismail recalls that when he first met you, you had an extensive record collection, among which was "the music of Nazakat and Salamat Ali Khan, two brilliant Pakistani vocal musicians. . . . Jim enjoyed Indian classical music as much as I did." How did you develop your interest in Indian music?

Ivory: My feeling for Indian music came out of working on *The Sword and the Flute* and from seeing Ray's films, especially *The Music Room,* in which the singer Begum Akhtar is featured. Indian vocal music slowly comes to be enjoyed in time; it's rather difficult for the Western ear to adjust to. It grows on you, however, until it surpasses all other enjoyment of Indian music. I remember Hyman Bloom, the artist, telling me that in time this would happen to me. I think it's a bit like the appreciation of opera in the West. Slowly you come to feel that the human voice is the most expressive, the most beautiful, of all instruments.

Long: Go back, if you will, to the way you work with Robbins.

Ivory: You know, I'm not a musician myself. I can't read a score and could never be the judge of performances on the whole. However, I've always liked all sorts of music and even fancy myself something of a connoisseur when it comes to certain kinds of period music, such as baroque, and some vocal music—not to mention Indian music. But it's an amateur's ear we're talking about. Dick knows that I'm not absolutely hopeless in matters of craft when we go to work. He accepts that.

Long: [*Laughs*] I imagine there are worse.

Ivory: Exactly. We usually plan the source music before we begin shooting if we can—the music that is actually being performed on screen by somebody, for instance, Lucy Honeychurch's Beethoven or Olivia Rivers's Schubert. Such instrumental music has to be very carefully prepared in advance, and the actresses—or actors—have to slave at it in order to seem to play convincingly. Dick is then their music master, all but knocking their knuckles, I imagine, and going like a metronome. Or sometimes it's a performance piece, like the little opera in *Jane Austen in Manhattan,* for which he composed the music entirely, arias and all, in an early classical style. Then the actors, who may not be singers, have to be taught to sing, or seem to sing, stylishly. So that's one side of it, but by no means the biggest job Dick has to do.

Long: That would be the actual composition of background music, I imagine. How do the two of you approach that?

Ivory: When the film is more or less edited—when we've cut it down to a manageable length—he and I sit together for several sessions and work out where we think the music ought to be. I have sort of a rough idea already; he often has a more exact one by then. Sometimes—rarely—our ideas don't coincide on placement. There are times when I think a bit of music is needed to smooth over rough edges in the editing that we can never really fix for some reason. Sometimes I feel, then, that we have the opportunity to make a virtue out of necessity. I explain these concerns; he listens, makes notes; I go away while he works out some themes that he already has in mind on the piano or the Kurzweil electronic keyboard. When I come back, he plays these against the film, which we watch on a video monitor. Naturally, this being Merchant Ivory, he's always being rushed; the tempo of finishing the film and preparing for the mix has now become for him what the shooting earlier on was for me. Everything has to be got ready: music composed—maybe twenty-five cues or more, some several minutes long—and then orchestrated, musicians and conductor and recording studio engaged. I don't know how he does it, but he always has. Strangely, though living so close to New York, we almost never record there.

Long: Why not?

Ivory: Oh, he doesn't much like the system there, dominated as it is by the musicians' union, and appallingly expensive. He prefers to go abroad, usually to London. Well, so many of our films have been made in England, have been British productions, that would be a natural after all. But we've recorded in Salt Lake City—very good musicians—and for a while in Dublin, where none of the musicians (also very good) appeared to be over twenty-five. [*Long laughs*] We just pick up and move. Naturally, Ismail and I want to be present at the recording. That's always a pleasure, a sort of culmination of it all, the whole film; and then we may have to confer, put our heads together when some cue needs adjustment. And Ismail wants to be sure that all those expensive violinists are playing loudly enough and that he's getting his money's worth! In that respect I'm like Ismail. I want Dick to give me music that will ravish everybody—as Satyajit Ray's music did. I want it, in combination with certain images, or sequences of images, to be literally ravishing—at least for people in a receptive mood seeing the film. I want them to clutch at their hearts if possible.

Long: When an actor or an actress comes to read for a part, what sort of things do you look for in reaching your casting decision?

Ivory: Whether in appearance and personality they have some kind of individual distinction. I don't want actors who aren't very much themselves. I take the talent for granted in most cases. They wouldn't be there meeting me if they were untalented, unless I was doing someone a favor. Of course they must seem right for the role. Sometimes it's an instantaneous decision, as, for instance, with Hugh Grant in *Maurice* and with Daniel Day-Lewis as Cecil Vyse in *A Room with a View*. Incidentally, I saw both actors for the latter role; Hugh said I didn't even glance at him; he was in and out of our office in seconds.

Long: How elaborately do you rehearse your actors before shooting a film?

Ivory: We are almost never able to rehearse before shooting except, of course, on the set the day we shoot. We're lucky if we can do a prior read-through. That's because in a film the entire cast is almost never assembled at the same time. *Mr. and Mrs. Bridge* was the exception.

Long: Do you allow them to improvise or to contribute ideas that may not be in line with your own conceptions?

Ivory: It's not possible to improvise dialogue when you're adapting authors like Henry James or E. M. Forster. But improvising action is a very different thing. I always welcome my actors' improvisations if they're consistent with the scene. If I am doing a contemporary film, then I hope they'll improvise dialogue, too. However, I obviously don't want improvised ideas that are inconsistent with my own ideas about the part, the scene, the story. If an actor insisted on something and it didn't do any general harm, I might, to be diplomatic, agree to shoot it. But then, if it was as bad as I feared, I'd just throw it away in the editing room. Usually actors are so unsure of themselves they are timid about suggesting radical changes.

Long: I've watched you directing actors on a set and was struck by your calmness, by the way you keep things on an even keel. You can seem quite detached. Have you ever lost your temper and stormed off a set?

Ivory: Once, but I went right back on again. I did it for effect many years ago but then thought, "Why am I doing this? I need to be on the set to have my way, not off it." This was during *The Wild Party.*

Long: When Shirley MacLaine and Jack Lemmon were preparing to make *Irma La Douce,* they are supposed to have gone to the Paris brothels to do their research. Have your actors, or have you yourself, done background research of no matter what impolite kind in preparing a film?

Ivory: A lot of research is, by nature, impolite. I know that actors do "research," but frankly I'm not very interested in how they do it. Ismail and I once went with William Shawn and Lillian Ross to "do research" in a jazz club in Greenwich Village for *Vertical and Horizontal,* which we hoped to but didn't make. Sitting there between them, I felt humiliated that they thought I needed to be "educated" in that way.

Long: Why should that have made you feel humiliated?

Ivory: I think it was mostly because a young woman who was about my age—Ismail and I were in our thirties—had been hired to guide our party from club to club. This seemed strange then, and now, because Shawn was apparently a habitué of that kind of Village musical scene. He himself was said to have been a gifted jazz pianist, and to have played the piano in Paris jazz haunts in the

1920s to earn a living for a while. Anyway, we were led by this girl—I think she was given ten dollars at the end—so we could experience the special ambience, observe the customers, hear the music. I don't know if you've read Ross's *Vertical and Horizontal*, but one of the characters in it was a young jazz musician who starts going to the psychoanalyst, Dr. Blauberman, and this causes him to give up his playing . . . But you were asking about actors doing research, not directors. We're digressing . . .

Long: Generally speaking, do your actors come to the set well prepared, having thought out their characterizations in detail, or do you have to give them quite a bit of help?

Ivory: Actors are generally very well prepared, are far more in touch with their parts than I can ever be. Especially English actors, who are fanatical about preparation. Americans are a bit more apt to wing it (and sometimes don't know their lines, *the* unforgivable sin of acting). Sometimes I have to do a lot of work with actors, helping them to shape the part, say their lines well. This is most often the case with very young actors or, sadly, very old ones.

Long: How conscious of the camera should an actor be, very conscious or hardly conscious at all?

Ivory: The more conscious they are, ideally, the better. Nothing is worse than to have to argue with an actor over the camera. Often they don't have a clue about what the camera sees but are fussing a lot, out of fear or vanity. The best thing is when an actor knows what the camera can do and exploits that to his or her (and the part's) benefit.

Long: What is it that makes a great, a magical, screen performance?

Ivory: I know it when I see it happening long before the film is finished. I watched Maggie Smith and Daniel Day-Lewis during *A Room with a View* and was certain they were doing something very fine. And during *Howards End* I had the same feeling about Emma Thompson. I think I even said to myself: "She will be nominated for an Academy Award."

Long: What sort of dealings have you had with agents?

Ivory: For a director, they're mostly of two kinds: those with one's own agent and those with the agents of the actors you'd like to hire—or not hire, that's a more delicate situation.

Long: Who are you represented by yourself?

Ivory: I've been very lucky to have been represented for many years by Creative Artists. My agent there is Rand Holston. He also represents Ruth and Ismail. Sometimes it's necessary for him to handle Ruth's affairs with *us.* He's absolutely unflappable and is possessed of such common sense he makes *me* look like a hysteric, which I'm not. I also have an English agent in London, Anthony Jones, at A. D. Peters. He, too, is unflappable; we've known him since he was a very young man and just starting out.

Long: What about other agents before you found Creative Artists?

Ivory: We didn't really have good representation until the days of *The Bostonians.* Christopher Reeve, knowing this, brokered our arrangements with Michael Ovitz at Creative Artists to get us in to that agency, which also represented him. Our later success with the Hollywood studios is certainly due in good measure to Rand. He opened doors after *A Room with a View* and guided us through some tricky negotiations with virtually every Hollywood studio in the last fifteen years.

Long: Do you deal with actors' agents, or is it Ismail who does that?

Ivory: I leave all that to Ismail. I wouldn't dream of getting involved; I'd say all the wrong things. Also, it's considered to be a form of lèse-majesté, I've noticed, for a director to speak personally with agents representing actors he might want to hire, except in very unusual circumstances. Anyway, as I said, for sure I'd get us in hot water. I'm sort of a pushover. But now and then I do come to know an agent fairly well, and then I'll call him up like any friend and perhaps ask his advice about something.

Long: Who makes the career decisions, an actor or his agent?

Ivory: Agents are powerless when faced with the determination of their talent. All they can do is damage control when their client decides to do a low-budget movie like one of ours, for little money. Similarly, they can rarely talk a client into doing a role that the client thinks is wrong. Sometimes the client is bent on making a bad choice, and there is nothing the agent can do about that either.

Long: Can agents be frustrating to deal with?

Ivory: Certainly. They can build a protective wall around the client you'd like to woo, send scripts to, telephone. When that happens, you have to find a way to reach your actor, and Ismail is incredibly resourceful in finding these ways.

This of course irritates the agent no end. But what else can Ismail do in that situation? The agents take their own time to deliver a script to somebody you're considering. They may even forget and leave it in a taxicab, as happened with the agent for Imogene Coca, whom we wanted to cast in *Roseland*. . . . But I have to admit that they are also loyal to old clients who get few parts or make little money for the agency by way of commissions. That's touching, in a hard-boiled place like New York or London.

Long: What do you like most about directing films?

Ivory: The life of the shoot—the eight, ten, twelve weeks it takes to actually shoot what is, after all, just raw material to be shaped and reshaped over and over in the editing room. But the intensity of that life is when a director really lives.

Long: What is the hardest part of directing films?

Ivory: Not losing hope as the film goes through the hands of one financier after another until the deal is made. The rest is easy. Except at the very end, when you project the film for the financier and don't know what his reaction will be. There's not a great deal he can do if he doesn't like it, but you want him to, most desperately.

Long: When you have completed a film, do you continue to live with it for a long time, still thinking of ways it could have been improved?

Ivory: Once a film is finished, there is no further tinkering with it; it's not a painting or a play or a piece of music. The expense in changing the tiniest thing is huge. So I don't think or worry about it at that time. Of course you do go on living with it, from festival to festival, from premiere to premiere, and then its release in DVD and so forth. And, yes, at a later time, I do think of the ways I might have done something differently, better.

Long: Have you changed your mind later about a film you have made, deciding that it was really better than you thought, or perhaps not good enough?

Ivory: Yes. Lately I've felt that *Surviving Picasso* could have been better, on the one hand, and that *The Bostonians* was better than I had remembered, on the other.

Long: How reliable a gauge of the reception of a film are your advance screenings for invited audiences?

Ivory: Not reliable, if you're being honest about it. One's friends rarely tell you what they really think. Years later a close friend will surprise you by saying, "Oh, I just *hated* that scene. Why did you leave it in?"

Long: You've been to innumerable film festivals. What has that experience been like? And what are your feelings particularly about the Cannes film festival?

Ivory: It's another aspect of the business, you might say. For me, it's never been that easy to get tickets to the films, then get dressed up, then get oneself to the Festival theater to see the films. After working all day with the press on one's own film, you mostly just want to take it easy, to escape. At Cannes we always have our own rented villa, and I hide out there as much as possible. I even dread Ismail's big parties. On such nights, if I could, I would be the first to go to bed.

Long: How do you feel about critics?

Ivory: I feel that the critics are always sitting in the front row of my audience, as it were—are definitely part of that audience. If you're lucky, they go out afterward and tell everybody how much they liked your film. They need to do that from time to time for a director of films or theater to have a productive, ongoing career. But beyond this sporadic praise, you're in danger if you take what they write too seriously. A critic who has written about you in ecstatic terms may in the next breath destroy some other director's film that you feel is little short of sublime. Or he may pronounce sublime, putting it next to one's own film on his shelf of favorites, a film you know is nothing but rubbish. What can you do when this happens, other than stick to your own opinion?

Long: Have you ever been attacked savagely? . . . Well, I suppose you were for *Slaves of New York* . . .

Ivory: That's not the only time. What about *Jefferson in Paris* and *Surviving Picasso?* When critics heap scorn on something you've just made and love dearly, you have to be thick-skinned, as Oscar Wilde appeared to be on one occasion when he declared, apropos of a play of his that didn't work, "My play was a success; it was the audience that was a failure." So you must tell yourself: "My film is a success; it is the critics who are a failure."

Long: But there are critics and critics . . .

Ivory: Unfortunately, many of today's critics do not seem to be writing for the moviegoing public. The most important audience for these reviewers is made up of other reviewers. Film criticism itself seems to have become one more form of show business, almost stand-up comedy. In the newspapers and on television these days, the reviewers are the performers that count, the *real* stars.

Long: Merchant Ivory seems to have been stuck with its own distinctive set of adjectives that critics apply exclusively when putting down your films.

Ivory: It's hard to imagine that those reviewers use such words in their actual speech: "decorous," "languorous," "stately"—as in a "stately pace." "Pallid" is another word they like a lot. And "wan." Perhaps they picked these obsolete words up from anthologies of Pauline Kael reviews. But she had an old-fashioned education; she knew what she was doing.

Long: What can you tell me about the famous remark the director Alan Parker made about your films, referring to them as belonging to the "Laura Ashley school of filmmaking"?

Ivory: Actually, he had drawn a cartoon about us for the English film magazine *Screen International,* which flourishes in a big way at film festivals like Cannes. The cartoon showed two middle-aged people putting their coats on at the end of one of our films. On the screen behind them it says, "A Merchant Ivory Production." One says to the other, "I don't like those Laura Ashley kinds of films." It made me laugh, and I tried to buy the original drawing, but somebody else got there first. The press picked it up, and it's hounded us down through the years. His joke will be remembered long after Parker's own films are forgotten, I think.

Long: Both you and Ismail are remarkably prolific. As soon as you complete a film, you begin the next one. Is this an ideal way for you to work, or is it dictated by the need to keep your film production company moving along?

Ivory: Well, of course one wants to go on as long as one can, as long as one has the energy. And, naturally, for our company to survive, we have to produce new films. My hope is that we will be able to do that with younger directors working through us on their own projects.

Long: When you and Ismail were making your early films, you were always in transit and were never in one place for long. Today, after a long and successful career, you have comfortable homes and New York apartments, but you still travel almost constantly. If I see you in New York, you may be leaving for your home upstate in Claverack, and a day or two after that you may be flying to Los Angeles. When summer arrives, you are sure to spend a few weeks in a cabin in the Oregon woods; and when you return to New York, you may soon be off to London or Paris or Venice or even Bombay. Don't you ever tire of traveling?

Ivory: Not really. Except for my weeks off in the Oregon cabin, my travels always have to do with my films—one about to start somewhere, one about to open somewhere else, one to be presented at a festival.

Long: By the way, I have sometimes wondered what you do when you go to that cabin in the Oregon woods. Do you swim or fish or commune with nature or . . . ?

Ivory: I've never fished in my life. I don't like to eat fish very much, and catching them has no interest whatsoever for me. I do swim, but my lake is cold. As for communing with nature, at my age one finds oneself simply sitting somewhere *in* nature, staring ahead either without a thought in one's head or else with thoughts far, far away from nature. No, at Lake of the Woods I see my old friends from high school and college, some of whom are extremely good company, or I import my company.

Long: Your home base has been New York City rather than Hollywood. What does Manhattan mean to you as distinct from what it means, say, to Woody Allen?

Ivory: I can't answer that; my Manhattan is not Woody Allen's. He's always lived in New York, whereas I came to it straight out of college on the West Coast. It was then the beckoning city of sophistication, and I was—and still perhaps am—as susceptible to its glamour as when I was twenty-four. Anyway, it's my home, for better or worse. I can't imagine living full-time somewhere else. I wish I'd made more films in New York, however.

Long: What about London? You're often in London and have a branch office there. What are some of the attractions of London for you?

Ivory: I like it well enough. I have many close English friends, and there is an interesting, very agreeable sort of social life, which is, in some ways, more interesting than that of New York. The English are always surprising me. And then there is the city itself, a sort of treasure house, like Paris—maybe even more than Paris. Things to see and things to buy, if you're so inclined.

Long: You have apartments everywhere, it seems, and you also have permanent offices—one in New York with a fine view, another in Paris.

Ivory: The one in Paris is a fifth-floor walk-up—it kills you.

Long: Another in Bombay.

Ivory: I don't know how permanent any of them are. Ismail is always threatening to shut one or the other down—just as he threatens to sell the apartments. Today it's New York, the next day Paris. Never London, however.

Long: Why is that?

Ivory: Because nearly every film we make now is based in Europe or India, so it's the London office that mostly deals with financial matters, production matters. Say, the lab or music recording—big things like that.

Long: Ismail can't run all these offices himself. He must have some help.

Ivory: He gets it in England from Paul Bradley. Paul started working for us there when we didn't even have an office, when we were making *Heat and Dust* out of the basement of the publisher John Murray, who publishes all Ruth Jhabvala's novels. Paul must have been very young—twenty-two or twenty-three. He looked like an undergraduate, but he had then—and still has, though more so—an iron authority and an unflappable manner. He was like those young men in English war movies who always knew in an emergency the right, sensible thing to do and say. Ismail's rages don't faze him, or my "artistic beastliness" either. He just goes on, has thrown his lot in with us for better or worse. And he has a great sense of humor, which you really need when you work for Merchant Ivory. Behind every one of our big English movies you will find Paul Bradley, moving men and matériel around (and money), until victory is assured.

Long: And in New York? Who is in charge there when Ismail is away?

Ivory: That would be Richard Hawley, an altogether different type than Paul Bradley—someone with a different fighting style; someone, you could say, who is never thrown off-base by the guerrilla warfare of the entertainment business in New York and on the West Coast.

Long: You didn't mention the English theater. When I lived in London, I went to the theater all the time and saw everyone perform there, including Laurence

Olivier in repertory. One night he was the father in *Long Day's Journey into Night*, and the next he was Shylock in *The Merchant of Venice*. You must have had acquaintances in the London theater or have known some of the leading figures.

Ivory: I've met some, mostly socially, as friends of friends. But since you've just mentioned Olivier, here is a little story about him. In 1985, while we were shooting *A Room with a View*, Maggie Smith and her husband, Beverley Cross, asked me for the weekend at their house in Fittleworth, in West Sussex. On the Sunday, we went to lunch at the Oliviers, who lived nearby. He was sitting in his garden under a big tree. By then he was pretty old and frail. He'd suffered from cancer and had also recently banged his shin against a bed and developed a clot, so that he had to wear shorts and keep the leg propped up on a stool. Maggie introduced me and explained that she was shooting a film with me. He was extraordinarily courteous and welcoming; he kept getting up to show his guests to their chairs, though it was obviously a struggle, and he even offered to go and fetch our plates of lunch, though he could barely totter. I didn't exactly help matters; in my haste to refill my glass of champagne, I knocked against the stool on which he'd rested his throbbing leg, but being such a great actor and perfect host, he stifled his cries. He told me an extraordinary thing, confiding perhaps as one director to another (or as an elder to a younger)—though I don't know which films of mine he'd ever seen, beyond *Shakespeare Wallah.* He said that the accomplishments in life he felt the happiest about were the two films he'd directed, *Henry V* and *Hamlet.* Those made him prouder, more satisfied, than anything else he'd ever done. This coming from the man everyone calls the greatest English-speaking actor of the twentieth century!

Long: Do you know other directors or spend time with them socially?

Ivory: In the course of my rather long directing career I've met many other directors, but apart from Satyajit Ray I've never become close to any of them. I have felt warmly toward some, and if I could have spent more time with them, I feel that they might have become personal friends: Louis Malle, Krzysztof Zanussi, Peter Weir, Jacques Demy, Martin Scorsese. It might have been possible to have had interesting discussions about work, actors, and just life generally. At Venice, before the fall of the iron curtain countries, I came to know Zanussi slightly; but at the end of our lunch together—before the end, in fact—

some Polish strong-arm men came to the table and signaled that it was time to go. He had warned us this would happen when he sat down. He flew off to Warsaw under escort, and I never saw him again.

Long: What is it apt to be like when two film directors meet?

Ivory: The orbits of film directors swing together and intersect for a few moments at film festivals and other official functions, and then you're off again on what might be thought of as a lonely trajectory. I've noticed that these encounters can be a little edgy; one feels that defenses are up, well in place. Remarks are apt to be carefully formal, a bit distanced, guarded. There will be a mutual exchange about having admired the other's recent film, with suitable expressions of modesty and self-deprecation. This must be the only time that directors are so modest: when they are talking to each other. [*Long laughs*]

Long: Is there any comment made to you by another director that you have always remembered?

Ivory: I remember how a very senior director put a junior colleague, myself, at ease. I once met Jean Renoir, and after I gave him news and greetings from Indian friends, he touched my necktie, which had a stylized paisley pattern on it of mangoes, and said, more or less: "When you eat an Indian mango, you taste all the succulence of India—just as, when you bite into an apple from Normandy, you can taste in its crisp flesh all the rich flavors of France." He spoke in English and no doubt had said this other times in French, much more beautifully than I recall it today. But I was wowed by it.

Long: Speaking of Jean Renoir, it's been said that your ancestor is Renoir and the humanist filmmaking tradition that he stands at the head of. Do you yourself think this is so?

Ivory: Perhaps it's true; it would be nice to think there's a line from Renoir and Ray to me. That would be one line perhaps. I think a parallel cinema has recently developed in China, actually. Today's Chinese films remind me of the humanist cinema of the past in the West. I think it would be impossible to make similar films in America in any sort of consistent way today.

Long: Your reading would be interesting, probably revealing. Do you have time to read very much?

Ivory: Yes, even while shooting I manage to read. This is mainly for pleasure. I don't really read in the hope of finding some book to make into a movie, though that is the assumption of many people.

Long: A final question. You've made so many films that celebrate other countries, other cultures, other worlds. Do you have affirmative, even patriotic, sentiments regarding your own country?

Ivory: Never so much as when I'm looking down at it from an airplane. Then I think of it—I may have been drinking—but sometimes I think of it almost with a kind of rapture as *my* country. I don't mean I feel *I* own it, or want to own, or possess, it. But it's my country. My own. And this is never so strong as in the big expanses of the West. But once I'm over the Rocky Mountains going east, I seem to lose interest. It's strange, seeing that I've lived my entire productive life on the well-ordered East Coast in and around New York and have a beautiful house in the Hudson Valley, which I almost think of as the House of Life, like that of Mario Praz. Yet somehow I'm more emotionally connected to the uninhabited, wild, desolate western deserts than to the more regular and tamed eastern part of my country. (I think that's why I loved Afghanistan so much, both on the ground and from an Ariana Airlines plane; it must have reminded me of home.)

Long: I didn't know you had such strong feelings about desert places . . .

Ivory: I look down on the long, long scratches on the red earth of Arizona from a height of thirty-five thousand feet, and I wonder: Where do these dirt roads go? Who put them there? What purpose do they serve? I feel as someone might feel who is flying over Mars and looking down on the so-called canals: How do those scratches happen to be there? And then when I see towns, some of them huge, I also wonder: Who lives there in this wild, cut-off, seemingly cursed place, with playing fields and swimming pools? What do the people do? What jobs do they have? But I don't want to omit saying that to look straight down on Manhattan at the end of my trip, especially at night, is also to experience a kind of ecstasy.

THE EARLY YEARS

Robert Emmet Long: Your films are cosmopolitan, urbane, but you were not a city boy, having been raised in the small town of Klamath Falls, in the timber country of Oregon.

James Ivory: Well, lots of American artists who have done all kinds of things have come from the most unlikely little American town; and have made their trek first from their little town to New York, and from New York to Europe, making their name along the way, or maybe even making it in Europe. I'm just one of those kinds of people.

Long: You've said that Klamath Falls was a "Wild West" town.

Ivory: It *was* a Wild West town. It was full of cowboys, it had Indians, it had stabbings in the street. But then they have stabbings in the street in New York. I've never lived anywhere where they didn't have stabbings in the street, except maybe Paris, which is very well policed.

Long: You seem to have certain qualities that some people at least associate with small towns, qualities that coexist with your sophistication. For example, you appear to have an essential down-to-earth quality.

Ivory: I hope. But would that not also be a part of sophistication? One of its components? Maybe even the main one?

Long: You give an impression of being genuine.

Ivory: Why thank you! But I think that has nothing to do with coming from a small town. Small towns everywhere can produce people who are not necessarily down-to-earth; and all sorts of down-to-earth people can come from the most sophisticated places in the world. Actually, I think small towns are best known for producing people who are narrow-minded, constricted types. But I had a sophisticated father and mother, and that helps a lot.

Long: I was going to ask about your parents. Your father seems to have been important to you. Do you find that you have any of his traits?

Ivory: Many.

Long: What do you share, do you think, with your father?

Ivory: I think he had a largeness of spirit, a breadth of spirit, which I would hope to have myself. Sometimes I find myself about to do something which is not admirable, and I think, "Now what would my father have done here?" His memory shames me sometimes at what I am doing, if it is some small-minded thing.

Long: He sounds like a very interesting man.

Ivory: Well, he *was* interesting. He came from upstate New York, from the town of Norwich. He went to France in the First World War as a cavalry officer and became a Francophile, which he remained till the end of his life. He liked good wine and sophisticated food and those kinds of things, without in any way being a gourmand or someone who ate a lot . . . he had a taste for French civilization, enjoyed the monuments and museums of Paris. He had French friends, kept them all his life, and I inherited them in fact. At Christmas-time and at other times, and always for my mother's birthday, we would go to San Francisco from Klamath Falls; and we would stay in a grand Frenchified hotel, the Palace Hotel, which was San Francisco's version of . . . I suppose it was a sort of cross between the Saint Regis and the Plaza hotels in New York.

Long: I had dinner there when I was in my twenties and living in San Francisco, and remember being awed by the dining room.

Ivory: Then you know what it was like, a wonderful hotel. . . . I'm afraid that if you saw it after the 1950s, you can't know what it was really like because it was utterly changed once the Sheraton chain took it over. But at least the Garden Court dining room is still there. It was in that restaurant and in that hotel, with its mirrored doors, marble floors, crystal chandeliers, and all of that—where along with the delicious "continental" food, I first tasted the luxury of big-city life, and its sophisticated vistas of this, that, and the other. San Francisco also had dazzling department stores like Gump's and the long-gone City of Paris, and legitimate theaters where we saw Broadway plays on tour, as well as a big Chinatown, where pharmacies sold things like dried sea horses. What was their use? Were they aphrodisiacs, cures for cancer? Sometimes I wonder why it is that I don't now go back to San Francisco more, because at least for me as a child and teenager it had the special magic of a sophisticated, worldly place. If you lived in Oregon and wanted the big city and bright lights, you didn't go to Portland, which was then pretty stuffy and dull. You went south to San Francisco, to "the City." Now it is almost reversed. Portland is a lively city, and San Francisco, I feel, may have lost what it had.

Long: Are there other traits that you think you share with your father? Did he have a code of living, for example?

Ivory: He was a Catholic, but a Catholic like President Kennedy was a Catholic, which meant that he went to Mass every Sunday, went to confession and communion twice a year, Christmas and Easter, and that's about as far as it went. But with that, of course, comes a whole Catholic way of thinking about right and wrong.

Long: He was an Irish Catholic?

Ivory: Irish Catholic.

Long: Did your father's being an Irish Catholic . . .

Ivory: He never made much of being Irish at all until he became elderly. I think that's because when he was young and growing up in Norwich in the first decade of the last century, the Irish were looked down upon, were considered brash newcomers. Exactly the way the Kennedys had been regarded when they first came to Boston. There was a kind of social stigma in all that which my father didn't like. He didn't go around proclaiming his Irishness. He didn't have to. He was a very attractive man. He was popular, very good-looking, very outgoing. He had what's called "the common touch," a great thing to have, and which Ismail has, for instance, and I shall never have, alas.

Long: He wasn't just a businessman.

Ivory: No, not at all.

Long: Although he was a very successful businessman.

Ivory: He was a very successful businessman. He had worked for Thomas Edison after the First World War. Edison hired bright young men who had an inventive turn of mind in the practical sense—young men who could invent things. My father was one of these young men that Edison hired, and he worked for the great man in wherever it was . . . East Orange, New Jersey, I think. Later in life he invented all kinds of lumber-making machinery and simplified the machinery of sawmills so that his own mills were very, very modern and right up-to-the-minute in terms of technology, as well as being safer. He could have a mill that employed only twenty men where the other mill owners who hadn't modernized had to manage with an old-fashioned mill that would employ a hundred men, where they sometimes had terrible accidents. And that's the sort of person he was.

Long: You haven't said anything about your mother. She was from Bogalusa, Louisiana. Was she religious?

Ivory: Not at all. If anything, the opposite. *Her* mother—my grandmother De Loney—and my mother's sister Eve, who I was very close to when I grew up, couldn't have been called atheists, I suppose, but you'd have to call them nonbelievers. My grandmother used to take her children (she had seven) on nature walks instead of to church (Presbyterian) on Sundays.

Long: That would have been very subversive behavior for a small Louisiana town in those days.

Ivory: And these days, even. I like to think that where I'm concerned—my religious beliefs, I mean—the work of a thousand years of Irish priests on my father's side was overturned by those three De Loney women walking in the outskirts of Bogalusa on Sunday mornings. They must have been pretty brave in another way, too, because my mother told me that the place was full of water moccasins and alligators.

Long: Her maiden name, De Loney, sounds French . . . a Norman name.

Ivory: It sounds French, but it's one of those English names that started out as French and became English in time. There are lots of English names like that, with a capital "De" in front of them—capital "D," not a small "d," as in France.

Long: Was she interested in the theater perhaps?

Ivory: Not in a great way. Nor the movies.

Long: Or in music?

Ivory: No, she didn't practice any of the arts.

Long: Didn't play an instrument?

Ivory: She played the piano. She read. She liked to collect. Old glass, and then later on she formed a collection of Japanese netsukes long before they became highly prized things . . .

Long: She kept house . . .

Ivory: She kept our house well without being . . .

Long: Were you hospitable people, with many friends at your house?

Ivory: Yes, there were almost always people invited for dinner, or so it seems to me. My mother was a good cook, though she didn't much like to cook actually. She made delicious things like floating island, which I guess I took for granted until I went to France in my twenties and saw such things on restaurant menus. I know we must have been the only people in Klamath Falls who ate artichokes in those days. None of my friends there knew what to do with them.

Long: Then you went to the University of Oregon, at Eugene, in 1946. Was your interest at that time chiefly in architecture?

Ivory: No. I was chiefly interested by that time in the movies.

Long: But you started at the university with a major in architecture, didn't you?

Ivory: Only as a means to an end. I had decided when I was sixteen, seventeen, something like that, to be a set designer for the movies. We had a friend, Sheldon Brumbaugh, an architect. He was a modern architect and a very, very good one; and as it happened he was doing some work on our house. I don't know how I got in conversation with him. I must have opened up, most uncharacteristically, and said that I would like to do sets for the movies, and asked him what would be a good way of going about it. He said, "Go to architectural school."

Long: Did he recommend any particular school?

Ivory: No. I don't think so. Or I can't remember. At first I wanted to go to Stanford, but my high school grades weren't good enough to get me in. It was 1946, and the veterans were coming back from the war that year, so every college was jam-packed. But I could always go to the University of Oregon, being an Oregon resident; it had a fine school of architecture and allied arts. I was really lucky in a way that my grades kept me out of Stanford, because I was much better placed from the point of view of architecture, art history, and so on at the University of Oregon. So I went there and started out in architecture for two years before giving it up and taking all kinds of courses—particularly in the history of architecture, which I was crazy about. I took up French, theater design, painting, printmaking, and writing—specifically, short stories. It took me five years to graduate instead of four because I kept switching my major.

Long: You went to Paris in the summer of 1950 with the idea of enrolling at the IDHEC, the French film school.

Ivory: That's right. But in order to do that I needed to know fluent French. I was going to take French while I was there, make a stab at it anyway. I went with three friends, and we all intended to learn French; but before we got very far the Korean War started. The only way to keep out of the Korean War (I was twenty-two) was to go to school or stay in school. I wouldn't have been drafted because I hadn't graduated yet. And also, if you then went on to graduate school, you were exempt. So I went back to Eugene, graduated from the University of Oregon's school of architecture and fine arts, and was admitted to the film school at the University of Southern California. While I was in the cinema school, I went to Italy to make my first film, about Venice. Before I could finish it, however, I was, in fact, drafted.

Long: If we can pause for a moment, your being at the USC film school placed you in Los Angeles, right in the neighborhood of Hollywood. Did you go to the studios much during that time?

Ivory: I went to the studios when I was thirteen and fourteen because my father and his partner, who lived in Los Angeles, sold lumber to MGM. From time to time we would go out to MGM, and I would be taken on a tour of the studios by somebody or other we knew who could do that sort of thing. This

was while I was in high school and even before high school. But I never visited the studios while I was at the USC cinema school. My teachers at USC
didn't believe in studio tours for us for some reason. I don't know why. The
curriculum was heavily slanted toward documentaries—"how-to" films, that
kind of thing.

Long: When you were at USC, did you belong to any cinephile society, or
have a circle of friends who were passionate about films and talked about them
frequently?

Ivory: There were people of my own age at the school who intellectualized
a lot about "the Cinema," but I've never been like that myself. It's never been
my kind of thing to talk theoretically about anything. I had friends, people I
liked and went around with, but in those days there really weren't those tight
groups of mad cinema addicts that would come later.

Long: Some people feel that the types of films Hollywood was making in the
1950s were boring. Did you feel that way, or did you find the general run of
those films to be interesting?

Ivory: Boring, then, if anything. Yet some great films were made there in the
fifties, and I probably didn't realize that I should be sure to see them. I'll tell
you what had happened by the fifties. It was the discovery of postwar European cinema. The movie industry was back on its feet again in England and
France and Italy, and began to make wonderful movies. That was what was
exciting to me, not—with some exceptions—the American movies I was seeing. It was the European movies I was seeking out. There was a good reason
to go to Portland when I had been a student in Eugene. I can remember to this
day seeing Cocteau's *Beauty and the Beast* in Portland's best art house in the
late forties, the Guild.

Long: Weren't you also going to European films in Eugene, while you were
an undergraduate at the University of Oregon?

Ivory: There was a little art house in Eugene around the corner from my apartment, and I remember what a great impression some of the pictures I saw there
made on me. One of these was Carl Dreyer's *Day of Wrath;* another was *Devil
in the Flesh,* a marvelous movie with Gérard Philipe and Micheline Presle; and
Olivier's *Henry V.* All these kinds of films were the ones that inspired me. The

Italian neorealist films began in the late forties and were going along strong in the early fifties, until finally evolving into Fellini and Antonioni. In the midfifties the Japanese cinema burst on the scene. You could only see it in Los Angeles by going to "Japan Town." *Rashomon* came, without subtitles; when we heard about it at USC, we rushed to see it and were agog at how new and marvelous it was. For me it was like watching Ray's *The Music Room* later on. *Rashomon* didn't need subtitles, it was so compelling. All this is what seems to me to have been really happening in the 1950s, not what was going on virtually on my doorstep at USC, in the Hollywood studios.

Long: This was also the period of the McCarthy witch-hunts and the House Un-American Activities Committee, which was scourging the American entertainment industry, but particularly the Hollywood film industry.

Ivory: I went to one of the hearings just to see what it was like.

Long: In Washington?

Ivory: No, in Los Angeles. They were grilling people who were to tell what they knew, or not tell what they knew, about their friends and colleagues. There was an appalling congressman, fat and red-faced, from Ohio, who was a sort of Grand Inquisitor. The investigation was centered on musicians the day I went.

Long: In 1952 you were drafted into the army and served for the next two years in Germany, an assignment that enabled you to travel around in Europe, to revisit Venice, and to spend more time in Paris. What was Paris like then? It was supposed to be a great place to be in the postwar period. Paris was bustling with creativity, French cinema was flourishing. The customers at the sidewalk cafés included men like Cocteau, Sartre, and Camus.

Ivory: All that was mostly wonderful for the French. People like Sartre and Camus sitting in the cafés didn't have anything to do with Americans, or other foreigners, for the most part. That was a rarefied world that one could merely read about and try to imagine. Certainly, when I first went there, all those people who made French art and letters at that time so great *were* very much around. But for someone like myself, it was a matter of just being a tourist, like tourists today, and wondering where you were going to stay, how far a dollar would go, whether you could afford two full meals a day or only one. Or how to cram in as many museums as possible. It was exactly the same as to-day, except that today such heroic figures aren't around anymore. Those fa-mous figures, that whole intellectual and artistic world in Paris that still ex-isted in the fifties when I was first there, and mostly could be seen in and around the boulevard Saint-Germain cafés, that's all gone. Now people spot movie stars out shopping.

Long: Didn't you live in San Francisco in the fifties, when the Beats were there?

Ivory: Yes, yes, but *very* briefly. I was making my film, the *Sword and the Flute* documentary, and staying in San Francisco around the time that Allen Gins-berg brought out *Howl.*

Long: Howl was published in 1956.

Ivory: But I never met any of the people who created the Beat movement. My young cameraman, Mindaugis Bagdon, was very aware of all that, though. I remember that I went to City Lights bookstore with him—only a few blocks away from where I was living in North Beach—and bought a copy (I still have it), which I enjoyed. If that's the word you can use for Ginsberg's *Howl.* Yes, I think it is. But it was not possible for . . . I mean, I didn't know anybody who could introduce me to those circles. Again, it was like standing a bit unawares on the sidelines and watching, being present but not present, at an interest-ing moment in American cultural history, just as in Paris. And, strangely, I never met up with Ginsberg in India, or even in New York City, where we both came to live more or less permanently.

Long: Did you live for very long in New York City in those early days?

Ivory: For a while when I was making my first two documentaries, I went back and forth between the East and West Coasts, because I was living in Los Angeles or San Francisco. I would go to New York to shoot in museums and collections, then go back to the West Coast to edit the footage there, and so on; I would bring the finished film here to New York and attempt to sell it. And that's what I did from '57 to '59. . . . No, wait, I actually moved here in '58 and stayed here.

Long: I remember hearing you tell someone that when you were a young man in New York, you stayed at the Plaza Hotel. That's living pretty high for a student.

Ivory: Well, that was not such a big deal. If you had a student card, it cost four dollars a night to stay there. Or you could stay at the Waldorf Astoria, or at a fancy hotel called the Savoy Plaza, which stood where the General Motors building stands now. The Statler Hilton was most favored by college students, who slept six to a room. All you had to do was present your student body card, and it cost four dollars, plus tax. Of course, these obliging hotels, which were all owned for a time by the Hilton chain, had to have rooms. If there was an empty room, you got it. If they didn't, then you were turned away.

Everything about this arrangement was fine, except the problem of what to do with your dirty laundry. It was too expensive to have it done by the hotel, so you had to wash your clothes in an obliging friend's apartment house. Once I was returning in a taxicab with a bundle of clean laundry, and when I stopped in front of the Plaza to get out, the Duchess of Windsor was waiting on the Fifty-ninth Street sidewalk with an elegantly dressed gentleman (not the Duke), who was hailing the cab. I very nearly thrust my bundle into her arms as I scrambled out, awed. She was amused and got into the cab smiling back at me. Don't ask me why she was traveling around New York by cab, I can't tell you.

Long: You must have been aware of the Plaza's status as an icon of East Coast culture.

Ivory: I had read F. Scott Fitzgerald and knew about the Plaza. I was a sort of connoisseur of hotels at that age [*Long laughs*] and loved their various atmospheres, so I particularly liked the Plaza. I remember talking my father into staying at the Plaza when he came to New York in the early sixties. My father was another person who *loved* good hotels and would only go to the best ones. I wanted him to stay at the Plaza because for me by that time it was full of memories of my early experience of New York. He came to town for the premiere of *The Householder,* and I got him a room at the Plaza, but he would only stay there one night. It wasn't good enough [*Long laughs*], and he went to stay at the Saint Regis, and that was OK.

Long: Now in New York in the fifties there were a lot of art movements going on; it was the time of the abstract expressionists . . . of all those painters out on Long Island—Jackson Pollock, Mark Rothko. And the poet Frank

O'Hara had a circle, not only of poets but also of painters. Did you ever brush against any of these people?

Ivory: I did. I did and . . . slightly later than that . . . I was a bit vague about who all these people were. I remember staying with a friend of Frank O'Hara's up in New Hampshire, and Frank O'Hara came to visit. He was a rather sharp-tongued, slightly older man to whom I did not have anything particular to say, or he to me. Nude bathing in a freezing creek was the activity that weekend, and I opted out, though—you may be surprised to hear—I was always throwing all my clothes off back then to run into the water. Another celebrity splashing about in the icy stream was Paul Taylor. Other friends took me to meet Larry Rivers at his house in the Hamptons, and Franz Kline at the Cedar Tavern, the painters' hangout in the Village. Both were on the face of it interesting and even fascinating men, the former especially. But, again, I had very little to offer them. I was a young filmmaker, messing around in Italy and India. I felt then that artists like that weren't much impressed by somebody calling himself a film director; it was a slightly suspicious calling, not serious. Anyway, what had I done so far?

Long: Did you go to the theater very much when you were in New York?

Ivory: Constantly. If everybody was talking about a hit play, I made it my business to get tickets. Fifty years later you have to drag me to the theater.

Long: Have you ever thought of directing for the theater?

Ivory: No, I have never really wanted to, but as I say, I went to the theater all the time when I first moved to New York. It seemed to be a sort of civic duty.

Long: It was a good time to go to the theater.

Ivory: Or was it? I wonder. Those plays seem to me pretty dated now, plays from the fifties that are revived all the time; I go now because I want to please some actor friend who is performing, but the plays don't seem as wonderful as I had remembered them.

Long: There were exciting young stage and film actors then—a long, long list that would begin with Marlon Brando, Montgomery Clift, James Dean . . .

Ivory: There have always been exciting actors. I don't want to sound . . . Luckily with every generation there are clusters of wonderful actors.

Long: Do you think those of today compare with those of the past?

Ivory: Sure.

Long: Did you know people getting started in New York when you yourself were, who didn't impress you particularly at the time but later became famous?

Ivory: I'm constantly meeting people who say, "Don't you remember we met . . . " and they can be very famous people, and I blurt out stupidly, "I'm afraid I don't." John Ashbery was an example of that. He remembers meeting me, but . . . I ought to have been more curious about what other people were doing. I regret that I wasn't more receptive sometimes. This is the second example of my snubbing a poet . . . both times to my regret.

Long: In those early years, did you ever doubt that you would make it? Were you ever despairing?

Ivory: Never. Not for a second. I've never had a period in my life when I felt that I was unsuccessful. Because I was always doing what I wanted to do, not slaving at something I didn't want to do. All of my early professional life, from the time when I met Ismail and before, when I was working on my own making documentaries, I was never thirsting to make feature films (although I was sure that one day I would make them), or feeling that what I was doing was just marking time until I got on to something better. My very first films were my own, and they were very absorbing. I was writing them and photographing them and editing them and the whole thing. I never felt that they were some sort of inferior work, and that I would move on to something better and more exciting and glamorous.

Long: Did your attitude change at all when you teamed up with Ismail and were confronted with some of the harsh realities of making your first feature films?

Ivory: When Ismail and I began to make feature films, it was of course more exhilarating, a more complex world altogether. They were so interesting in themselves that I was never filled with self-doubt, even when we had all our problems, of raising money and so forth, and strings of flops. . . . Year after year we would make a film, and it would flop, and the next one we would make would also flop. But I never felt that I was unsuccessful, or that I was wasting my time. There's a streak in me . . . and it's good that I am like that, that I feel like that, I would be an awful drag otherwise on Ismail, who is so incredibly optimistic and ebullient, and a go-getter. . . . I've always had a kind of mindless faith in what I could do, or could do with someone like Ismail, and I never, ever doubted it.

Long: When *The Householder,* your first feature film, was released, you were about thirty-three or thirty-four, correct?

Ivory: No, thirty-five.

Long: And this was a defining moment in your life.

Ivory: Well, I didn't see it as that at the time. I didn't realize that it was a defining moment. It was fun, and we were doing it . . .

Long: And you became, in John Pym's phrase, "the wandering company." Thomas Mann sometimes refers in his fiction to artist figures as "gypsies traveling in a green wagon." In Germany, with its great burgher class, an artist is necessarily alienated and a gypsy.

Ivory: That's very true. That's a good description. And not just in Germany.

Long: You may have had something in common with your touring players in *Shakespeare Wallah.* Have you ever thought, by the way, of doing a film from Shakespeare?

Ivory: Yes, I have.

Long: Any particular play?

Ivory: Only one. *Richard II.*

Long: Now that is something I would like to see. . . . But let's go back to your meeting with Ismail, and your becoming partners in a filmmaking venture. How long has it been that Merchant Ivory films have been in existence? Do you date your anniversaries from the time that you and Ismail first met in New York and decided to become a filmmaking team, or from the release of *The Householder* in 1963?

Ivory: Before the release we had to *make The Householder.* I would say that making *The Householder* was what made us and made the company.

Long: You've passed your fortieth anniversary, then.

Ivory: Well, yes. Ismail and I met in '61 . . . in the spring of '61, and by the end of the year we had embarked on *The Householder.*

Long: You've said that when you first went to India, you fell in love with the country. What attracted you most about India?

Ivory: You have to recognize it in my movies. If you see my Indian movies, then you get some idea of what it was that attracted me about India and Indians. It's not that I am dodging the question. It's just that any explanation would sound lamer than the thing warrants. The mood was so great and overwhelming that any explanation of it would seem physically thin, and so I think the only way . . . I put all my feeling about India into several Indian films, and if you know those films and like them, you see from these films what it was that attracted me to India.

Long: What was New Delhi like in those days compared to what it is like today?

Ivory: People think it's horrendous now, with the pollution, gigantic overcrowding, and all the rest of it. But when I first encountered it, it was, I don't know, a wonderful place, a beautiful city that was modern and old, with great atmospherics of light. And with very handsome, lively people who were easy to get to know.

Long: Did you know much about India when you first went there?

Ivory: No, I was wide-eyed and ignorant. . . . I was the same there as I was when I first arrived in Paris or Venice. I didn't know anything. I mean, I was receptive, I did learn a lot. Where India is concerned, I am a very self-educated or self-taught person. Once I met Ruth and her husband, and Ismail, and Shashi Kapoor, and so many other friends, then, of course, they taught me plenty. But until I met them, for instance, during my first trip to India, I didn't really have that many close friends and had to manage on my own. It was only when I went back for the second time and began to work with Ismail that the place really opened up.

Long: Were you interested in Indian architecture before you went to India?

Ivory: I became interested in Moghul architecture only when I first actually saw it. Before that I had only seen pictures of it. When I got to India, I began to visit the great Moghul monuments, and of course the Hindu ones too. But that's an ongoing thing with me. I've still not seen some of the greatest Indian sights after all my trips. Ajanta and Ellora, for instance. And now when I go there I mostly spend my time reacquainting myself with the places I first saw forty years ago.

Long: Satyajit Ray enters into the making of *The Householder.* How did you ever win him over into helping you make your first film?

Ivory: Ray wasn't a forbidding man in any way. He was a very friendly, encouraging kind of man. I had seen *Pather Panchali* at the San Francisco Film Festival and was bowled over by it. That was when I was making my second documentary, *The Sword and the Flute,* about Indian miniature painting. I had never been to India. The closest thing to being in India that I had known up to that time was seeing Renoir's film *The River.* Then I moved to New York and saw the second film in Ray's Apu series, which was *Aparajito.* In time I was given a grant by the Asia Society to make a short film in Delhi, which would be about the city, about its history, about Delhi the place—a kind of portrait, like my first film in that respect had been, the Venice film. I met Indians in Delhi who told me that Ray had made not only his trilogy but also two other films, one of which was wonderful, called *The Music Room.* I said, "How can I see it?" I was on my way to Calcutta at that time, and they said, "Just call him up, he's in the phone book."

Long: The "Apu trilogy" had already brought him worldwide fame. It's amazing to think of your being able to just ring him up on the phone.

Ivory: That's what I did. When I got to Calcutta, I just called him, and he answered the phone. I told him that I was an American filmmaker making a documentary in India and had heard about his film *The Music Room,* and was there by any chance a print around, or could he arrange it for me, and this kind of thing, and he said, "Sure, I can fix it up right away." We agreed to meet, and I did meet him in a coffeehouse in Calcutta, where he was pacing up and down because at that very moment his film *The Goddess (Devi)* was being seen by the censors, and he was afraid (it was an absolutely scathing look at religion turned to superstition run amok) that the censors wouldn't like it. He smoked madly, and we drank coffee and stuff, and then somebody came running in and said that the censors had seen it and there would be no cuts. Everything was fine.

Long: So then you were able to see *The Music Room?*

Ivory: He arranged for me to see *The Music Room* out at the studio in Tolleygunj where he had his editing room and where he would occasionally shoot something. He and I saw it together. It had no subtitles, so he sat next to me and explained the story as we went along. I was absolutely bowled over by that movie as well, still am to this day, and I see it again and again. I have a tape of all the music (and I think I have a tape of the whole sound track), which I play in the car. When the film was finished and the lights came up, I told him that I loved his film, that it was a marvelous thing, and so on.

Long: Did Ray say how he himself regarded the film?

Ivory: When I asked him why *The Music Room* had never been shown in the West, he said, "Oh, you know, I don't think it's all that good. Technically it's sort of awkward." Then he said that he had shown it at the Moscow Film Festival, and the Russians had dismissed it as "decadent." But he did wish that it might be shown in the West, and his New York distributor, Ed Harrison, did eventually take the plunge. However, that's a whole other story.

DOCUMENTARIES,
1952–1972

Robert Emmet Long: Were there others in the United States and abroad making documentaries like yours while you were at the USC film school in the early fifties?

James Ivory: There weren't that many, perhaps, but enough to make up a kind of subgenre. That was a time when people liked to make films about artists and works of art. One of the attractions was that they didn't cost much money to make. You had to choose a theme carefully and then usually concentrate on one work of art, and explain it and analyze it. Your audience was in museums, schools, and once in a while in theaters. Those were the days when shorts were still shown along with a feature in art houses.

Long: Were there some memorable documentaries being made using artworks as their subject?

Ivory: There was one called *Image Médiéval,* which was very good. It was made from illuminated manuscripts . . . wonderful film. There were others. A terrific film on syphilis I saw that was made by George Stoney, using all kinds of prints and photographs. People would use works of art to tell other kinds of stories. I remember there was an interesting guy in the USC cinema school named Ray Wisniewski who made a film using Aztec works of art—all sorts of Aztec sculpture and painted pots and so on. It was called, I think, *The Feathered Serpent,* about the god Quetzalcoatl. In the midfifties Henri-Georges Clouzot made a well-known documentary about Picasso, which was called *Le Mystère Picasso* and was photographed by Claude Renoir, the grandson of Auguste. It was a period in which that kind of thing was being done, and it was

quite a respectable way of working; it was a viable way to begin because, as I
say, you didn't have to spend a lot of money on it. You found an interesting
way to shoot the works of art, and you could postulate anything you wanted.
You could tell a sort of history, as I did in my Venice film, or describe a *kind* of
art, as I did in *The Sword and the Flute,* or concentrate on a living master like Picasso or Alexander Calder. More recently Philip Haas has done this, too, concentrating on the contemporary British artists.

Long: I'd particularly like to know about the very first film you ever made,
the documentary *Venice: Theme and Variations.* It was your initiation into filmmaking. You've said that when you began the film you "didn't know anything
about Venetian painting, or the history of Venice as such." What, then, possessed you to do the film?

Ivory: I really, rather selfishly or self-indulgently, I suppose, wanted to go
back to Venice. I went there for the first time when I was twenty-two. I stayed
only four days, but I was absolutely dumbstruck by the
place—its beauty, its atmosphere, and the sheer idea
of such a magical city on the water. When I was back in
Southern California following my Italian trip and en-
rolled at the USC film school, it kept haunting me. What
a wonderful, fantastic place it was! I schemed to find a
reason to go back there. So I concocted the idea of
making a film about it, although I couldn't exactly say
what form it would take.

Long: But even at the beginning it was to have something to do with painting . . .

Ivory: I had seen the many gigantic paintings in Venice, which often told
the story of Venice: a kind of allegorical, or even historical, account of the
city, its rise and fall . . . not so much its fall but certainly its rise. And having seen these pictures, without any technical expertise to back it up, I had
the idea that I could also perhaps tell the story of Venice on film by showing these grand paintings by artists like Veronese and Tintoretto, and by later
artists as well. I drew up a proposal for the faculty at the USC film school,
and they agreed to accept the film as my master's thesis. There was no fund

to underwrite the making of the documentary, but my father put up the money for it.

Long: Was there much money involved in the making of this film?

Ivory: Not a lot. I had to buy a tripod and camera (a 16-millimeter Bolex), some film stock, and a light meter. That was about it. I didn't prepare myself any better than that; I should have, but I didn't. I went back to Venice for six months, and it was as wonderful as I had remembered. And it was wonderful shooting there, wandering around with my camera. There were places where I needed assistance, such as when I worked in the Accademia Museum—the main picture gallery of Venice.

Long: Why was that?

Ivory: I was filming some of the paintings I had seen earlier, which had excited me—or inspired me—but I found it practically impossible to do it well without a more elaborate setup. If I panned across a picture, I needed an assistant to follow focus. I didn't have anybody like that. I needed people to help me with the lighting. I needed electricians. These paintings were vast, and being dark they swallowed up vast amounts of light. I rented six huge lights from a defunct film studio in Venice called the Scalera Studio and brought them into the museum and set them up. The Accademia gave me people to help me with the lighting. I also needed more light when I was shooting the Byzantine mosaics in Saint Mark's Basilica. I really couldn't photograph them very well. Some of them were on ceilings or in completely out-of-the-way places. These Venetian churches were almost totally dark, and there was no way for me to light them or to bring enough lights in there. So I would say that about three-quarters of my idea about telling the story of Venice through its art was unrealizable for me.

Long: You went unprepared.

Ivory: I went as an amateur, but what came out of it, with luck, was something very nice. It was an amateur's first film, basically. I spent the whole winter in Venice and then returned to California and began to try to put together all that I had shot. My teachers at USC were aghast because I had failed to grasp, or even notice, the difference between silent speed (sixteen frames per second) and sound speed (twenty-four frames) in motion picture photography. I had

shot everything at silent speed. Perhaps I imagined I was being more eco-
nomical with my film stock. Or, again, as I had no sound recording equipment,
I must have thought the word "silent" referred to what I was doing. A lot of
the exterior scenes of Venice, for instance, having been shot at silent speed,
looked like old movies. At Saint Mark's Square you saw the crowd walking
across very fast. But this faster speed was actually helpful in more abstract exterior shots, as with gondolas. You know, if you see a gondola crossing a la-
goon at sound speed, it may take a long time, but with the "faster" speed of
silent film it is actually a better shot. The gondoliers seem to be poling along
more energetically. I gradually discovered all of this as I went along.

Long: But you went back to Venice again.

Ivory: I had a second chance to go back to Venice when I was drafted into
the army. I was sent to Germany instead of Korea; by that time the Korean
fighting was over. While I was stationed in Germany, I made trips to Venice,
taking along my camera and equipment, and corrected some of my earlier mistakes and shot more footage—this time at sound speed. But my original idea
for the film wasn't going to work somehow. I really couldn't exploit the big
pictures, like Veronese's gigantic wedding feast in the Accademia, which was
a disappointment, a loss even.

Long: So now the documentary was to be about certain artists' views of
Venice that capture the city in the passage of time.

Ivory: Yes. This new idea came about after discussions with my faculty adviser at USC, Lester Novros. Before I was drafted into the army, he had viewed
most of my footage and saw possibilities in it. He was a very good teacher and
a professional filmmaker himself, specializing in documentaries. So I went to
work on this new idea, made a storyboard (painting all the pictures myself),
which was allowed to be pinned up on a huge board in Novros's offices, and
which I kept arranging and rearranging. Finally we came up with a scheme—
one which required some additional shooting. Luckily, there are many Venetian pictures in American museums, as well as many others depicting Venice
by different artists, such as Whistler, Monet, and Saul Steinberg. After I got
out of the army, I went back to work. So finally we had something of the rise
of Venice, but we had no golden age (which would have been Tintoretto,

Veronese, and Titian), and then we had the decline. That was a rather magnificent omission, as a friend of mine pointed out. There was a very interesting rise and a very interesting, you could say, fading away of Venice's grandeur, finally arriving at what we see today with Saul Steinberg.

Long: I understand that you knew Saul Steinberg personally.

Ivory: Well, I eventually met him. I found out where he lived in New York, and I called him up. I don't know who gave me the telephone number. I wanted to show him what I had already shot from his Venetian drawings that had been reproduced. I didn't really shoot directly from his works at first. I took some out of books, and I put these into the film without even asking his permission. At any rate, when the film was more or less finished, I showed it to him, and he liked it very much. He invited me to dinner at his house on East Seventy-first Street, and there was this extraordinary meal where there were many famous people present. Janet Flanner and John Betjeman, the writer Niccola Tucci, Anthony West, Betty Parsons, people like that. I was put down at one end of the table with the wives of the famous men, but I can remember piping up from time to time with some observation, and all these famous faces swiveling in my direction, in surprise, I suppose, that I had something to say. It was almost as if the cat had spoken. It was my first New York dinner party of that kind.

Long: Did you see him again after that?

Ivory: Steinberg liked me and allowed me to see all of his drawings that he had put away; he had a lot of stuff about Venice which hadn't been published. And so I did some more photography, and I put that in my film as well. We remained good friends for the next few years, and I saw him off and on for the rest of his life. In fact, we got involved in another film project later on which was never completed: a trip across America from New York to Santa Monica, by way of his drawings. He had done many fine, moody watercolors of various parts of the country: New York of course, the Midwest, the South, California. Some of his views were even through a car windshield. All of this I actually shot on 16 millimeter. Several thousand feet. But when I asked him to actually draw for the camera, photographing his pen going in the ink bottle and so on and then on to paper, he refused. He said it would bore him to do that; it would not be spontaneous. So I had to give up the project midway, since I felt his existing drawings of America were not enough. Years later he told me, on reflection, that he had been wrong and that he wished he'd cooperated. By that time I was doing features, one after the other, and his own art had developed in ways that were less figurative and much more abstract. I still feel that he was America's greatest living draftsman at that time, and that he is much underrated. I once advised the publisher of a leading art magazine in New York to go to a show of new Steinberg drawings, and he exclaimed: "What? That cartoonist?"

Long: There's a scene you use from Steinberg's *Piazza, San Marco, Venice, 1951,* which enlivens the film considerably and has a strong cartoonish quality, together with a sense of modernity, élan, and mystery. In a way Steinberg even steals the film.

Ivory: Well, as I've said, I've always thought of Saul Steinberg as one of the greatest draftsman/artists of modern times. I put him way up at the top, and I don't think of him merely as a cartoonist who did the occasional *New Yorker* cover. He reminds me in the kinds of things he did of Paul Klee and sometimes of Picasso. He could draw abstract ideas and states of mind, a bit like Magritte, but much wittier. I wasn't putting him in the film for funny, cartoony reasons. I did think we ought to lighten up the film at the end with him because what he did in Venice was also expressive of modern life generally. His particular take on modern Venice seemed to be sharper than anybody else's. He was only interested in Venice as a subject for two or three years and then dropped it. I don't know of anybody else since who's done anything on Venice as interesting, or who is on the same level of sophistication. . . . Of course you have to remember that his drawings, when you isolate small bits of them and blow them up . . . bits taken, say, from a huge panoramic view of a lot of people in Saint Mark's Square . . . a close-up of two men arguing, or a tango musician, or whatever . . . they completely fill the screen, and the effect is very dramatic. As imagery it's as dynamic as a Picasso drawing, very strong. That was true of many, many artists that I photographed for the film. Of the eighteenth-century artist Guardi also. The figures that Guardi drew in Saint Mark's Square, how full of life they are! They had such immediacy and at the same time are so abstract. Just some squiggles, like figures on a Chinese scroll.

Long: How do you feel about Venice today? Do you often go back there?

Ivory: As often as I can. I'm always happy when one of our films is invited to the Venice Film Festival. Then I go and stay as long as I can. As at Cannes, we rent some sort of palazzo and fill it up with friends, and Ismail gives big parties, which end up running out of food because so many people crash them—though it's never as bad in that way as at Cannes. Perhaps it's because people have to get to our palazzo by boat. Anyway, Venice is still up on my A-list of favorite cities, along with Paris and New York. See how faithful I am! Only San Francisco has slipped a bit in my affections.

Long: You were inspired to make *The Sword and the Flute* documentary when you came across a collection of Indian miniature paintings at Raymond Lewis's art gallery in San Francisco. Was seeing these miniatures your first exposure to this kind of painting?

Ivory: My very first. And I can't help asking myself: What if the previous client of Raymond Lewis had been someone with an interest in, say, Japanese woodblock prints, which Ray also specialized in, and hadn't asked to see his Indian miniatures? And what if, after viewing them, all spread out on a big table, he had left an hour before I'd come in there and not just a few minutes, and there had been time to put them all back in their drawers? But no—this is Fate at work—the gallery was littered with them, sort of gleaming on every available surface. Maybe I'd even passed that collector on the stairs going out. He changed my life as surely as anything ever did—probably in the most profound way of all. Seeing those miniature paintings on that day had an effect on all the rest of my days.

Long: Had you been drawn to other kinds of Indian art, or to Indian literature, or even Indian religion?

Ivory: At that time I knew virtually nothing about India and its history, or its art and music. It was a new world for me entirely. If I'd seen an Indian miniature somewhere, I probably lumped it in with Persian painting—as most people do.

Long: You photographed a number of different Indian miniature paintings

from museums and private collections, but was there any collection of particular importance to you, or any individual who provided you with guidance?

Ivory: There was the Raymond Lewis collection, of course, in San Francisco—
all of it for sale. He also dealt in European old master and Japanese prints. He
gave me some guidance as to subject matter, dates, schools. In those days—
the mid-1950s—the whole subject of Indian miniature painting was yet to
come under the scrutiny of art historians. There was a lot of guesswork, both
as to schools and as to dates. Outside of Ray Lewis's collection, there were very
good pictures at the Freer Gallery in Washington, D.C., in Boston, and at the
Met. But the connoisseurship came later on.

Long: In preparing *The Sword and the Flute,* did any special problems come up?

Ivory: One of them had to do with the actual miniatures that I was using in
the film. My knowledge of them was limited, and my initial selection was also
limited. I didn't always have the best pictures—exactly like a novice art collector with uninformed enthusiasm who goes out to put
together a collection of something or other. I didn't realize that there were often better examples of what I was
shooting out there.

THE SWORD AND
THE FLUTE

*An evocation of contrasting
worlds, both Muslim and
Hindu, secular and spiritual,
of Indian miniature painting.
1959. Documentary. 16
millimeter; color; 24 minutes.*

Long: So what did you do?

Ivory: I kept shooting and reshooting—upgrading—
as I learned more. My eye became more discerning. Like
a collector's, in fact.

Long: You had the advantage of having accompa-
nying music by Ravi Shankar and Ali Akbar Khan,
which was very stirring and heightened the excitement of viewing the miniatures. How did you happen to meet them, and how well did you know them
by then?

Ivory: The first long-play records of Indian music came out in the United States
at exactly the time I got interested in Ray Lewis's pictures and was deciding to
make a film out of them. I bought the records—only three or four were available at first—and listened to them a lot until my ear became accustomed to this
new kind of music. Then Ravi Shankar turned up in Los Angeles in order to
play concerts, and I somehow got in touch with him. It wasn't any more difficult

than meeting Satyajit Ray was to be a few years later. Great Indian maestros are very open—openhearted, open to ideas. Or at least mine were.

Long: How big are the miniatures? It is hard to tell because you can enlarge them when you photograph them. But a scene in one of the paintings shows a figure giving an album of his miniatures to the ruler, and it is small enough to hold in his hand.

Ivory: They can vary in size, say, a playing card, up to a foot in height or even more. The tiniest are hardly bigger than a postage stamp—little Moghul drawings, for instance, or minute portraits of a ruler. If they're very fine in execution, they do hold up to enlargement.

Long: The Sword and the Flute is only twenty-four minutes long but seems longer because there is so much richness to absorb. What reaction was there when you first showed it publicly, and where was it seen?

Ivory: I think I first showed it in the two California cities where I'd done the most work on it—Los Angeles and San Francisco. Then New York. Everyone loved it at once. That kind of painting was as new to everybody else as it had been to me.

Long: It's an extraordinary film. The paintings you show in it belong to an exotic world remote from us in time, but I've also felt something modern about them. For instance, the artists work with very bold primary colors, especially reds and blacks, which you also see in the work of Matisse and Picasso. And sometimes these bold colors, together with rugged landscapes and the stylized leaves of trees, make me think of Gauguin. Did the Indian miniatures, in fact, exert an influence on modern artists?

Ivory: I don't really think so. As I said, they weren't so well known in the West until recently, though it's interesting that Rembrandt did some drawings after Moghul miniatures he'd seen in a European collection. Also the Hapsburgs were collectors of Indian eighteenth-century drawings, which they papered all over the walls of one of their palaces in Vienna.

Long: One of the most prominent features of the documentary is your interest in storytelling. Isn't this something it has in common with the Venice film?

Ivory: I felt that, as far as I was able, I had to enlighten my public. There wasn't room in such a short film to really elaborate on the artistic and philosophic

basis of many of the pictures I used; I had to sketch it in somewhat roughly—
the worlds within worlds contained in the Rajput pictures, which usually had
a religious as well as a secular content. The content of the religious pictures
was unvarying, from school to school, period to period, the same as in Western art—or as in, say, the life of Christ, scenes from the Old Testament, or
Greek and Roman antiquity.

Long: Your interest in storytelling is also reflected in the dramatic contrast
you set up between the two different schools of painting in the miniatures—
the Rajput and the Moghul, both of which came into being in the sixteenth
century.

Ivory: With the Moghul pictures I was on surer ground. They were almost
entirely secular, had often been painted to record some event or the exploits
of the Moghuls as they pacified India. Exact portraiture was important, but
being Muhammadan, the more populous scenes were rarely of a religious nature, perhaps because of the strictures of Islam on image making. Both in Per-
sia and in India all sorts of usually forbidden image making went on, but as I
say, though there might be a poetic content to some Moghul works, it was almost never devotional, unlike Hindu—or Rajput—painting. For convenience
you could say that Rajput painting tends to the spiritual, while Moghul depicts
the more immediate material world. But also, Hindu painters worked for the
Moghul emperors, painting their many albums, just as Muhammadan painters
did not shrink from doing Hindu subjects that were basically devotional—
and, to them, idolatrous. There was a great synthesis in Indian art then. It was
a golden age in many, many ways. And the synthesis existed in life generally,
in all sorts of ways in human relations.

Long: One of the most fascinating moments in the film for me was when
you show a miniature painting of foreign visitors at Akbar's court, who include
a Jesuit missionary and an English gentleman in Elizabethan garb, complete
with an elaborate white ruff and a plumed hat. One suddenly understands that
Akbar was a contemporary of William Shakespeare and that the miniatures
we are seeing at that point in your film were painted when Shakespeare's plays
were first presented at the Globe Theatre in London. But would it be fair to
say that *The Sword and the Flute* is less concerned with the linkages of history

than with making a statement about two Indian schools of painting, and perhaps also with enthralling the viewer?

Ivory: I think my concerns were to show something that had come to interest me, that I thought beautiful and mysterious: the whole world of Indian miniature painting and its relationship to Indian life then, and to Indian mythology. I was less interested in an exact historic presentation of how these complementary schools of Indian painting had come about. I've never been much interested in that sort of thing.

Long: I can't help but wonder if you may own some Indian miniatures yourself. Do you?

Ivory: Yes, indeed. A few of them even show up in *The Sword and the Flute*. How could I resist buying them? I'll tell you a story about this: I bought two miniatures from Ray Lewis in 1956. They were from the same eighteenth-century album, called a *ragmala*—that is, depictions of poetic moods. Their combined cost was two hundred fifty dollars; more than thirty years later, one of these was stolen from me and has never come to light. A couple of years back there was an auction of Indian miniatures at Christie's in New York, and two more pages from the same album were being sold. All four had been photographed for *The Sword and the Flute*. I bought one of them at Christie's—was the successful bidder—and had to pay ten thousand dollars for it, plus the premium and the New York City tax. But I'm awfully glad to have it and should have bought it in 1956. It shows an old holy man with long, long hair and beard sitting among rocks by a waterfall in the wilderness. The painter has worked all sorts of strange faces into the design of the rocks. It's a fine thing and sort of replaces the one that was stolen, which showed a mostly naked woman in communion with friendly serpents, also sitting among rocks (with strange faces).

Long: When you received grant money to shoot films in India and Afghanistan, what made you decide to focus your attention on Delhi in your next documentary, *The Delhi Way*?

Ivory: It was the idea of Paul Sherbert, the head of the Asia Society in New York. He and his associates, who passed out money for grants, had seen both my film on Venice and *The Sword and the Flute*. So a portrait of Delhi was a natural and would combine the techniques of both films. I didn't have to be persuaded.

Long: As I understand it, the roots of the city go back to before 2000 B.C.; by the time the British arrived in the nineteenth century, seven cities had already flourished on the site. In view of your antiquarian interests as a child, was one of the attractions of Delhi as a film subject that it was a modern city which was not only old but also immensely old?

THE DELHI WAY

A portrait of the ancient capital of Delhi, with live-action and archival footage, nineteenth-century photographs and engravings, and Moghul miniature paintings. 1964. Documentary. 16 millimeter; color; 50 minutes.

Ivory: I suppose that was mainly it. It is old in the way Calcutta and Bombay are not, and old in the way Rome is, another city that has always fascinated me. I went to see *The Gladiator* twice; none of my friends could understand why, or why I voted for it for Best Picture at Oscar time. The evocation of ancient Rome in that film was stupendous; I could relate to it as to one of my own films. The set designers had great flair. Even if purists could say that something—some detail—was wrong, it was still imaginatively right. I was thrilled by it—as I was with the sinking of the *Titanic* (but only the sinking) in James Cameron's film, which I also voted for at Oscar time for Best Picture (over the objection of friends who cried, "Oh, no, Jim, you *can't!*"). But I've gotten way off the subject . . .

Long: When you shot the film, you were capturing Delhi at a particular moment in time, that is, in 1960, or about thirteen years after India became an independent nation. The city's population was then about two and a half million. Today it is something like twelve million. If your documentary were made today, would it be significantly different from the one you made in 1960?

Ivory: Sadly, yes. Delhi is one of the most polluted cities in the world—on a sort of cosmic scale, like Mexico City is said to be. From the air there is a dense brown haze spreading for miles and miles, far into the desert, where it merges with the cloud over Jaipur, in Rajasthan. Apart from that, life on the ground seems much the same, has the same interest as always, and for the same reasons. The streets are packed with people and traffic, scooters and rickshaws and huge, overloaded trucks and dilapidated, overloaded buses blowing out

Ivory shooting some performing bears and "bear wallahs" from the Red Fort in New Delhi, India, 1960, for his documentary *The Delhi Way* (1964).

clouds of diesel exhaust, amidst which stray cows make their way, or stately bullocks, with lordly testicles: India.

Long: Mira Nair's movie *Monsoon Wedding* not only is set in present-day Delhi but also is a valentine to Delhi as a city with a splashy vitality, a breathtaking skyline, brilliant sunsets, great music and dance, and a warm humanity. This is quite a different view of Delhi than the one in your own more reflective documentary.

Ivory: My film concentrated more on the Delhi of the British Raj, and the Delhi of the Moghuls and the aftermath: in other words, a very Muslim culture. Mira Nair's film is about well-off Punjabis (mostly Hindu and Sikh), about the new Delhi of postindependence, and the new people who took over the city and now dominate it. Today Muslims are somewhat beleaguered, even in Delhi, and very few signs of the British Raj remain, apart from architectural ones. And of course the English language.

Long: How would you say that Delhi has a distinctive character of its own, as compared to, say, Calcutta or Bombay?

Ivory: I always used to think that to take a plane between those two cities was a bit like flying between Boston and Los Angeles—roughly speaking, between the life of the mind and the life of the senses. I don't know if I would feel that way now. It's been years since I was in Calcutta.

Long: In his 1970 film documentary *Calcutta,* Louis Malle roamed all over the subcontinent with a cameraman and a sound engineer, filming at random with a 16-millimeter camera. Malle called India "that paradise of the exotic" and said that his exposure to it "really changed my life." When you roamed through India and Afghanistan with a camera a decade earlier, did you also feel that your travels were a life-changing experience?

Ivory: You know, these kinds of insights come later, if at all. I can't say that roaming around Afghanistan changed my life; it was a short detour, a side trip. Obviously, setting foot on Indian soil for the first time was to dramatically alter my life, but in 1959, knowing Ismail and Ruth lay ahead. They, together with India, changed my life. When I turned up in India for the first time, I was maybe like all those wide-eyed young Englishmen who went out to India in the eighteenth and nineteenth centuries to make their fortunes. I didn't make any fortune, but it was very much my *good* fortune to find Ismail and Ruth.

Long: Early in *The Delhi Way* two images appear that might be quotations from Satyajit Ray—a sepia-toned scene in which a train moves along a field in darkness, and a moment in which, at the break of dawn, a vast number of birds take flight against the backdrop of an ancient building of monumental scale. Why would you be invoking Ray, if you were, at the beginning of the film?

Ivory: These kinds of images are quintessentially, inescapably Indian. It wasn't that I was consciously invoking Ray. That would have come later, after the discovery of what I had shot (I never saw my footage until I went back to New York), and when, very consciously, I could experiment with music in the editing room, trying out this and that against the images. Then I was certainly thinking of Ray.

Long: Between shooting the earlier and the later footage for *The Delhi Way,* you made *The Householder*. Both of these films have Delhi as their setting. Is the perspective you bring to the two films similar, or is it in some way different?

Ivory: The Householder was a narrowing of the focus on workaday life of contemporary Indians, moving closer up to it; moving from the streets of *The Delhi Way* and from shooting anonymous strangers, into the bedroom, where we concentrated on individual lives and their intimacies and came to know what our subjects were thinking.

Long: There is quite a bit about the Raj in *The Delhi Way*, making it your first foray into the subject. The modern part of the city was built by the British, who created New Delhi on a grand scale, with great parks and gardens and very broad avenues that led to the imposing Viceregal Palace. You have also re-created the period of the British Empire in India by photographing prints and paintings of the 1857 Indian Mutiny and incorporating ancient footage of the royal visit in 1911, complete with British troops passing in review on horseback before King George V and Queen Mary. Was the Raj period one of the highlights of the documentary for you?

Ivory: I think it was, without my quite knowing it. At that time I had almost never been to England and knew almost no English men or women. I seemed to have little curiosity about them. But staying on and working in India led to making many English friends, and their Indian connection was something *I* connected with. I never questioned their right to be there. The pros and cons of colonialism meant nothing to me. As an American, I think I even asked, feeling a kind of smugness, why the Indians took so long to throw the British out. When I first came to read *A Passage to India*, I never burned with fury at the awfulness of the English in India. Now I do.

Long: The Delhi Way presents a myriad of images evoking contradiction and contrast. We see scores of civil servants bicycling to their offices to begin a day's work, while a solitary, nearly naked beggar sits by the roadside, nodding by a tree. At a height above the city we see an ancient mosque overrun on all sides by a swarming market center. In a Moghul miniature we see the legendary Peacock Throne, encrusted with jewels, and then a billboard celebrating the latest Bombay movie star. What response to this portrait of a city are you calling up on the part of the viewer?

Ivory: To share in my own delight, I think: the ever-changing Indian urban scene, which is endlessly fascinating and is a mixture of timeless India and an encroaching modernization—even Americanization—of the place.

Long: You also spent time in Afghanistan, which in more recent times became a Russian and then an American battleground. I wonder if you would comment on your wanderings with a camera in Afghanistan at the beginning of the 1960s.

Ivory: I probably wouldn't have gone there at all if there hadn't been a small catch to the Asia Society grant. I was supposed to make *two* documentaries with my twenty thousand dollars, and their idea was that I should go to a neighboring country for the second one. That meant Pakistan, Ceylon, or Afghanistan—the latter being the most distant and most different from India, I thought. As it was getting hot in Delhi—it was May—I quite pragmatically decided to go somewhere cool. But I had no preparation at all. And no plan or scenario. There was one city in Afghanistan that was not impossibly remote, and that was Kabul. There were few comforts, virtually none of the luxuries the traveler can find in India, like well-run hotels and delicious, subtle meals. The language was a dialect of Persian, so communication, too, was difficult. But still I went and somehow enjoyed myself. I decided to make a film about all the people living along the Kabul River and its tributaries. I knew nothing about these people—mostly farmers and nomads—or the river. Like a kind of specimen hunter with a butterfly net, I would light down among my subjects and start filming. Nobody seemed to mind; I seem never to have transgressed or to have given offense. I knew not to photograph the women, except as mysterious figures shrouded in the billowy yards of their chadors, from afar. Unlike my experience in India, I made no close friends. I wanted to, very much, but no one came forward. Seen now, my footage is evocative. It shows Afghanistan somehow idyllically; the shots are like the corners of Persian miniatures, off beyond the main figures, and in the margins next to the text: old men in turbans sitting by a torrent or pulling purple fruit down out of mulberry trees and staining their white beards; crowds of other men at Bakra Iid haggling in a bazaar, or crossing the Kabul River on a swaying footbridge of planks and rope, the long, long sleeves of their silk coats blowing in the wind;

workers painstakingly making brick as in ancient times, near a ziggurat-shaped kiln out of which clouds of black smoke billowed. When I got back to New York, I could find no way to shape this material into something coherent. It exists as a purely visual record of a lost world. I had no sound crew to record the sounds, speech, and music that would have made it immediate. Twenty years later the Russians invaded. You know all the rest.

Long: Adventures of a Brown Man in Search of Civilization is a fifty-four-minute documentary of yours about the Indian writer-scholar Nirad Chaudhuri, who was then living in Oxford. Why did you think, when the BBC approached you about doing it, that Chaudhuri would be a good subject for a documentary?

Ivory: It was also to be my first film outside India, apart from my earlier documentaries. I suppose making a sort of "profile" film of this delightful Indian gentleman seemed to be a sort of easier transition. The film was maybe as eccentric as he was, with its non-stop monologues, the alternate scolding of the undergraduates he encountered during the filming, or his cranky/touching attempts to improve their minds, lift them up—all the while showing off, sometimes in his red velvet frock coat, waving and pointing his tiny hands in the air.

Long: Ruth knew Chaudhuri at least a bit in Delhi, and you and Ismail had met him once or twice, so you must have had some idea of what he was like. As the central figure in the documentary, did he turn out to be any different from what you had expected?

ADVENTURES OF A BROWN MAN IN SEARCH OF CIVILIZATION

A portrait—or profile— of the diminutive but super-charged Indian writer Nirad Chaudhuri, shot in London and Oxford. 1972. Documentary. 16 millimeter; color; 54 minutes.

Ivory: Actually, we were barely acquainted, so I didn't know what I was getting into. He was a great favorite of Ruth and Jhab, her husband. He used to invite them to elaborate dinner parties in his little flat perched on the Old Delhi city wall. He brought out vintage French wines—God knows where he got them—and made toasts in Latin. All this sort of thing was reported in detail to us. And then I read *Autobiography of an Unknown Indian* by the time we were hired by the BBC to make the film (I think they contributed five thousand pounds).

Nirad Chaudhuri, dressed up for a dinner party in London,
1971, during the filming of *Adventures of a Brown Man in
Search of Civilization* (1972).

Long: You've said yourself that Chaudhuri, as he appears in the documentary, is an eccentric. He is a tiny, delicately built man, barely five feet tall, who
pronounces on a variety of subjects as if he were infallible. When he saw the
documentary, how did he feel about your presentation of him?

Ivory: You may not know that the film was first broadcast by the BBC on
April Fool's Day, 1973. This made him cackle with laughter, but I think he liked
it well enough. You know, he would hold forth on various grand topics—maybe
he was trying out ideas for some book—and once in a while he'd get something wrong, some fact or other which by some miracle I knew about. But you

could not correct him or introduce your own ideas on these topics. He seemed not to hear you and to roll right on, or wrong on, I should say.

Long: In one sequence he walks down a street gesticulating and explaining his views on Indian and English culture, accompanied by a *very* tall Englishman; and together they look like a giant and a dwarf. I know you feel that you treated Chaudhuri respectfully, but can you say that there isn't a very droll quality in this scene?

Ivory: Well of course it's droll—and he was aware of this possibility and certainly played along. Why else wear an eighteenth-century velvet frock coat to a modern dinner party? He was having fun, or it was his own contribution to the fancy-dress of swinging London then. He loved to puncture the ideas of the young men he was meeting; one of them was the articulate George Trow of the *New Yorker,* representative of a decadent America, who was skewered in midsentence by Chaudhuri but was too polite to contradict his elder.

Long: You not only directed the documentary but also wrote the script. I wondered what you had him say, since he seemed to be improvising, to be unscripted throughout the picture.

Ivory: I couldn't tell him what to say or prompt him; we just set the camera going, and he'd perform, spinning out all sorts of fantastical ideas. For instance, that he gave up a vegetarian diet at age fifty in order to have the physical strength to write, and that a writer can only produce if he has this source of protein. He would run down Indian classical music, talk about its repetitiveness, which was also due to the musician's poor diet. But he must have known that many North Indian maestros aren't vegetarians and exist on a diet of kabobs, rice, and energizing dal.

Long: How would you rate Nirad Chaudhuri as an actor playing himself?

Ivory: Well, as I've said, I can't think of a more delightful old man that we've ever put on the screen. But he is exhausting, too. You have to listen to him very carefully to get what he's saying. He had a habit of putting the stresses on the wrong syllable in English sometimes. He used not only big words with many syllables he could get wrong but also words that one hears only rarely. So it could be almost like listening to a foreign language.

Long: I couldn't make out everything he said because the sound track wasn't

all that clear, although I imagine that with the advances in audio technology today the sound will be perfectly clear when the documentary comes out on DVD.

Ivory: We had a perfectly good English sound man. If there is any problem,
it's because of Chaudhuri himself. It's just a pity that in his hurry to speak on
so many topics we sometimes miss what he's saying. As his obituary in the
New York Review of Books pointed out, he was the last of his kind: the last of the
great freelance intellectuals of the twentieth century.

Long: When you made the film in 1972, Chaudhuri was 76 years old, and
one might have thought that he was at, or nearing, the end of his career. Yet
he continued to publish books in his 80s and 90s and had published a book
only two years before his death in 1999 at the great age of 101. This little man
was like some powerful engine, and you have to ask: Where did all that energy
and confidence come from? Did you ever meet any other Indian men who were
like him?

Ivory: No. Once Ruth and Ismail and I had lunch with him and Mrs. Chaudhuri in Oxford when he was in his eighties. He was very excitable that day. He
kept hitting Ruth on the back—he was seated next to her—by way of emphasis. Afterward we had to lie down in our car before we drove back to London,
he had so exhausted us.

Long: When Chaudhuri died, an extensive obituary on him appeared in the
New York Times, in which V. S. Naipaul was quoted as saying that his first book,
The Autobiography of an Unknown Indian, "may be one of the great books to come
out of the Indo-English encounter. No better account of the penetration of
the Indian mind by the West—and by extension, of the penetration of one culture by another—will be or now can be written." Would you agree with this
assessment?

Ivory: One would not dare to disagree with anything V. S. Naipaul says,
would one?

Long: One might; he isn't omniscient. But here is something I would like
to know about. When the picture opens, Chaudhuri is being measured by a
Saville Row tailor for an elegant suit. Tell me about this episode.

Ivory: Well, he expressed to us that he'd always wanted a bespoke suit from
a Saville Row shop. It was one of his dreams. So I think we blew five hundred

pounds on that suit, but shot the whole ritual of being fitted, of picking out the cloth—he knew a lot about good English woolens—as an episode that would show him off at his best. Then it turned out that the tailor as a child had known Rabindranath Tagore, which startled and amazed Chaudhuri.

Long: During the conversation at the dinner party, the camera zooms in for dramatic close-ups of domestic objects: a pair of scissors that suddenly look as if they might be a work of art, the strikingly vivid face of a clock, and a number of startlingly beautiful porcelain figures—a lion, a zebra, and a tiger. Were these objects already on the mantle, or did you come across them somewhere and decide to place them there?

Ivory: They were there: the kind of civilized objects to be found in an upper-class English house that he would covet himself—he adored good china and brought a whole dinner set of the best Lenox back from his stay in America. He said it was superior to English china.

Long: You take Chaudhuri through a series of setups—a dinner party, a stroll through the streets of Oxford, a drive around Trafalgar Square, a visit to a cemetery. In the cemetery scene, Chaudhuri visits the grave of Max Müller, the German Sanskrit scholar and Orientalist about whom Chaudhuri is writing a biography. Müller is an interesting figure for you to call attention to, since he is a counterpart to Chaudhuri: Müller was a Westerner fascinated by India and the East, while Chaudhuri is an Indian fascinated by England and the West. But visually isn't the cemetery scene stolen by those ancient tombstones . . . from what period?

Ivory: They weren't so ancient. What I liked was the overgrown, weedy look of the place, with the very tall grass, so that Chaudhuri was lost in it, only his hat skimming along above the grass, as he was accompanied by the very tall undergraduate, who loomed up over him like a giant. The name of that undergraduate is Richard Macrory, and he's now a distinguished environmental lawyer and the chairman of the board of Merchant Ivory Productions, U.K.

Long: Another feature of the film that is visually striking is the Oxford campus, which an English critic accused you of falling in love with. Whether or not, the Oxford scenes seem an anticipation of the far more elaborate Cambridge setting in *Maurice,* no?

Ivory: I had never been to Oxford in any sort of useful way before, or filmed there, hadn't professionally ever stepped foot in England until then, so of course I would try to bring out its beauty—Oxford *is* very beautiful, just as Cambridge is. How awful to be accused of falling in love!

Long: What the critic—John Gillett in *Sight and Sound*—actually said was "there's a shared, ironically romantic reaction to Oxford by the American film-maker and the Indian writer." But what is striking about *Adventures of a Brown Man* chiefly is Nirad Chaudhuri; you can't take your eyes off him, for one thing. For another, he contains a stupendous contradiction, for this master of learning and elucidation also makes one think of a child, an impression heightened by the presence of his heavyset wife, who could as well be his mother.

Ivory: If only one could *understand* what he is saying better! He's really saying some very inflammatory things.

Long: Chaudhuri is the precursor of the princess in *Autobiography of a Princess* insofar as he lives in a self-imposed exile in England, but you couldn't have known then that *Autobiography of a Princess* would follow soon afterward. Aren't Chaudhuri's descendants, in some respects, the characters in recent movies about Indians or Pakistanis who live in London and are caught between two worlds?

Ivory: Not really. The characters in such films are not writers or intellectuals. I've seen that other Indian intellectuals—people like Ved Mehta and V. S. Naipaul, neither from the same generation as Chaudhuri—seem to be perfectly at home in the West, where they prefer to live for many reasons. In a way, they are Chaudhuri's spiritual heirs. But the middle-class or working-class Indians and Pakistanis in today's London are there mostly for economic reasons. They are in flight from Indian poverty and in some cases anarchy. In a generation or two these immigrants will produce their own intellectuals, their own savants, who will go to Oxford and Cambridge also, and in turn write tomes on civilization.

FEATURE FILMS

INDIA

Robert Emmet Long: You had been to India, met Satyajit Ray, and shot your documentary *The Delhi Way,* as well as your footage in Kabul. At that point, you returned to New York.

James Ivory: I shot *The Delhi Way* and brought it back to New York to edit, and then I decided that I really needed to do more work on it, that I hadn't got all I wanted—and at that point I met Ismail. I introduced him to some people here in New York who wanted to make a feature film in India. One of them was the anthropologist Gitel Steed. She had written a script called *Devgar* set in a village in Gujarat where she had once worked as an anthropologist, and she wanted very much to film it. She got together with Sidney Myers, a wonderful filmmaker, who was going to direct it; and I, in a rather foolhardy way, said that I would actually shoot the film, which I wouldn't have known how to do, though I didn't realize it then. Ismail was going to produce it. He went to India first, and I came along later because I wanted to go on working on *The Delhi Way.*

Long: But you didn't make the film, I know, about the village in India.

Ivory: The Steed film collapsed because Ismail couldn't raise all the money for it. He raised some of it, but he couldn't get all of it. He had suggested casting Shashi Kapoor, Durga Khote, and Leela Naidu—all of whom were later to be the stars of *The Householder.* It also turned out that Ismail had read Ruth Jhabvala's *The Householder* when he was working in Los Angeles. Supposedly he wrote in his diary that he would make her novel—the fourth—into a film, though none of us can find that historical document. He got *The Householder* out and reread it, I guess, and gave it to me, saying, "Let's make this." I had no sense of what was involved in making a feature film, or what you had to do. I had never worked with actors really, or anything like that, but I said, "Oh, yeah, let's do it."

Long: And you did it.

Ivory: The time comes when you finish one stage of your life, and you go on to the next stage. When you are in high school, you take it for granted, if you are lucky enough to be born under that star, that you will be going on to college—or at least I did. That will be your next stage. The first stage of my film-making life was making documentaries all by myself; the second stage seemed to be going into feature films, and I never questioned that. I didn't know what they would be or who I would make them with, or what kind of stories I would tell. Of these things I had no idea. Stage two came rather quickly, rather too soon, maybe. We made *The Householder* in two versions—in English and in Hindi—and by some miracle we sold the finished picture to Columbia Pictures for worldwide rights.

THE HOUSEHOLDER

Merchant Ivory's first feature, based on Ruth Jhabvala's fourth novel, set in Delhi. Prem Sagar and his strong-willed young bride, Indu, learn to live together. With Shashi Kapoor, Leela Naidu, and Durga Khote. 1963. Feature. 35 millimeter; black-and-white; 101 minutes.

Long: The Householder cost $125,000 to make, and part of it came from your father. How much did he lose, and how did he feel about losing it?

Ivory: He didn't lose, or rather he didn't lose very much, because, as I said, we sold the film to Columbia Pictures, and the money he put in came back to him out of the money from Columbia.

Long: I think you've told me that your father thought of the money he invested in the film as being *your* money.

Ivory: That's right. Some of it, anyway. He thought of it as a portion of my eventual inheritance. Later on, there was a tallying up of how much I had taken and how much my sister had taken as advances on our inheritance. It was understood that if I took something then, there would be less later. He was, of course, happy that we had sold the film to Columbia Pictures. That, he thought, was a great thing. We were paid for it in "frozen" rupees, which were then invested in *Shakespeare Wallah*, a more successful film, and he was happy to be backing that successful film.

Long: You spoke of the frozen rupees previously.

Ivory: Yes, they were earnings in India of the American film companies, which by Indian law could not be repatriated but could be used in India for production. This practice became the financial base of our operation there in the 1960s, and Ismail exploited that situation very ingeniously.

Long: Did your father back any of the other films?

Ivory: He died around that time.

Long: But he lived to see you succeed.

Ivory: He lived to see the success of *Shakespeare Wallah*.

Long: That was great.

Ivory: He lived for a year or so after that. There were terrific reviews in magazines like *Life, Time,* and *Newsweek,* and all that kind of thing, and so he saw all of that . . .

Long: Would you have done anything differently if you could make *The Householder* again?

Ivory: That isn't a question that can realistically be asked because . . . you know, it was a first feature film. I had never broken down the scenes with the actors and cameraman, and I didn't appreciate the relationship of the director to the actors. All that I had to learn as I went along. Having now done other movies, of course I would do things in a different way. At the time I had no choice. I had to manage. It was like being thrown into a river; you had better swim. That's what I did.

Long: Were there things you learned about moviemaking from *The Householder?*

Ivory: Everything. I had to learn everything . . . not everything I *was* to learn, but at least I went through every single step of the process. I was not involved in the script. That was written by Ruth—out of her head. Having written the novel, she didn't have to go back to it and work out scenes from it for the movie. She just wrote her screenplay out of her memory of her book. I wasn't involved in the script at all.

Long: But you were involved with everything else.

Ivory: With everything else . . . finding all the other actors apart from the three leads, and of course constantly being present at the shooting, and everything in postproduction, which up until then I knew nothing about. I had been in editing rooms because I had edited my documentaries, but I had never edited a feature and didn't know what a big job it is. Editing the documentaries, which were without sync sound, was not at all the same as feature sound editing, which now loomed up like a huge additional task that I knew nothing about.

Long: Your having made the film in different language versions must have created other complications for you.

Ivory: An important thing about making *The Householder* which most people don't realize is that we shot the two versions of it simultaneously. If the actors were fluent in Hindi but not in English, we would do the Hindi scenes first to break them in. On the other hand, if they were more at home in English, we would begin shooting scenes in English. It doubled the time of shooting because I would do, maybe, three or four takes in English, and then another three or four in Hindi. And it doubled the editing time.

Long: How did you manage to direct the film without knowing Hindi yourself?

Ivory: I didn't know Hindi, but I had very good help. I had people around me . . . a very good assistant who was himself a writer and spoke Hindi fluently, and of course our actors would correct themselves (and each other) if they made mistakes. Ismail was there on the set sometimes to correct these mistakes. But on the whole, most of the crew could not correct the actors because they—the crew—were all Bengali speaking. They had all come from Calcutta. They spoke Bengali and English, so when it came to assisting me with the Hindi version, they were of no help. My assistant director was a Bengali— Sailen Dutt. He knew Hindi, although not all that well.

Long: It must have been a great help to have Ismail there.

Ivory: Yes, it was. Sure. He was always around, always trying to raise more money to pay people. Eventually our money ran out, and we didn't finish our shooting. It was also getting very, very hot when we ran out of funds. We had a few more scenes to do, but we packed up. It was mid-May, and the temperatures were in the high nineties in Delhi. Later, by the time the monsoon rains came and it had cooled off a bit, we'd edited quite a lot of film. We could see

Prem Sagar (Shashi Kapoor) pleads with his landlord (Pincho Kapoor) for a reduction in his rent in *The Householder* (1963).

what we really needed; when Ismail had raised more money, we went back and shot the remaining scenes.

Long: Could you talk a bit about Shashi Kapoor, your male lead, and where he was at this time in his career?

Ivory: Shashi was just starting out. He was a member of a famous acting family and had two famous brothers. His oldest brother, Raj Kapoor, was the biggest Indian movie star. A second brother, whose name was Shammi Kapoor, became a kind of comic actor and a movie star as well. Shashi was the youngest and had been in one or two films previous to ours. He was a great guy and wonderfully good-looking and a very good actor. In a way he was almost too good-looking for the part he was playing. . . . You felt when you met him that he was too much of a matinee idol to really be convincing as the put-upon teacher, Prem Sagar. But somehow I think he managed, he pulled it off. Audiences found him very affecting.

Long: When Shashi Kapoor was cast for the lead, did you already know him personally?

Ivory: I remember when I first met him, with his English wife, Jennifer, at a party in Bombay. They seemed so vital and beautiful—and so beautiful together. I certainly didn't know any actors when I arrived. I had no way to tell who was and who wasn't good, who would be salable in terms of the box office in India, who would interest financiers. So it was pretty much Ismail who had to put the cast together—at least the principals. He knew Shashi, and there was a young girl, Leela Naidu, who plays the wife, Indu, whom Ismail knew about. She had been in a successful film that had caught his eye just before we were ready to start our picture.

Long: Who were some of the others in the cast?

Ivory: There was Durga Khote, who plays Prem's mother and was then, I guess, in her late fifties. She was a famous ex–leading lady. I think that she had starred in films in the silent days almost, and everyone knew her. Other members of the cast were assembled from here and there. The most difficult character for us to find was the swami. We couldn't find anybody in Bombay who seemed right and whose English was good. So we then got a Bengali named Pahari Sanyal, whom I had seen in a Ray film, *Kanchenjunga.*

Long: How is the swami to be taken? Later ones are satirized in your films.

Ivory: No, this was a serious treatment. This was a true, benevolent soul who was giving good advice.

Long: You said that Shashi Kapoor, to return to him for a moment, was a "great guy." He was a close friend of Ismail's, wasn't he?

Ivory: He still is. We all became very close friends. To this day we almost—in fact we are—like family members.

Long: By "great guy," do you mean that he was outgoing and sociable?

Ivory: You know, a large, generous-hearted soul. His wonderful wife, Jennifer Kendal, was an English actress, and they were in Shakespeariana together, the Shakespearean troupe founded by her parents, Geoffrey and Laura Kendal.

Long: For such an agreeable film, *The Householder* contains a number of unpleasant characters—the martinet headmaster, the incredibly pompous elder teacher.

Ivory: Some of these people weren't really actors, you know.

Long: They weren't?

Ivory: They weren't professional actors at all. We cast them because they looked right—and we hoped would *be* right. I mean, they *did* look right, like the headmaster, Ramesh Thappur. He was an editor of an intellectual New Delhi weekly and a political writer, a well-known character who had been in some movies but was not really an actor. The other teacher, Harendranath Chattopadaya—God knows what you would call him, a sort of performance artist? Later on, he can be seen in Ray's films, where he's also over-the-top; he was irrepressible. Many of our people, as I say, were not really actors.

Long: The characters all seem to live in their own limited worlds. It's a theme of the film, isn't it, that these characters are not communicating with each other?

Ivory: Well . . .

Long: The headmaster's wife who claims that the teachers are exploiting her husband when he is really exploiting them, and that sort of thing; and Prem's drunken landlord who is indifferent to Prem's pleas to reduce his rent, citing the high cost of the imported Scotch he drinks; and the pompous elder teacher, Mr. Chadda, who intimidates and humiliates Prem at the school. Surrounded by such people, Prem feels cut off and alone.

Ivory: Well, it's like that anywhere. It's not just India. How is that different from anyplace else?

Long: Ruth's early novels set in India are filled with self-centered people who cannot make contact with others. *The Householder* belongs to that period and reflects what might be called the comedy of self-involvement.

Ivory: I think you're right about a failure of understanding among the various characters, but the film is also about the system under which these characters live. It was a system where there are various stages on the totem pole, higher or lower . . . and this sort of thing can be seen operating within the family as well. You have the tyrannical mother, you have the young husband trying to act as he thought a husband should act, and a young wife who is fed up with all of this and decides to go home. She has had enough of the mother and son. They're all trying to get on with each other, but they each have their own ideas of the way things ought to be.

Long: The mother is a good example of a character who is wrapped up in her-

Prem and Indu (Leela Naidu) returning from their friend's wedding in the final scene in *The Householder* (1963).

self. She's sobbing into her sari and feeling sorry for herself, and she's not considering for a moment what she is doing to the young couple . . . that she may be driving them apart.

Ivory: But I think *The Householder* . . . If I had had more experience as a director, and if the actors had been more professionally trained . . . I think that I would have approached it in a different way. A lot of the performances in *The Householder* seem too broad. There's no modulation in them. The mother-in-law is the best example of that. It could have been a much more subtle creation if I'd known how to do it. I wasn't really aware while we were doing it of the effect of the overacting and overperforming on the screen.

Long: What would you say was the chief problem that confronted you in making the film?

Ivory: It was particularly unfortunate that while we *saw* our rushes, we had to watch them silent. We never saw rushes with sound for months and months, so that I had no idea of what these actors were sounding like, that they were sometimes overacting. It could have been a far more subtle style of acting, as well as being more homogeneous. As I say, a number of people in it weren't really actors; some were stage actors, some were Bengali actors who didn't know how to speak Hindi. Ernest Castaldo was a Broadway actor, out of the cast of *West Side Story,* and he, too, was sometimes too broad, or rather too theatrical, for a film.

Long: Oh, yes, very much so. But then it was his first film, as with you?

Ivory: Yes. Had we seen the rushes with sound . . . had Ruth seen them with us (as you know, she loves seeing rushes), I'm sure she would have said, "You've got to pull them down a bit, they're all over the place." But we weren't able to. In those days there was no way. One doesn't realize how difficult things in India were in terms of working on location in another city, away from the film centers of Calcutta and Bombay, where we could have arranged for a screening room to have the picture and sound projected together. That didn't exist in Delhi. All we could do was to rent some time in a theater and watch our mute rushes. That was a *great* drawback.

Long: We haven't even talked about Ray's part in the making of your first two films. *The Householder* and *Shakespeare Wallah* have the distinction of your having had Satyajit Ray as a contributor. He supervised the music that went into *The Householder* and influenced the editing. For *Shakespeare Wallah* he wrote and recorded a magnificent musical score. I can't think of the film without remembering Ray's haunting music. What was it like having Ray as a collaborator?

Ivory: It was a dream come true to have him accept the job of composer. I knew that (a) I would certainly love the music he wrote and (b) it would be professionally scored, under his supervision. He wrote it in about ten days, sitting at his upright piano in his Calcutta apartment, where he must have come up with the main theme:

SHAKESPEARE WALLAH CUE   Satyajit Ray
                                  Transcription by George Brooks

fine

This, he said, represented the mood of philosophical resignation implicit in the story of the traveling English actors. Our melody has a strong emotional relationship with the *rag* Kafi, though it may seem very Western.

Long: What is a *rag?*

Ivory: In Indian musical terms it means a mood, or an emotion, and is expressed in a few basic melodic notes, out of which some vast composition can develop. There is usually a poetic or devotional context, and a *rag* is also tied to the seasons and the hour of the day.

Long: Did you have the same problem with *Shakespeare Wallah* that you had with *The Householder* in not being able to view your rushes?

Ivory: Yes. We went to a run-down cinema in a hill station below Simla and watched our flickering, dark images on a patched screen. It was so dark that the cameraman, Subrata Mitra, was tearing his hair.

Long: But the acting styles in *Shakespeare Wallah* seemed a lot smoother.

Ivory: I know, but in that film we had, you know, professional English actors . . . though even the Kendals were sometimes over-the-top. But when they were over-the-top, it was in their Shakespearean scenes, never at other times. Geoffrey Kendal was doing an old-fashioned Victorian or Edwardian *Hamlet,* for instance, that has probably long since disappeared from the English stage. I'm glad he couldn't hear himself in the silent rushes doing an old-fashioned and perhaps sometimes even hammy *Hamlet* and *Othello.* It would have made him self-conscious, whereas what he did was finally exactly right. He may have consciously been striving for a somewhat outmoded performing style. But I wouldn't have known the difference, in any case.

Long: When you were making *Shakespeare Wallah*, did it ever occur to you that it would be considered an exceptional, a notable film?

Ivory: No one thinks like that. Everyone I've ever known who is a serious writer or director or actor is in despair all the time. They are constantly exclaiming about their work, "Oh, my God, what *is* this?" No one is sitting around saying, "This is going to be a great book or this is going to be a great film" (unless it's the financiers, who may be whistling in the dark); and the people who are foolish enough to think like that are usually going to be seriously disappointed.

Long: Why do you suppose *Shakespeare Wallah* made such a strong impression on the public when it appeared?

SHAKESPEARE
WALLAH

The passing of the British Raj is embodied by a strolling company of Shakespearean players in an India that no longer has any use for them. With Shashi Kapoor, Felicity Kendal, and Madhur Jaffrey. 1965. Feature. 35 millimeter; black-and-white; 120 minutes.

Ivory: It was a delightful idea to begin with, an interesting and intriguing idea. Nobody had seen anything like that. I mean, the Indian films that had come to this country were exclusively Ray's films, and those were all in Bengali with subtitles, and mostly dealt with present-day Bengali life in and around Calcutta. The last film that had dealt with the issue of the British Raj even mildly had been Renoir's *The River*, and that had been about a decade earlier, in the early fifties. Here we were in the midsixties, and I think that by then the Renoir film had probably been more or less forgotten. People just found *Shakespeare Wallah* very striking. It was felt that there was something poetic and out-of-this-world about it.

Long: Shashi Kapoor stars in *Shakespeare Wallah*, as he had in *The Householder*, but the characters he plays are really quite different. How would you compare them?

Ivory: Prem Sagar was meant to be a kind of woebegone, poor schoolteacher with a pregnant wife, but there was nothing woebegone about Shashi. He always was, and I suppose was even more so in *Shakespeare Wallah*, a splendidly handsome man, full of life, and full by that time of success. By that time he had become a real movie star; crowds would come to look at him if he was around and all that kind of thing. In *Shakespeare Wallah*, Shashi was playing a kind of shallow but exuberant playboy that his English girlfriend falls in love with—a more suitable kind of part for his personality, and even more so a few years after that in *Bombay Talkie*, where he did indeed play a movie star. He was at the peak of everything by then.

Long: Felicity Kendal was terrific in *Shakespeare Wallah*. Did she have a lot of offers to appear in other movies?

Ivory: Strangely enough, no, she didn't. I don't know why not. As in the film, she left India. She made the break with India in the same way the girl Lizzie does in the film. She went to try her luck in England, and she had a lot of luck straight on. The first thing she landed was a role in a play opposite John Gielgud, which was made for TV. And soon after that she began getting leading parts on the stage. She had a very good agent, and she just took off. By the mid-1970s she was already a household name in England. Her forte is comedy, light comedy. Of all the young women we've introduced in our films, hers is still the greatest success story. In the United States she's less well known.

Long: I understand that Ruth wrote a sequel to *Shakespeare Wallah* called *A Lovely World,* in which Lizzie would be living in the trendy world of London in the 1960s, but that Filmways, which commissioned it, decided not to go ahead with the movie. Could you tell me something about the screenplay she wrote?

Ivory: What happened in that story was the opposite of what actually happened to Felicity Kendal. Felicity became successful almost at once. She married a young actor whom she later divorced, but in our screenplay, the Lizzie character is trying to decide at the end of the story whether she wants stability in marriage outside the theater or whether she wants to go on, almost from hand to mouth, trying to be an actress. So she opts for stability and the life offered by an older man and gives up the stage. But all through *A Lovely World* she's homesick for India—homesick for her parents, homesick for her old life. She spends all her time with Indians when she's not looking for work, wants to be with them, prefers their company to others. That was the sort of story it was.

Long: *Shakespeare Wallah,* your first major film, was concerned with the acting profession, but soon after that you made another film, *Bombay Talkie,* also about actors, and a little later *Jane Austen in Manhattan,* again about actors, in this case in rival theater companies in New York. Your recurring interest in the acting profession puts you in the company of certain other filmmakers—of Ingmar Bergman and Federico Fellini, for example; of François Truffaut and Joseph L. Mankiewicz (in *All About Eve*). There's also Marcel Carné's 1945 film, *Children of Paradise,* about the life of a theater company in nineteenth-century France. Is *Children of Paradise,* by the way, a film you happen to like?

Ivory: Absolutely! It's been a while since I last saw it, but I've seen it more than once. I remember a poster, which was put out by the Academy Cinemas in London the year after *Shakespeare Wallah* came out and was plastered everywhere in the tube; it announced "a season of classics," and one of the classics was *Shakespeare Wallah,* while another was *Children of Paradise.* I still have that poster. I remember someone laughing and saying that *Shakespeare Wallah* was perhaps an "instant classic," but I didn't care.

Long: Both pictures were about theater companies and how all the people involved in them fared.

Ivory: Yes.

Long: One thing that struck me in comparing *The Householder* with *Shakespeare Wallah* was how much bolder the imagery was in *Shakespeare Wallah.*

Ivory: They were two very different kinds of movies. *The Householder* involved a small domestic world, with all the action concentrated pretty much in a one-room flat, in a house in New Delhi. There were a few excursions outside the house, but most of the dramatic action was in that house, upstairs or downstairs, or in Prem's school, whereas in *Shakespeare Wallah* you had the world of a wandering theater company that traveled across India, and that's a very different kind of thing. In *Shakespeare Wallah* you had all kinds of opportunities for wonderful images. There were not that many in the other film.

Long: But that's it. The thing you notice about *Shakespeare Wallah* right off is its great visuals. It is as if your visual sense has been freed to express itself fully. Of course, as you say, *Shakespeare Wallah* gave you opportunities for this play of imagery that the earlier work had not.

Ivory: It came out of the strolling company itself, traveling to all these interesting Indian sites: Rajasthan, Lucknow, foggy romantic hill stations,

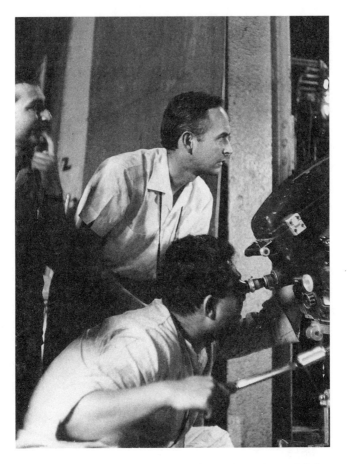

Ivory with cameraman Subrata Mitra during the making of *Shake-speare Wallah* in 1964. Actor and first assistant director Prayag Raaj watches the shot.

Simla—how can you go wrong? We also took advantage of those places in ways which seemed new. The production of *Antony and Cleopatra* that the troupe does for the maharaja at his palace . . . you would not expect to see something like that. We took some liberties there in the way we staged the play in order to exploit that palace.

Long: How is that?

"I am dying, Egypt, dying." The Buckinghams (Geoffrey Kendal and Laura Liddel) stage *Antony and Cleopatra* in the palace at Alwar in Rajasthan, in a scene from *Shakespeare Wallah* (1965).

Ivory: It was a very run-down palace, in Alwar, a minor state in Rajasthan, and full of smelly bats; nobody had lived there for I don't know how long, and there was hardly any lighting. The story called for a decrepit maharaja, so we had to find a decrepit palace. And we chose to stage the play outside in the court, which is where, in fact, they would have had other kinds of performance—music, dance. Anything of that sort would have been held outside, perhaps under a tent. It wasn't far-fetched, but it was more beautiful than

The Buckingham troupe arriving at Gleneagles, their hill station hotel, in a scene from *Shakespeare Wallah* (1965).

you'd normally find, because the old palace itself, with its carved walls and airy balconies, provided an appropriate background for Cleopatra's Egypt, a place sumptuously oriental.

Long: The scene of the arrival at Gleneagles was . . .

Ivory: Gleneagles was a decrepit place, too, an old-fashioned hotel in Kasauli that was a collection of strung-together, tin-roofed guest cottages. It was considered by the British a good, homey place to stay, and we stayed there ourselves. But it was on its last legs, really, about to slide down the hill.

Long: The arrival in the rainstorm takes the form of a processional, and there is another processional in the film where the Madhur Jaffrey character, Manjula, is carried in a sedan chair by men who are dressed in white.

Ivory: Let me explain that. Those chairs were used in the mountains. We didn't make that up. People were carried around in "carrying chairs" because the terrain was steep. There would be two men—*palki wallahs*—one in front, one behind, to carry you up and down the mountains so that you didn't have to get out and climb. We made a sedan chair like the ones in old photographs for the film; by the time we got there, it was really a custom of the past, a holdover from colonial days during the British Raj when English people were carried up and down the hills. Manjula's sedan chair in the film wasn't some sort of fantasy thing that I created . . . as if she were Cleopatra being carried by slaves. It wasn't that. It was a realistic touch.

Long: She's holding an umbrella, isn't she?

Ivory: Well, no, someone is holding it over her. In India an umbrella is always a symbol of royalty, and of course movie stars are today's royalty.

Long: The procession is seen in silhouette against a silver sky. It forms a striking picture that makes you think of her as you would, say, a queen. You see her at this moment as a formidable antagonist for Sanju's affection.

Ivory: She was supposed to be a reigning movie star. However, physically, she was not quite right for that role, and everybody knew that. The crew particularly was disappointed on the first day of shooting with the appearance of Madhur Jaffrey; she wasn't a buxom and curvaceous Indian movie goddess in the way they were used to. But of course Madhur gives a smashing performance.

Long: There is a memorable scene where Sanju and Lizzie are engulfed by a dense white mist. They kiss and there is a blackout—or whiteout—for a moment, and then they emerge again from the mist. It has a magical effect. I imagine that this is a moment that takes them out of time . . . when they kiss. Was that your intention?

Ivory: No, but you may think that if you like. I'll tell you what happened. All that fog came from smoke canisters that the Indian army gave us. And it was a good thing the film wasn't being made in color because the smoke was yellow. The couple are walking together in a wooded area, they turn and embrace, they begin to kiss, and then they are completely covered by "fog"—which happened naturally. Somehow we had got it right, the prop men had placed the canisters just so, and the wind stirred the smoke, again just so, and the embracing couple seem to disappear in the mist.

Long: It happened accidentally? It certainly gives the impression that it had been planned that way.

Ivory: No, it happened accidentally. The fog just drifted around them, and we thought that was fine, that was wonderful. We congratulated ourselves!!

But then it wouldn't go away, and we had to stand there and shoot and shoot while the "fog" completely hid them and nothing was happening on the screen. Then eventually it cleared, and when it did clear the cameraman zoomed slightly forward to get a tighter frame. But we had this long, long piece of film when you couldn't see anything. So we cut that out and dissolved between the two halves. It all seemed a perfect sort of fog effect, with everything happening exactly when you want it to. But, in fact, it wasn't like that.

Long: Were there any other problems with the shot?

Ivory: While all of this was going on, the cameraman was bitten by a dog. [*Long laughs*] Felicity's little dog was running around barking and bit him on the ankle, but Subrata didn't lose his nerve or stop shooting. He kicked the dog into the underbrush and went right on.

Long: For a variety of reasons, I feel the presence of Satyajit Ray in the background of the film.

Ivory: He's in the foreground. After all, his music is there.

Long: More than the music alone. The kind of poetic realism and the imagery . . .

Ivory: Well, after all, we were using his cameraman, Subrata Mitra, and Mitra had done great, great films of Ray's, and so it is bound to resemble . . . to visually resemble Ray's films. Both Satyajit and Subrata were at the height of their respective arts then, and I was the lucky recipient.

THE GURU

A great master of classical sitar playing attempts to mold his resisting disciple, a young British pop star. With Michael York, Rita Tushingham, and Utpal Dutt. 1969. Feature. 35 millimeter; color; 112 minutes.

Long: The Guru, an excursion into the world of Indian musicians, is unique in the repertoire of your films. You had by then come to know Ravi Shankar and Ustad Vilayat Khan. How well did you know them?

Ivory: Ravi Shankar I first came to know when I began to search for the music for *The Sword and the Flute.* I met him in Los Angeles in 1957, and he was very responsive. Three years later I met Ustad Vilayat Khan in India, partly because of my interest in Ray's *The Music Room,* for which he'd done the score. So I asked him to record some music for *The Delhi Way,* which he did. It isn't difficult to get to know the great Indian musicians. They're very open, not standoffish. They invite you home at once, feed you, you meet their wives and children. You become almost intimates in a short period of time. Or at least I did. It was my close-up immersion in their worlds that led in time to the idea of *The Guru*. Another great musician was added to the brew, and that was Ustad Ali Akbar Khan, the sarod player. If you're reasonably perceptive and discreet, you do pick up a lot in India, you know, in even a short time. You've got all your feelers out, waving in the charged air.

Long: I believe that you had been contemplating a film about an Indian musician, a maestro, and a devoted but not necessarily talented disciple. The idea was based on the real-life relationship of Graeme Vanderstoel, an Australian friend of yours, and Ustad Ali Akbar Khan. Could you elaborate on that?

Ivory: Graeme became a kind of unofficial *chela*, or disciple of Ali Akbar—helping him arrange his concert tours in America, doing all sorts of things for him. And there are always many tasks to be done if you give yourself wholeheartedly over to serving any kind of Indian master, or guru.

Long: Ismail presented the idea to Twentieth Century Fox, which expressed an interest in backing the picture if the disciple of the musician-guru was a Western pop star—a conception inspired by George Harrison of the Beatles having gone to India to study the sitar with Ravi Shankar. Had you thought about a George Harrison figure yourself previous to this?

Ivory: Not really. But it was all there in the newspapers and magazines. Ruth thought it would be easy to imagine the disciple as a Western pop musician. This was all a new phenomenon; we read about its developments eagerly and just used what we wanted. Its topicality pleased Fox, of course, and we didn't feel compromised by it at all. It's a misconception, however, that Fox suggested the disciple could be an English rock musician. That was our idea.

Long: Michael York plays the English pop star Tom Pickle, who studies the sitar with Utpal Dutt's Ustad Zafar Khan—a mismatched pair, since Pickle never really comes to terms with the spiritual discipline involved in mastering the instrument. According to obituary tributes to George Harrison in the *New York Times* following his death two years ago, the Harrison-Shankar relationship was just the reverse of the one between Pickle and his guru in the movie. Harrison became deeply informed about Indian music (and culture), and he

Utpal Dutt as the sitar virtuoso in *The Guru* (1969).

and Shankar became close friends who staged concerts together. Did you know of the extent of the Harrison-Shankar friendship when you made *The Guru?*

Ivory: We didn't know the extent of it, and I doubt the newspapers writing about the relationship both then and now actually "got it." George Harrison, already very famous, came as a disciple to the most famous of all Indian musicians, a man so secure in his art and the esteem of his countrymen that it would seem there could be no possibility of friction arising out of any misunderstanding he and his student might have. Then, George Harrison might have found it easier to accept his guru's ideas about a disciple's true role; his personality might have been more low-key than Tom Pickle's, less prickly. *Our* guru had never been abroad, and wanted to go and concertize beyond India; he hinted to Pickle's agent about this. However, I can imagine that Ravi Shankar, notoriously sensitive to slights real and supposed, might have had

a lot to put up with from his protégé, a Beatle, no less. Ruth's understanding
of all this was very exact; I don't agree that Ravi Shankar's relationship with
George Harrison had to be without friction. Though Tom Pickle and the Ustad were neither so famous, both sets of men—the real and the fictional—had
more in common than the romantic and idealized accounts that came out after Harrison's death would lead one to believe.

Long: Ruth regarded it as an ill-fated picture, almost everything about it. "The
people who came out hated India, and they didn't get on," she remarked. "Jim
was worried and anxious. Nothing went right. . . . It was as if the hand of doom
was on it. No scene really gets going. They just lie there heavily. The clothes
were all wrong. . . . Sometimes what you write just doesn't take off; it doesn't
have some inner quality to make it rise. Something's missing. There are some
nice scenes. . . . But that's about all." What happened?

Ivory: I think it was a case of the authentic being smothered by studio expectations—it was Twentieth Century Fox. They wanted stars, and then the
stars in turn wanted all their usual prerogatives: special makeup artists, special food, a say in their costumes. So there was a layer of artifice, like a layer of
too much makeup on a face. There were awful flare-ups between the English
actors and the Indian crew. The actor playing the guru, Utpal Dutt, was put
in prison for sedition on the first day of shooting and had to be pried loose by
Ismail.

Long: Michael York's performance as Tom Pickle (what a name!) is puzzling,
for he never seems quite "there." Even when he is mobbed by crowds of manic
teenagers, even when he rides on their shoulders, he seems curiously affect-
less and absent from what is happening.

Ivory: I guess he wasn't really right classwise and was also perhaps tempera-
mentally unsuited to playing a popular working-class musician. He was perhaps too nice a guy—one felt that somehow. The rough-and-tumble of a rock
star's life wasn't anything he knew much about personally or could imagine and
project (any more than I could). Ismail wanted to cast Mick Jagger, and sent
him the script, but Jagger told us a couple of years ago that he never got it.

Long: While out on the water with the English girl Jenny, played by Rita Tushingham, Michael York sings a song he has thought up himself, and he can hardly

carry a tune. Doesn't this undermine his credibility as a famous musical performer?

Ivory: Oh, I don't know. He's supposed to be sort of making it up, trying it out as he goes along. It wasn't supposed to be any kind of a performance. It's almost speaking the lyrics, which are all about being on a sacred river in India, rather than singing them. I liked it.

Long: Rita Tushingham plays a young, middle-class girl who is in search of spiritual enlightenment in India and in the end finds that it has a dark, horrifying underside. She is naive and impressionable, but the trouble is that she is never more than a type. Outlined heavily with kohl, her eyes are at all times wide open and staring. And her romance with Pickle by the end comes too easily, and too predictably. Jenny seems a thankless role for an actress who was so moving and real in *A Taste of Honey.*

Ivory: Again, Rita was wrong classwise; Michael too middle-class, Rita not middle-class enough. So there was a strain in her work and in her line readings. Add to that the fact that she seemed not to be very much at home in India, was frightened by it for herself and her child, who she'd brought along. Her husband had nothing to do but moan—what the English call "whingeing"—and criticize. And she got into a spectacular row with the cameraman, Subrata Mitra, and they ended up not speaking. Or, rather, he wouldn't speak to her. He had been "insulted" by her, he said. He was lighting her close-up and had asked that she be present for the last-second fiddling with the light meter, instead of her stand-in. He turned away from her suddenly, with the light meter still raised in the air at the level of her face, and she chose that moment to sit down. He turned back—I can still see him—and she wasn't there. Well, in his mind that constituted an insult to his work and was a deliberate rudeness, which was just nonsense. From then on he wouldn't speak to her, passing all his instructions to her through me or the assistant director. After several days of this she got fed up and complained to her English agent. We were facing one of those crises that can overwhelm and destroy a film. She issued an ultimatum: he must speak to her, behave normally. And he would not. If he'd been fired by the studio at that point, the film would have collapsed; he owned all the camera equipment. Ismail and I begged him to speak. I think if he hadn't

Rita Tushingham, as the talentless Jenny, is about to prostrate herself before her newfound guru, watched by his suspicious senior wife, played by Madhur Jaffrey, in *The Guru* (1969).

agreed Ismail would have had him blinded, or put his eyes out with his own two thumbs in the classical way. [*Long laughs*] He relented finally, and the crisis ended without Fox learning about it (as with the case of Utpal Dutt being imprisoned). It had been arranged that Mitra would speak to Rita on the set, and we were all waiting for this to happen. For some reason Faye Dunaway was there that day paying us a visit, sitting relaxed on the sidelines in a cool white pantsuit. I wonder if she knew anything about all this. And still we waited. Finally Mitra, holding his light meter, said to Rita pleasantly, "It's not so hot today as yesterday, is it?" And that ended the standoff. Altogether, *The Guru* was not an easy movie to shoot . . . and there was worse to come.

Long: You had an opportunity to use Mia Farrow in the role but turned it down. Could she have done any more with it than Rita Tushingham?

Ivory: She was much more the kind of middle-class girl that was apt to go off to a place like India and become besotted by a guru—in fact, she more or less did just that, by attaching herself to the Maharishi. And in those days Mia Farrow had a very English sort of accent. No, she would have been just right. Only I'd never heard of her when Fox suggested her name, and did know (and very much liked) Rita Tushingham.

Long: I think it was generally felt that the most engaging figures were the Indian characters, particularly the Ustad, played by Utpal Dutt. What was Dutt's standing in the Indian film world?

Ivory: He wasn't that well known. He was a famous Bengali actor-manager, a figure from Calcutta's politicized theater world, but not a film star. Satyajit Ray suggested him for the Shakespeare-loving maharaja in *Shakespeare Wallah,* where you first saw him. We also cast him in *Bombay Talkie* as a corrupt film financier. Ray used him a lot also in his later films. He had started out as an actor in the Shakespeariana troupe in the 1950s, with Jennifer, with whom he was briefly in love before she married Shashi.

Long: At the end Tom Pickle and Jenny leave for England, having learned not who they are but who they are not; but what has the guru learned as we see him walking alone along the beach?

Ivory: That the ways of the West are mysterious and unknowable, inscrutable and dangerous. He seems to be heaving a sigh of relief that the plane has taken them away (as we ourselves did).

Long: Madhur Jaffrey is, as usual, wonderful, as both a sufferer and a termagant. I once asked Cyrus Jhabvala about her, and he replied facetiously, "She's tiny and she's made of steel." What other qualities would you say she projects?

Ivory: Her portrayal of an elder wife who has produced only daughters seems very real to me. She's vulnerable and can convey that very successfully. She

Mustani, a visiting holy woman played by Zohra Segal, enters the guru's Mumbai apartment shouting blessings in *The Guru* (1969).

has a very nice scene with Michael York in which she asks him all sorts of questions about the younger, more beautiful, and pregnant second wife.

Long: There are various forms of humor in the film, including a beauty pageant in Bombay with Ismail playing the MC, but the dominant mode of humor is satire. The Ustad is your most brilliant as well as elaborate rendition of the guru figure. But there is also the guru's guru, an elderly man of starvation leanness played by Nana Palsikar, who smokes a hookah interrupted by fits of coughing and asks his guru disciple why he had not brought him his sweets. Your seemingly neutral yet humorous portrayal of the guru's guru is one of the best things in the movie. What can you tell me about Nana Palsikar?

Ivory: Well, I didn't know a great deal about him when we cast him. He looked exactly right and was a good contrast to the much plumper Ustad. He was said to be a very good actor, which I took on faith. Physically, he reminded me a lot of Cyrus Jhabvala, Ruth's husband. Or the Cyrus to come, let's say; that was thirty-five years ago.

Long: In addition to this satire, you also had the visual advantage of the old Bikaner Fort and the stirring music of Ustad Vilayat Khan. But reviewers didn't think this was enough and treated the film dismissively. How do you regard the film today?

Ivory: I think I wrote in your book about us something like this: that *The Guru* is the most mysterious, because mostly unseen, of our films; that it was Merchant Ivory's version of a sixties trip kind of movie, and that it holds up as well as many of the others of that genre which have survived. Certainly one of the reasons for that would be the marvelous visual look of the film our prickly cameraman created, and its beautiful sitar music by Vilayat Khan. Also, the Benares locations were very beautiful.

Long: About *Bombay Talkie,* I suppose an obvious opening question would be to ask why the film is called *Bombay Talkie.*

Ivory: Because when we made it in 1970, sound films in Bombay were still called "talkies."

Long: It has a very striking opening in which the credits are shown. It begins with a view from above of an intersection of broad avenues in the heart of Bombay, where six men in white garments are running along one of the streets holding up a large red billboard with the film's title, *Bombay Talkie,* on it. And following this we see other billboards with posters in garish colors of members of the cast. It's an unusual and stylish opening, and I wonder if you were the one who dreamt it up.

BOMBAY TALKIE

A melodrama set in the Bombay film world, in which a best-selling American writer of sexy novels ensnares an Indian matinee film idol. With Shashi Kapoor, Jennifer Kendal, and Zia Mohyeddin. 1970. Feature. 35 millimeter; color; 105 minutes.

A billboard created for the 1971 Indian premiere of *Bombay Talkie*.

Ivory: I did, but it didn't take all that much dreaming about. Indian cities are plastered with garish billboards for films. There will be several huge colored faces of the stars. Sometimes the colors are psychedelic—the villain might be acid green, the leading lady bright pink, and so on. So we did that with our own actors, followed by the crew as well, including Ismail, Ruth, and me.

Long: Bombay Talkie was an original conception rather than an adaptation, and it was written by you and Ruth. Was the idea of the film yours, and if so how did it come about?

Ivory: More or less mine, and seconded by Ismail. There were some preliminaries during which the idea was tossed about by the three of us; but I remember it developed very quickly. Basically it was to be a melodrama, involving an Indian movie star and a Western lady novelist, within the Bombay film world. At its center was the idea of casting Shashi Kapoor and his actress wife, Jennifer Kendal, as the leads.

Long: Why did you want to make a melodrama?

Ivory: Ruth saw it as that: it was to mirror popular Indian films, and in turn the best-selling novels the leading lady churned out—also melodrama.

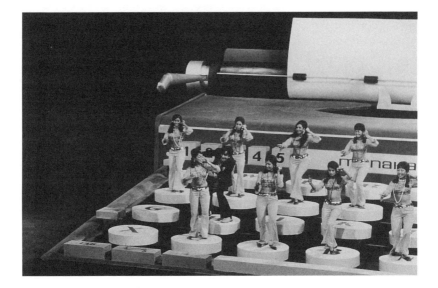

Shashi Kapoor, the movie star Vikram in *Bombay Talkie* (1970), during a dance number on a giant typewriter.

Long: In making the film you had the advantage of having Ismail as your partner; he had grown up on Bombay films and knew that world. Was he enthusiastic about the project?

Ivory: Very much so. He had many useful contacts and old friends who could help us—one of whom, Nimmi, a retired movie actress, became a kind of muse for him, as well as the dancing star, Helen. Most of the authenticity of location and detail comes from Ismail. He had very good casting ideas for many of the smaller parts.

Long: The opening Bollywood sequence, Ismail maintains, came from a dream you had of a Busby Berkeley dance routine on the keys of a giant typewriter, with Helen leading a chorus line. Is that the way this happened? And do you often dream about making movies as well as make them?

Ivory: I do dream up things in my sleep—literally. And I'm attentive to those ideas that might present themselves from out of my subconscious. As I remember, however, the idea for the giant typewriter came from my seeing a Bollywood musical number in which chorus girls were sitting inside giant champagne glasses kicking their legs over the side.

Long: Ismail even appears briefly in the picture as a young Indian film producer who takes the newly arrived English novelist, Lucia Lane, on a tour through the studio. He has always been a handsome, photogenic man. Did he ever consider a career as an actor?

Ivory: Wistfully, perhaps. Not seriously. He would have tried it out if someone had given him the chance. He speaks of that in his book *My Passage from India*—how when he arrived as a penniless unknown in Los Angeles, he had an A and a B plan. "A" was hopefully to set up as a producer, and failing that, to follow his B plan and go into the movies playing Sabu parts.

Long: Did Jennifer Kendal and Shashi Kapoor play together as a couple before *Bombay Talkie* was made, or did they afterward?

Ivory: This was their only film as lovers, but both had been actors in the Shakespeariana company of Jennifer's parents. Jennifer played leads, Shashi young hotheads like Mercutio. And they later acted together in the Som Benegal film *Junoon,* set during the 1857 mutiny. She was an English *memsahib,* he a mutineer who falls in love with her young daughter, played by their real daughter, Sanjana Kapoor.

Long: Jennifer Kendal is splendid as Lucia Lane, the bored and restless bestselling novelist who is out to break up Vikram's marriage. She is a kind of Circe figure who turns men into swine. In *Bombay Talkie* she manages to ruin two men, Vikram and Hari, the screenwriter-poet. Would you say that she is not only the central but also the most complex and interesting character in the film?

Ivory: To me, certainly. But I think in the West a character like that is greeted with a certain amount of impatience by audiences: selfish, self-dramatizing, with a streak of masochism so that she's repeatedly acting against her best interests. We quickly get bored by such ladies on the screen, as in life. I learned that the hard way.

Long: If the Vikram character is less involving, isn't it because he is putty in the hands of Lucia Lane?

Ivory: Perhaps. Or is it because he's so self-indulgent, living dishonorably, but at the same time with a strange and confusing sense of his "honor" as an Indian man that is continually compromised by Lucia's demands? She keeps angering him, embarrassing him; she stamps off, then runs after him, and the cycle resumes. We ought to have learned from *Bombay Talkie* that audiences tend to reject stories in which all the main characters seem unredeemably bad. But we did not, and ten years later launched *Quartet*, to face a similar rejection. Ten years or so after *that*, we tried again and made *Slaves of New York*, and that too failed to interest the public.

Long: It seems to me that there is something of Chekhov in *Bombay Talkie*. There are so many characters who are stymied in some way; no doors open onto fulfilling futures for them. There is a poignant note of yearning for an ideal that can't be realized. Isn't it true that the atmosphere of longing is unusually important in the film?

Ivory: Yes, that seems true, and we have Ruth to thank for that. It is a nice observation.

Long: Apart from the story the movie has to tell, it also offers the enticing prospect of catching Bombay itself on film. I am thinking, for instance, of the Taj Mahal Hotel and its stunning staircase. You fell in love, I believe, with that staircase.

Ivory: That staircase is certainly the most stunning public space in Bombay; the hotel itself appealed to me as a director almost as a colorful character would. We always felt that the Taj Mahal Hotel was indispensable. It helped that I stayed there during the shooting. That way I had more time to discover the place and work out my shots.

Long: There is an extraordinary episode in the film where Lucia Lane celebrates her birthday with Vikram and Hari. We see them in a carriage with brightly colored balloons that drift away across a very green lawn and the street behind the moving carriage. It is the middle of the night, and the streets are totally empty. There is almost complete darkness except for a tall highway lamp and the first light of dawn breaking in a violet sky. Theme music accompanies the journey of the carriage along the street, but it really surges at this point, highlighted by the sounding of a dreamy, wistful horn. Critics have sometimes spoken of a quality of nostalgia in your films, and in this scene, certainly, it can hardly be missed.

Ivory: But whose nostalgia? Not for an Indian. It was like a scene from a Lucia Lane novel. The streets were empty, but they should not have been. As the festive carriage rolled by, we should have seen hundreds of sleeping forms on the sidewalk—the homeless lying like so many corpses under dirty sheets. We could have had that typical image of Bombay, but I didn't think of it in time.

Long: The commercialization of romance plays a central role in the picture. Lucia Lane is the author of a successful novel about Hollywood, *Consenting Adults,* that is reminiscent of Jacqueline Susann's *The Valley of the Dolls.* Did you and Ruth have her, or someone like her, in mind when you created Lucia Lane?

Ivory: Absolutely. Or at any rate, an English equivalent. Who would that have been? Not Barbara Cartland. She was somehow more wholesome.

Long: As an Indian film idol, Vikram is also a purveyor of "romance," and thus he and Lucia play similar roles in their different societies, East and West. They are romantic escapists in the work they do and in the lives they lead. Isn't it their narcissism, their deep self-involvement, that dooms their affair?

Ivory: Self-involvement, certainly. I felt that Vikram was trying to be better but did not have the intellectual equipment to know how to go about that. And Lucia constantly brought out the worst in him.

Long: Their romance is complicated by the presence of another male character, Hari, who also falls in love with Lucia. He is a Bombay screenwriter and frustrated poet who writes stilted verse plays and insists on seeing Lucia in an idealized way. His rage at Vikram when he repudiates Lucia precipitates the tragedy of this trio of characters. What connects *Bombay Talkie* with your films just preceding it is the failure of transcendence; isn't that, by the way, a frequent theme in Ruth's novels, both early and late?

Ivory: Yes, but in this case it is in a lurid, melodramatic mode.

Long: But *Bombay Talkie* isn't entirely a tragedy; there is a certain amount of humor in it. The most obvious instance of this humor is seen in the figure of the guru at the ashram, who shows home movies of his "conquest" of Los Angeles and plays Ping-Pong with gleeful complacency.

Ivory: The home movies were real home movies taken at Agnes Moorehead's house at one of those quasi-spiritual events that were concocted from time to time by the young Ismail. This one was a *mahurrat*—the celebration at the beginning of an Indian film as the first shot is taken, when the camera is draped with a marigold garland and a coconut is broken. All this is very Hindu, in fact. We have one for every one of our films, wherever we are. We can always find a coconut, but the marigold garland is harder to come up with.

Long: It was a little hard to know what to make of those home movies, but the guru in any case is evidently a fraud. Lucia joins his ashram at one point and plays a flirtatious game with him. Strolling around the porch of the building with his followers pacing beside and behind him, and running on with opaque comments about the holy life, the guru darts a glance at Lucia that reveals his awareness of her in a sexual way. Another deflation of a character occurs when an Indian gentleman of venerable age pursues Lucia down the corridor of the Taj Mahal Hotel, attempting to get her to sign his copy of her sexually provocative novel. Are there any genuinely spiritual characters in the film?

Ivory: Oddly, one would have to say it was the ill-fated Hari. He seemed to be the only character who was remotely self-aware, who had any imagination about their predicament, and any sense of humor about the antics the threesome were involved in.

Long: Bombay Talkie was treated roughly by critics, who felt for one thing that it moved too slowly, a charge sometimes made about certain of your other films. How would you respond to it?

Ivory: It probably did move too slowly for most people, particularly if they ran out of patience with the story and characters. None of my films are exactly noted for their speed, but in some the story is involving and maybe even moving, so the slow pace is forgiven.

Long: You've said that *Bombay Talkie* is a personal favorite of yours. What is there about it that you particularly like?

Ivory: Sometimes one makes something that is wacky and atypical. One has a special affection for such products, I think. Visually the film was stunning, and its effects came out of the oddity of the story and situation rather than from anything picturesque in a conventional way. The terrific look Mitra got often came out of ugliness. He used to complain to me on a new set of *Bombay Talkie,* "Oh, it's so ugly, so vulgar!" And I would tell him to exploit that very quality. This seemed to satisfy him, and he ended up shooting maybe his very best color

film. He also had two of the most beautiful Indian stars to light: Shashi Kapoor
in his glory, and Aparna Sen in hers. She played Vikram's barren wife, Mala.
Do you remember her from Ray's *Two Daughters?* She was the beautiful tomboy
bride who ran away on her wedding night to play with her squirrel.

Long: In 1974, when you and Ismail were in India, Ismail decided to revisit
his friend, the Maharaja of Jodhpur, who had helped him earlier to gather material for a documentary he was making with Anthony Korner on royal India.
It was during that visit—you also went along, with Ruth—at the Umaid Bhawan Palace that you conceived the idea of a film that was to be *Autobiography of
a Princess.* Can you tell me something about the Maharaja
and the Maharani of Jodhpur and their world?

Ivory: That was only two or three years after Indira
Gandhi had stripped the "native princes," as they were
called by the British, of all their privileges and their privy
purses. Many of them had vast estates, foreign and Indian investments, masses of jewelry, houses in Monte
Carlo . . . *they* were okay. Others had nothing but run-
down palaces and armies of dependents. The Jodhpurs
luckily belonged to the first group, and they also entered
politics.

Long: There was an archive of miscellaneous film
footage of royal India at the palace in Jodhpur. This had
been discovered by Ismail and Anthony Korner, who was a school friend of
the maharaja. Was this footage to be set off by modern interviews with the deposed rulers?

Ivory: Well, that was the idea at first. But in time I sort of inherited all the
footage, and Ruth and I used it to make another kind of film—mostly fictional,
but with the old footage and modern interviews with the princes woven
through it.

Long: You compiled an illustrated book in 1975 called *Autobiography of a
Princess; Also Being the Adventures of an American Film Director in the Land of the
Maharajas.* It includes excerpts from interviews you yourself did with Gayatri
Devi, the Maharani of Jaipur, in which she talks about her lifestyle and that

AUTOBIOGRAPHY
OF A PRINCESS

*A maharaja's daughter with
a romanticized view of her
father is reunited in London
with his disillusioned male
secretary on the occasion
of the maharaja's birthday
anniversary. With James
Mason and Madhur Jaffrey.
1975. Feature. 16 millimeter;
color; 59 minutes.*

of her family, and also about the new laws being enacted by the Indian government, rescinding the perquisites, allowances, and even the titles of the maharajas. You make it seem as if excerpts from your own filmed interview with her had appeared in a British newsreel. But didn't the dispossession of the maharajas happen long before this?

Ivory: No. Only in 1971. And it wasn't a newsreel. We concocted a fake TV program about the deposed princes, who were heard lamenting their new powerless state and the loss of their twenty-one-gun salutes and special license plates for their Rolls-Royces. It's not an especially flattering portrait. But Bapji, the Maharaja of Jodhpur, wasn't self-pitying at all. He was hardheaded and quite soon positioned himself in the central government, was sent abroad as an ambassador, and so forth.

Long: A number of the photographs, paintings (including a life-size one of Queen Victoria), and settings shown in the book also appear in the film. The footage of "the cenotaphs of the dead queens" outside Jodhpur appears memorably in the movie; how do you feel this powerful image is relevant to the story you are telling?

Ivory: Well, a cenotaph in India is constructed at the place where the body of an important person was burned. A monument is built over the spot, more or less grand. The group of cenotaphs we showed resembled—in Cyril Sahib's (and Ruth's) mind—a flock of prehistoric birds come to roost in the desert. It suggests vultures. This is the place where the royal ladies were brought when their lives in the purdah palace were over—and where the princess would end up maybe. She gives a little shudder in the film when this image appears.

Long: Then there are those colorful art deco rooms we see in the film, which might seem out of place in an Indian palace but actually were not. Would you comment on this?

Ivory: The Umaid Bhawan Palace was built in the 1930s and '40s as a famine relief project by the then-maharaja; he wanted something up-to-date, as many of his fellow princes did. It's the last great Indian palace to be built. It's now a hotel, and all those amazing rooms can be visited, or even let.

Long: There is a sequence with an old, partly toothless Indian lady who sings and accompanies herself on a harmonium, which Ruth liked particularly. Why did you want this sequence in the film?

Ivory: The old woman was a songstress, an aged courtesan, who would, when younger, have been called to the palace to perform for the men. Her name was Bari Moti Bhai. She sings with gusto in a cracked voice, her arthritic fingers on the harmonium and dancing around her head in the last vestiges of professional coquetry. She was happy—or so the princess felt—with her mat to sleep on and a few old pots to cook in—because she still sang like a bird at eighty-five and her heart was full. . . .

Long: As Ruth envisioned it, *Autobiography* was to be a single character film with an Indian princess relating her story, but you persuaded her that a male character would also be needed, someone she knew at her father's court. For this figure you drew partly on the experience of E. M. Forster, who had been the private secretary of a maharaja in the early 1920s. Was it you or Ruth who thought of Forster in this connection?

Ivory: Both of us drew on that, and on J. R. Ackerley's *Hindoo Holiday,* which also has a bright, young—and gay—English hanger-on at court, ostensibly helping the maharaja in some way, and helping to keep him amused and au courant. The same figure turns up in *Heat and Dust* as Harry. Now, *don't* get the idea that any of these bright young Englishmen had physical affairs with their maharajas. They might have liked to, and have pined away in their own version of a purdah palace, thinking of their handsome, magnetic, and sensual employers, until they finally got disgruntled and went back to England.

Long: Autobiography is unique among your films insofar as it uses only two actors, James Mason and Madhur Jaffrey, whom it places within the confinement of a single room. But it doesn't seem like a filmed theater piece; it feels very cinematic. Is the fact that the action takes place in such a limited space meant to add to an impression of a constriction in the lives of the characters, Cyril Sahib and the princess?

Ivory: Well, no, though their lives are certainly constricted, or become constricted in time. We continually go out and see what it is those characters are talking about. And then we keep coming back to the room where they are having their little reunion, back to the two aging characters and their reminiscences. We keep showing what it is they most remember about life in princely India decades before. The film "opens up," as they say, because of all the archive footage in which many kinds of glamorous and exotic events, as well as horrific ones, are shown, not just discussed.

Long: With her film projector the princess shows scenes of her father, the maharaja, and his entourage in India in the 1930s and '40s, but what the viewer sees is a strange jumble of fragmentary scenes that don't make much sense. Wouldn't she realize that what she is showing isn't coherent?

Ivory: To her it is perfectly coherent; she remembers every frame of it and is ready to relive it: home movies with weddings and whatever, parties and pig stickings and celebrations. Of course she has seen them and seen them and seen them. But in the mind of Cyril Sahib it *is* just a jumble. He didn't know half the time he was in India what great events they were celebrating. There's a bit Cyril thinks is a royal procession, with someone being carried in state somewhere, but in fact it is a corpse being carried to be put on a funeral pyre. So everything like this is all mixed up in his head.

Long: What about the sequence near the end where the maharaja's involvement in a sordid sex scandal in London is dramatized briefly. It's surprisingly like some silent movie melodrama. Isn't this out of key with the subtlety of the rest of the film?

Ivory: It isn't out of key. It was supposed to have a sordid, tabloid quality. It was an ugly blot, something horrid, a lurid headline. It is only out of key in relation to the almost sanctified picture the princess had of her father.

Long: Why is it that the princess has not returned to India to live?

Ivory: She talks a lot about her "freedom"—how it will be taken away from her if she returns to her father's state, and how she'll just be locked up in purdah, closed off from everything. So she opts for a life abroad. But it is a life alone.

Long: When the princess and Cyril meet at the princess's London apartment, they both in their different ways have been living in a kind of exile from what was. But they also have something else in common; although this is supposed to be a happy occasion, an inner anger that each harbors toward the other lies buried just beneath the surface of their supposedly cordial reunion.

Ivory: It's not so buried and comes out in the course of the film. She tries to provoke him, accuses him of disloyalty to her father. By the end of the film they seem to be mutual accomplices almost in some dark deed.

Long: Cyril has never forgiven the maharaja for having led him astray into a useless and wasted life, and the princess has never forgiven Cyril for his not having come to the support of her father when the sex scandal broke.

Ivory: Right, and she can't now forgive his not writing the appreciative, the glamorizing, book that she wants him to do about her father, a sort of history of the rosy days she remembers (very selectively) and wants to save for posterity.

Long: The truth is that the maharaja was a sybaritic prince who damaged both of them. He undermined Cyril's morale and his chance to lead a life having some purpose in it. You know, Cyril seems like quite a number of characters in Ruth's fiction—the English characters who come to India and are so overwhelmed by its "heat and dust" that they lose their sense of identity.

Ivory: This was Cyril's complaint. It had all been fun at first, then it turned dark. He said he felt as if he were "rotting" there in the maharaja's palace, that he had lost himself . . . that his life had become empty and pointless.

Long: Cyril's life at Turton-on-Sea involves a significant loss of color and seems dominated by guilt—guilty isolation and penance. The irony of the princess is that she is too much like her father, is very self-centered, willful. She willfully refuses to recognize her father's faults. *Autobiography* runs to only sixty minutes, the same length as the reunion itself, yet it manages to be a very accomplished and subtle study of character. Isn't this one of Ruth's favorite films?

Ivory: And mine. I tell people: if you want to really experience our Indian movies, look first at *Autobiography of a Princess,* then see the others.

Long: In casting the male character for *Autobiography of a Princess,* Ismail claims that you first considered Ralph Richardson, John Gielgud, and Laurence Olivier. How seriously were they considered, and were they ever contacted?

Ivory: They certainly were; scripts were sent to all of them. I wanted Ralph

Ivory with James Mason and cameraman Walter Lassally on the London set of *Auto-biography of a Princess* (1975).

Richardson the most, but they all turned it down for one reason or another. Then Ismail impulsively sent it to James Mason, who had always been *his* choice for the part, and Mason—luckily for us—accepted it at once.

Long: The greatest thing about it of all perhaps is the acting of James Mason and Madhur Jaffrey—he so weary, so hesitant and inward, a man worn down and groping in the dark; and she with her almost coquettish cordiality and her inner hostility. Their performances are so perfect, so flawless, that they must constitute one of the finest acting duets in your films.

Ivory: Yes, I think so. Perhaps the only duet as such. Both were perfect, though when we began I couldn't imagine the glamorous James Mason in such a part and had to be literally forced by Ismail to accept him. Then he arrived on the first day, already in character, and sort of crept up the stairs to our set, after which he held us spellbound by those long ruminative soliloquies, which he'd got letter perfect. How did he do that? During them he'd sometimes pause for a moment; I felt he was then preparing for the next flow of words by a sort of instantaneous review in his mind of what was to come.

Long: *Autobiography of a Princess* and *Hullabaloo over Georgie and Bonnie's Pictures* have in common that they each have a connection with the Umaid Bhawan Palace in Jodhpur. *Autobiography* made use of its film archive to sketch the maharaja and his world in royal India; but in *Hullabaloo,* more importantly, the palace is the showcase setting of the film. It is a magnificent palace that seems to stand off by itself in a far-stretching, uninhabited landscape. What was especially attractive for you about this place?

Ivory: At first I guess I didn't like it very much. It was new, mid-twentieth-century. I had snobbish notions about how Indian palaces *ought* to look. Its vast art deco concept and decoration were lost on me. And then I suddenly got it and understood the concept, which was as traditional as the Taj Mahal: a high central dome in the center with a tower at each corner. It had been built as a public works project by the Jodhpur family in the midst of a famine—just sort of madly plunked down on a boiling hot desert in an imperial gesture. It began to fascinate me.

Long: Your cinematographer, Walter Lassally, has been described as catching brilliantly "the light, mood and even the heat of a languid Indian countryside, framing dreamy figures in the delicate fretwork of a palace window drifting through the shadows of magnificent rooms." One is conscious of this at the opening when a young woman in a brightly colored sari is shown walking alone, rather mysteriously, through the gardens of the palace. Is she Bonnie, the maharaja's sister?

Ivory: Yes—or Bonnie's ancestor, I guess you'd say. We dressed her in the

HULLABALOO OVER GEORGIE AND BONNIE'S PICTURES

A fabled collection of Indian miniature paintings and how its owners—a young maharaja and his sister—thwart some high-minded Westerners who have plans to "save" it. With Larry Pine, Peggy Ashcroft, Saeed Jaffrey, Victor Banerjee, and Aparna Sen. 1978. Feature for television. 16 millimeter; color; 83 minutes.

style of an Indian miniature painting and showed her how to walk in a certain way, holding the edge of her sari out to hide her face. But you hardly had to teach the great Aparna Sen things of this kind.

Long: There is also supposed to be a female ghost of the palace, a young Englishwoman who died there in the period of the Raj, seemingly from "an excess of happiness." We see her in the garden at the end, apparently blessing the spirit of harmony and happiness that has descended on the film's characters. Yet Ruth herself had become disenchanted with the "heat and dust" of India at the time she wrote the screenplay.

Ivory: Well, *Hullabaloo* was a sort of fairy tale, about picture collecting and skullduggery in an oriental palace. It was a whole new mood for everybody.

Long: I'm told that Ruth really didn't want to write the screenplay for *Hullabaloo* at all, and that the writing of it did not come easily for her. What was there, do you know, that made her resist the work?

Ivory: This seems too extreme a view. We'd asked her—or she'd come up with—a sort of tongue-in-cheek idea that had to be just right—you know, like a soufflé—and it wasn't always easy to do this. How to find the exact balance between realism and fancifulness?

Long: There's also a story that when you were shooting the film on location at the palace, you still had not figured out what your denouement would be, and that you were shooting in fact from day to day without knowing what would come next. Didn't this put you under terrific stress?

Ivory: Well, not really. What was stressful was trying to write down her dictation over the terrible telephone connection between Delhi and the wilds of Rajasthan. I was afraid I'd miss something, and she was never sure I hadn't. The line kept being cut off. In those days the telephone service in India was more than primitive.

Long: *Hullabaloo* is widely regarded as the best of your early Indian films, with the exception of *Shakespeare Wallah;* yet you and Ruth supposedly do not consider it as one of your favorite Merchant Ivory films. What reservations do you have about it?

Ivory: Well, I have some, but who gave you that idea? I mean, it was a light, funny sort of little movie made for television which then unexpectedly clicked with the public and the critics. It was never meant to be a major opus or any-thing like that.

Long: It has often been compared to Henry James as a subtle and sophisti-cated comedy of manners. Was either of you ever conscious of James while you were making the film?

Ivory: I don't remember ever summoning him up; with Ruth, however, he's never very far away, like her beloved Chekhov.

Long: Georgie is played by Victor Banerjee, who had been featured as Dr. Aziz in *A Passage to India* and appeared in some of Ray's films, such as *The Chess Players.* It struck me that he looks very much like the Maharaja of Jodhpur in the photograph of him in your book *Autobiography of a Princess.*

Ivory: Yes, he does a bit: or maybe Maharaja Ram Singh of Jaipur, who reigned in the nineteenth century. Again, he was suggested by Satyajit Ray, and it was pretty much his first actual lead in any film. He was from a family of zamindars—feudal landowners, I guess you'd call them, so his royal manner came naturally to him.

Long: There is Saeed Jaffrey, the former husband of Madhur Jaffrey, as Shri Narain, the suave curator of the Tasveer art collection; and Larry Pine as Clark Haven, the scion of a peach-canning fortune, who has a rather cold-blooded passion for collecting art. But most of all there is Dame Peggy Ashcroft as Lady Gwyneth Pugh ("Lady Gee"), who acquires ancient Indian art for a British mu-seum like the Victoria and Albert and is marvelous. All of these characters are involved in a game of wits to obtain the Tasveer collection. Was it you or Ruth who had the idea for this film? The use of the Indian miniatures makes me wonder if it wasn't you?

Ivory: We were approached by Melvin Bragg of London Weekend Television about making a film for them. There was only one stipulation: it had to be about the arts in some way. None of us wanted to make a documentary, so we came up with the idea of *Hullabaloo,* which Bragg liked. It was my idea, all right, to bring in Indian miniatures. Why not? we thought. But it was a joint decision to go to India to make a film, and again Bragg was happy with that. In fact, he may initially have suggested it; I don't remember any more.

Long: The "Georgie" and "Bonnie" in the film's title comes from their Scot-

Peggy Ashcroft, as Lady Gee, examines a miniature painting offered for sale by Shri Na-rain, played by Saeed Jaffrey, in *Hullabaloo over Georgie and Bonnie's Pictures* (1978).

tish governess's having adopted these names for them when they were small. But it is certainly far-out that a maharaja and his sister should have these Scottish names—and the names, in fact, of wee children.

Ivory: Why do you say "far-out"? It's all far-out. You are forgetting—or maybe you don't know—how much aping of English manners, speech, dress, and so on the Indian upper classes indulged in. Now they try to seem American.

Long: The Christmas party with Georgie dressed up as Santa Claus, and an elderly, stony-faced nun leading a group of Indian schoolchildren in an Indian-accented rendering of "Jingle Bells," belongs to the same mad spirit as the title. It is comic because so incongruous. But I wondered why they would be celebrating Christmas. Aren't these characters Muslims?

Ivory: Maharajas are not Muslims, for one thing. They're Hindus. A Muslim prince in India is called a nawab—like the Nawab in *Heat and Dust* played by Shashi Kapoor. But this is being pedantic. What's more important is the aping of English upper-crust manners by these people. Also, Catholic nuns often ran the private (and exclusive) convent schools in India—and still do.

Long: The theme of the past versus the present runs through the film. Georgie and Bonnie are the inheritors of the past, including its art, yet they feel its constriction and would also want to leave it. Georgie practices not painting but photography; he photographs blond-haired Western girls and aspires to be a freelancer. In the party scene from a generation earlier, the palace's past seems very romantic. But doesn't the impulse in Georgie and Bonnie to break free of their tradition-bound past at the palace undercut the implication of a sublime past?

Ivory: But we don't really regard the tradition of princely India as being sublime, do we? The whole point of *Autobiography of a Princess* is that it was far, far from that. Similarly here. Under the veneer of glamour lay a bloodthirsty history of a feudal state in Rajasthan, in which the ruler was an absolute master. He might be someone like Saddam Hussein, cutting off people's heads in a temper tantrum, and then the English would depose him. Or he might be somebody like Georgie, fooling around with English girls and photography or other harmless hobbies, in which case he would be left alone.

Long: There is, I think, a shared interest in the past versus the present in *Autobiography of a Princess, Hullabaloo over Georgie and Bonnie's Pictures,* and *Heat and Dust.* Are they in any sense a Merchant Ivory trilogy?

Ivory: Aren't trilogies supposed, in the best of worlds, to be a grand, overarching story in which there is some masterful theme, common characters, and resounding climax? As, for instance, Ray's trilogy about Apu? I think our three films set in princely India don't satisfy the criteria.

HEAT AND DUST

Two contrasting and interlaced stories from Ruth Jhabvala's novel, set in the British Raj of the 1920s and in modern India. With Greta Scacchi, Shashi Kapoor, and Julie Christie. 1982. Feature. 35 millimeter; color; 130 minutes.

Long: Heat and Dust was adapted for the screen by Ruth from her own Booker Prize–winning novel. How did she feel about the movie compared to the novel?

Ivory: I think she liked it very much. She was at the first public screening at the BAFTA [British Academy of Film and Television Arts] theater in London and seemed very pleased.

Long: I notice that she follows the novel to the letter, whereas in some other adaptations you have made you took what you wanted and did not hesitate to make changes.

Ivory: Yes, she pretty much followed the novel; if I remember, we might have juggled the flashbacks to the 1920s around a bit in the editing room. She originally wrote both stories out and then cut them up and dealt them almost like cards pinned to the wall in storyboards. She said she would never have worked like that if she wasn't so used to being in an editing room.

Long: You've been quoted as saying, "It's the hardest film I've ever made. . . . It's a very abstract story, much more so than any of our other recent films. It's more literary than most scripts, and because all the details and layers of thought and explanation have to be translated into dialogue and action some of it is very hard to play." Were you thinking of any scenes in particular?

Ivory: I suppose I was thinking of the transitions between the present day and the 1920s. Sometimes those were made according to written passages heard from Marcia's letters from Olivia, sometimes because the parallel stories were being enacted in the same place. Or the time of the year—the time of heat and dust storms—dictated how we moved ahead. It's funny, because I no longer recall the film as being all that difficult for me. I enjoyed making the film, despite our shaky finances: it brought me back to India, and it turned out that I hadn't in any way lost my enthusiasm for the place, my feeling for it. Also, by then, I had fully subscribed to the appeal of the scientific, even scholarly, approach to making a period film that had first excited me during *The Europeans.* "Getting it right," as Martin Scorsese puts it: costumes, interiors, dialogue, makeup, odd social or visual tidbits that make the thing "right," or authentic.

Long: Autobiography of a Princess and *Hullabaloo over Georgie and Bonnie's Pictures* both prepare for *Heat and Dust* in their interest in the period of the Raj. Don't they, however, take different views of it?

Ivory: Well, really, *Hullabaloo* is very much post-Raj. It's about modern India, though it has a light, almost fairy-tale quality. It's entirely an "entertainment," a kind of comedy having to do with the heist of some valuable art. *Autobiography*—also set in princely India—is far more serious. I don't think of either as being "Raj" films exactly. The English played subsidiary roles in both, or English concerns were not paramount.

Long: Reviewers tended to feel that the contemporary parts of *Heat and Dust*

Musical cushions, a scene in *Heat and Dust* (1983). Shashi Kapoor, the Nawab, on the left; his guests Olivia (Greta Scacchi) and Narry (Nickolas Grace), center.

were less involving than the earlier parts set in the time of the Raj. Do you think that assessment is fair?

Ivory: I understand it. The 1920s sequences were more glamorous, unusual, romantic even. And we introduced a whole new cast of players, apart from Shashi Kapoor and Madhur Jaffrey, that had not been seen in our films before; the 1920s section had more atmosphere, was more foreign, and in a way confirmed expectations. The modern sections, by comparison, seemed humdrum, even with Julie Christie in them. They showed a rather run-down, noisy modern India that people are afraid of perhaps: a place of poverty, often with frightening sights—the modern, negative conception of the country that Westerners, and especially timid Americans, have.

Long: Did you find that women were particularly drawn to the film? After

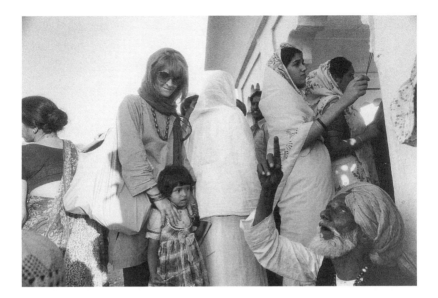

Anne (Julie Christie) visits a shrine in a scene from *Heat and Dust* (1983).

all, it's about women's experience in India. It seems almost the reverse of a movie like *Gandhi*, which came out a year earlier and in which the men were the movers and shakers and played a dominant role. The women in *Gandhi* were shunted into the background.

Ivory: Heat and Dust was a great hit in England as well as the rest of Europe, but perhaps it did mostly appeal to women for the reason you say. It was finally a story with many fine feminine portraits.

Long: It appeared in the same time frame—around 1983—not only of *Gandhi* but also of *A Passage to India,* and of two major television series about India— *The Jewel in the Crown* and *The Far Pavilions.* When you decided to make *Heat and Dust,* did you have any inkling that the movie would be in the vanguard of all these pictures about India?

Ivory: No. But the success in the United States of *The Jewel in the Crown* prepared people for the others. You know, Americans have never really had that much interest in India, and that big TV series broke them in more than all the films of Ray—or our own Indian films—together.

Long: Ismail has commented on the fact that before Ruth adapted *Heat and Dust* for Merchant Ivory, another producer was to have made the film, and the English playwright David Mercer to have written the screenplay. The project, which did not work out, was to have had Omar Sharif and Glenda Jackson in the leading roles. Would they, in your opinion, have been good choices?

Ivory: Of course not. At least not for us. With our long Indian past, and with Shashi Kapoor, who was exactly the right age, we would not need to cast an Arab, wonderful as he is. As for Glenda Jackson, well, she might have been a very good Anne, for all I know, but when we took over the project, we soon—or Ismail soon—came up with the idea of Julie Christie.

Long: Your first choice for the role of Olivia was Alice Krige, the girl from *Chariots of Fire.* Why Alice Krige?

Ivory: She appealed to me . . . and then we had not yet found Greta Scacchi. Our finding her was almost accidental.

Long: Twenty-two at the time and barely a year out of drama school, she made her film debut in *Heat and Dust.* What was she like at that early point in her career?

Ivory: She was one of those actresses who, upon meeting, I instantly decided to give the part to. She satisfied all the necessities: young, beautiful, with a somewhat odd kind of beauty, sexy or sensual, well-trained, well-spoken. A half-Italian English rose. What could be better, more spectacular?

Long: There were a number of stunning shots of Greta Scacchi wearing a white dress and holding a white parasol, against an expanse of rust-colored Indian landscape. I wonder if these tableaux of her as a figure in white were meant to have connotations of innocence, or if white was merely the costume of well-bred young Englishwomen of that time.

Ivory: Englishwomen did wear a lot of white then, not understanding, or caring, that in India it is the color of mourning, of widowhood.

Long: Julie Christie, who plays Anne in the modern story, was actually born in India—on her father's tea plantation in Assam. She became an international star in the 1960s in films like *Darling* as the liberated, rule-breaking young Englishwoman. In *Heat and Dust,* however, she's not really all that unconventional. It's her great aunt Olivia who broke the most sacred rules of English-Indian relations in the civil lines at Satipur, who was the unconventional one. What is it that these two women, Olivia and Anne, have in common?

Ivory: Both sink or disappear into Indian life and find their fulfillment there. Olivia would never leave; Anne undoubtedly would, taking her child with her.

Long: Olivia goes at the end to live alone in the Nawab's lodge in the snow-covered mountains. What is it that she discovers there?

Ivory: Discover doesn't seem the right word. She had been ostracized by the English in Satipur; she couldn't live there any more, yet she didn't want to leave India, or the Nawab, so she went to stay in a mountain chalet in Kashmir. Her music must have been a resource for her; she would have been very lonely. Anne tells us that she saw the Nawab infrequently. She must have developed great inner strength.

Long: Jennifer Kendal returns to your films in *Heat and Dust* as Mrs. Saunders, wife of the mean-spirited and irascible Dr. Saunders. In *Bombay Talkie*, as Lucia Lane, she had been a kind of femme fatale, a man-killer. Here she is a morbid neurasthenic, the product of too many years spent in Satipur. And she is splendid. Why didn't she appear more often in your movies?

Ivory: A good question. I suppose it's because she was raising a young family, and then, after *Bombay Talkie* we concentrated our energies on films in America. When we came to make all our English films in the mideighties and nineties, she was gone.

Long: The character of Chid in *Heat and Dust* seems a descendant of Ernest in *The Householder,* the young and very naive American who travels to India in search of a spiritual awakening. Doesn't Chid exist too much as a type who serves to illustrate a point? Don't we know from the beginning that he will fail?

Ivory: His body fails before his resolve, or his enthusiasm for India and the path of the sadhu. Chid undermines his health, which often happens to Westerners who take up the spiritual life in India. Inevitably they get hepatitis, aren't treated for it properly, and sometimes die out there.

Long: Reviews of *Heat and Dust* were generally favorable, and Vincent Canby's was in particular. There's a passage in the review, however, that was rather puzzling. He speaks of "Jhabvala's wise, multilayered, essentially comic adaptation of her own novel." I wondered why he considered it "essentially comic." It moves at a rather measured pace and tends to be reflective. It's not a light-hearted film.

Shashi Kapoor, the charismatic and seductive Nawab of *Heat and Dust* (1983).

Ivory: No? I felt it was. More so than *Autobiography of a Princess,* which had many common features. Anyway, the *Times* always calls our films "comedies," and I'm glad they do. *Howards End* was a comedy, *The Remains of the Day* also.

Long: There was some criticism elsewhere of the Nawab-Olivia relationship as being "passionless," as failing to convey sexual passion. What is it that makes Olivia so fascinated by the Nawab that she is willing to throw over everything for him?

Ivory: The Nawab represents India and all it stands for and, by extension, the Orient. No doubt people who are not drawn to all that cannot understand the passion of people, both men and women, who are. In the one sex scene between the Nawab and Olivia, the former's attack is undoubtedly a bit comic; he can't unfasten her weird English garters and fumbles with them. Indian film critics were affronted by the Nawab's seeming lack of experience.

Long: Heat and Dust is remarkable for putting India on the screen in a large way. Images occur throughout the film that are surprising, and you might almost say "breathtaking." Visually the film is a triumph, and this would surely help to account for its success at the box office—more so than for any previous Merchant Ivory film. In its scope and visual excitement, doesn't it anticipate your large-canvas period films that come soon after it?

Ivory: It did have more scope, certainly: two time periods that were interlaced, the look at the inner workings of an Indian ruler's court, or life—the darker side of it hinted at, the glamour in the foreground. In that way it was like *Autobiography of a Princess,* with its references to violence, madness, dissipation and endless boredom, sudden, unexplained deaths, heat, dust, riots.

Long: Heat and Dust did well, but I believe there was some problem, some horror, with your American distributor, Universal Studios. Would you talk about that?

Ivory: It was a usual story. Universal took the film for distribution in America because a young executive in charge of acquisitions was crazy about it and successfully wooed us. But then, on the eve of the film's release in New York, he left Universal to become a producer himself, and his replacement didn't care that much about the film. This often happens, sometimes in the middle of the making of a film. The replacement assesses the situation and decides that if the project should turn out badly, he will be held responsible. However, if he maintains a distance, no one can hold him accountable. And though *Heat and Dust* was a great success in Europe, American lack of interest in India in the early 1980s was certainly a reality that a distributor would have to spend a lot of money to change. So the film just sort of faded away here, like our earlier Indian films. No one was willing to push it at Universal, make it a success in the United States like *The Jewel in the Crown.*

AMERICA

Robert Emmet Long: Savages is an unusual film for you; the four Indian feature films that precede it are realistic works, while *Savages* seems like pure fantasy. Also, instead of having a single protagonist or pair of protagonists, you divide your attention among a group of Mud People who then become civilized people, no one of which dominates the work. I can't think of any other film in which you have done this.

James Ivory: That's true. Perhaps only *Roseland* is in a way like that. That, too, shows some sort of "enchanted" world, where time is supposed to stand still; in *Savages,* on the other hand, time is compressed. Thousands of years pass in an afternoon.

Long: What is touching about this group of characters is that they have such a tenuous life. They become civilized people only briefly, during a single day, and they are gone again, back into prehistory. Yet I don't remember any reviewer commenting on this quality of group poignancy. I find it more touching than the decline and fall of Jolly Grimm in *The Wild Party.*

SAVAGES

A Stone Age tribe stumbles upon an abandoned American mansion. The rise and fall of civilization as seen in the course of a weekend house party. With Thayer David, Louis Stadlen, Anne Francine, Salome Jens, and Sam Waterston. 1972. Feature. 35 millimeter; color and black-and-white; 106 minutes.

Ivory: You can be touched by the decline of any group, or people, in history; you have to possess some kind of historical consciousness for that to happen. Not everybody is interested in history. In fact, very few are.

Long: I just said that *Savages* seems like pure fantasy, but within the fantasy you *do* sketch the manners of the upper-middle-class or upper-class social life in the American Northeast between the world wars. And in your own neighborhood, since you have a house near the Hudson, a large house with white pillars in front, not too far north of Beechwood, the mansion where you shot *Savages.* Have you ever taken much interest in the architecture and social history of this region?

Ivory: Beyond forays into Westchester, and then to Beechwood to make our film, I never ventured into the upper Hudson Valley until 1974 or so. I don't know why. Talk about the decline of a group being poignant! The old Hudson Valley gentry are the epitome of Rise and Fall. It's George Trow who first made me aware of all that.

Long: Perhaps the most important "character" in the movie is Beechwood itself, the neo-Georgian mansion on the Hudson that you came across one day. In your Indian films, deteriorated but architecturally magnificent palaces were so evocative that they were also virtual "characters." What was it about Beechwood and its grounds that attracted you?

Ivory: It really was one of those enclosed worlds "frozen in time," as they say—a large, deserted mansion, still filled with fine things, into which vines were creeping through doors and windows, where the closets were still filled with the clothes of long-dead owners, and desk drawers with their abandoned checkbooks. Much, much food for thought for someone like me!

Long: Beechwood seems to have a life of its own. Its lights flicker on and off at a dramatic moment like the lights of Gatsby's big house when he is about to be reunited with Daisy Fay. One thinks of F. Scott Fitzgerald a bit because of the evocations of the 1920s in the film and the life of the very rich in America. Did you ever think of Fitzgerald while you were planning or making the film?

Ivory: There wasn't a day when we didn't.

Long: How did you decide what the Mud People would look like when they are encountered at the opening?

Ivory: I saw ads for Canadian Club whiskey in magazines, in which explorers dressed in pith helmets and smart khaki outfits met up with New Guinea Stone Age "mudmen" in the jungle. These primitive people were smeared with mud and wore the kind of masks we made for the movie. After they put their spears down and shook hands with the curious intruders, the latter were seen back at

Margaret Brewster, as a Mudwoman, before her transfor-
mation into the tart-tongued Lady Cora in *Savages* (1972).

their camp relaxing with highballs of Canadian Club, reminiscing over their interesting day. All this was presented in the ads completely straight-faced.

Long: The Mud People at the opening seem a bit like farcical figures in a silent
movie. Isn't there humor here?

Ivory: The humor is there. How can you ask? It comes partly from the deadpan title cards explaining what was going on, like "In the forest, where perfect spheres are unknown, the arrival of a croquet ball causes astonishment,"
or "Tribal elders are often distinguished by pebbles in their teeth although such
is not the case here." Audiences did laugh when they saw things like that on
the screen—maybe nervously.

Long: The dense forest in which they live tends to be dark, and it is shot in sepia tones, as if it were a souvenir from the past; but Beechwood appears in clear, bright daylight. If I am not mistaken, you are interested in observing the qualities of light in which the estate is seen at different times and from different angles. It is more complicated than the forest world and maybe seems to stand for civilization; it has been constructed from the human eye and brain, and it has a history. The Mud People are in awe of it.

Ivory: The Mud People emerge from their dark jungle, yes, into the brighter world of civilization, represented by the house. It is also when we go from black-and-white photography into color. But "qualities of light," as such, weren't really all that much on our minds—unless you want to say that for a cameraman how light is photographed—especially daylight—is never very far from his mind.

Long: Doesn't Beechwood also suggest the idea of art? It has beautiful grounds on which well-to-do characters play croquet on summer afternoons; and inside we see a harp, together with oil paintings on the walls, including a remarkable one of a beautiful youth that a female savage licks lovingly with her tongue. There is even a life-size gilded sculpture of Minerva, the Roman goddess of wisdom and patroness of the arts.

Ivory: Yes, and the flowering of art and literature, a golden age, is represented by the long soliloquy spoken at the dinner table by Penelope, the "high-strung" girl played by Paulita Sedgwick, about the Villa Miramar and its owner, the painter Andrew Chatfield—all imaginary. After that hushed moment, it's all downhill.

Long: Julian Branch, who seems to be in residence at the house, is a rising young musician-songwriter and protégé of Carlotta, the hostess; in the course of the film he sings, accompanies himself at the piano, and at the end plays a mournful or soulful cello. How does Julian Branch figure in the larger scheme of the movie?

Ivory: He was meant to be the artist, or "creative," figure, and at the end, during the Decline, he withdraws into a contemplative solitude and plays his cello as everything goes to hell. Rather like a monk in the early Middle Ages.

Long: So we have the awestruck Mud People following the source of the mysterious croquet ball that comes sailing through the forest to the place where they are about to perform a ritual sacrifice, and their arrival at Beechwood as if by means of a time machine. This was wholly your conception, wasn't it?

Ivory: Pretty much. But much elaborated by the two scriptwriters.

Long: You had George Swift Trow and Michael O'Donoghue prepare the screenplay. Did you do any work on the screenplay yourself, apart from offering your guidance?

Ivory: My guidance, as director/instigator, was more or less continuous, and when George Trow took off before finishing the script (I think he wasn't finally all that interested in scenes where people revert to barbarism), I had to pitch in to help Michael O'Donoghue, who stayed on valiantly to the end. I ought to point out that when we began to shoot, the two screenwriters hadn't finished the screenplay. The last third of the film is much more O'Donoghue's work than George Trow's. Luckily, we had quite an elaborate and well-worked-out treatment to go by, but it lacked dialogue.

Long: I've read the screenplay recently and found it quite intelligent—sharper and more subtle than some people might think on a casual viewing of *Savages.* Were there any problems between the two collaborators, particularly since George Trow just up and left, as you say, partway through the shooting to work on another project?

Ivory: No problem that I know of. They loved working together, trying out jokes on each other, and savoring the elaborate dialogue they were thinking up. But George Trow had a subsequent history of abandoning film projects he was involved in, or had even instigated. I think he got bored easily, and a little rebellious, a little resistant, to all the paraphernalia and personnel of moviemaking.

Long: Savages is essentially a comic work. It seems like a haywire kind of drawing-room comedy at times, and it contains elements of farce, as, for example, when the Mud People go through the bedroom wardrobe, puzzling over garments they find and beating on a gentleman's black top hat as if it must be some kind of drum. You have also called *Savages* "an absurdist comedy." Would you expand on that?

Ivory: We had to call it something, and "absurdist" was a very current word back in the early seventies for dramatic works that couldn't quite be pigeon-

Left to right: Asha Puthli, Neil Fitzgerald, Ultra Violet, Eva Saleh, and Margaret Brewster. As the decline commences, the Mud People, now transformed into civilized men and women, return to their narcotic leaf chewing in *Savages* (1972).

holed. And perhaps "absurdist" diluted another frequently used adjective to describe *Savages*—"sophomoric."

Long: I see absurdist comedy in the film in the many things that don't quite make sense. Why does Otto Nürder go waltzing off across the lawn at a mad, whirling pace with the bully called Archie? Why does Lady Cora, in the double-seated lawn swing, peel the leaves off a cabbage that is then snatched away and tossed from character to character like a volleyball? Why does an athletic young man wear a dress, and why do the others fail to notice it or find it out of the way? Did you contribute any of these oddnesses in particular?

Ivory: Everybody was contributing various kinds of oddnesses all the time. So did the actors (Ultra Violet wearing her backless evening gown front to back, for instance), so did I, and so even did the no-nonsense cinematographer, Walter Lassally.

Long: There is an absurdist feeling, too, in the non sequiturs of the conversations that are held. Lady Cora and Sir Harry seem at times to be conversing to each other about completely different things. It seems to me that Margaret Brewster as Lady Cora and Neil Fitzgerald as Sir Harry are among the drollest pairings in your film archive. Had they ever appeared together in a film before?

Ivory: Not that I know of. When Neil Fitzgerald finally saw the finished film, he was horrified and tried to sue us, saying that he'd been tricked into making a pornographic movie. He didn't like the shot of himself licking the air in the boiler room. But if that's lewd, he, after all, agreed to do it.

Long: You drew your cast from actors in the New York theater. Did they work out well for you?

Ivory: Mostly. They were very good and really got into their parts. Only Salome Jens had trouble playing her Woman in Disgrace. She fought the notion, somehow.

Long: Sam Waterston plays James, the sensitive Limping Man who drowns in the swimming pool while the poolside people neither notice nor care. You didn't discover Sam Waterston, but when you cast him in *Savages,* he was basically a stage actor and at a very early point in his film career. Two years later he played Nick Carraway in the film version of *The Great Gatsby* and became a movie star. Ismail has subsequently used him in *The Proprietor,* and I would think he would be a good character actor for you in other films.

Ivory: Well, he plays a big role in *Le Divorce*—that of the American professor Chester Walker, who visits his endangered daughters in Paris. He's the best, the richest—in terms of style—high-WASP actor we have in the United States. I think there's no one better at projecting worldliness or a kind of clearheaded sophistication. He lives in the wrong period almost, because today's American directors don't seem much interested in those qualities.

Long: Tell me about the fetching Asha Puthli, who plays the forest girl among the Mud People and the housemaid at Beechwood. Is she Indian?

Ivory: She is, from a South Indian Saraswati Brahmin family—the highest of the high. She's first seen in *The Guru* as a bright young thing at a party. Asha

Ismail Merchant (left), as Ivory (center) grapples with the left/right issues facing him on the first big Merchant Ivory dinner table scene during *Savages* (1972).

was vaguely connected with Andy Warhol's world but is primarily a singer with an amazing but untrained voice. She also appeared in a Louis Malle film, which I think was never released.

Long: I was struck by Louis Stadlen as Julian Branch and Thayer David as the rapacious Otto Nürder, but all the actors were good. The characters are all types, but they are strongly defined and come fully to life. Isn't the dinner party, where all the characters come together, a pivotal scene in the picture?

Ivory: What do you think? Everything led up to it, and then away from it. But I include the scenes immediately following it as part of this long episode: foretelling the future in the rotting fruit, the radio broadcast about the sinking ocean liner, and the "Steppin' on the Spaniel" dance sequence which followed that.

Long: There are certain things I wondered about. How did you decide to shoot a sequence with split screens, so that there was something happening on four different screens being shown at the same time?

Ivory: You know, with me, it's usually that I have some shots that are visually nice but lacking content or real dramatic interest, and I don't want to throw them away. So I pile them one on top of the other: the eye can take in more than one idea at a time, as we know. Sometimes these different shots, by accident, complement each other and even have some overall relevance.

Long: It can be argued that the "civilized" characters are not really civilized. Although they have the semblance of polite society, their sexual obsessiveness makes them reminiscent of their Mud People former selves, and they also exhibit a "primitive" drive for power over others. This is particularly true of the bully Archie and of Nürder, the capitalist-imperialist who is a bully on an international scale, a wielder of power in colonial Africa. Later in the film, civilization enters into a period of decline and fall. Some people feel that this passage of the picture is less focused than the earlier parts, less sharp and involving. What would you say to that?

Ivory: That's right, and it's because at exactly that point George Trow left us. The end of the film is quite slapdash, except for the final scene when all the savages return to the woods. That's strong, creepy, and if the viewer is historically tuned in, sad.

Long: I notice that a number of patterns and motifs run through the movie to give it structure. The toy railroad train running along its tracks at the beginning anticipates the later references to the railroad's incursion into the tropical forests, where the more advanced people will wipe out the primitive ones, who are in their way. And the idea of a people who have been extinguished is also relevant to Beechwood itself. The original occupants of the estate have disappeared, or time has expunged them, and the house, like the between-wars period it evokes, intimates the idea of transience—the fate of man. Although *Savages* is a sophisticated comedy, it is also edged with poignancy and a very moving sense of loss.

Ivory: This may be true—usually I have to be hit over the head with "patterns and motifs" before I recognize connections that are obvious to nearly everyone. It's been too short a time; 1972 is only yesterday. Give me another thirty years to mull it over, and then get back to me.

Long: I found it interesting that while you were making *The Wild Party,* you

had occasion to call on George Cukor, who came to Hollywood just at the time
the film is set and went on to become a veteran director under the studio system. What impression of Cukor did you have at that time?

Ivory: I needed to join the Directors Guild of America [DGA] for *The Wild
Party* and had to be nominated by somebody. Christopher Isherwood and
Henry Fonda's wife, Shirlee, who were friends of Cukor's, suggested him. That
seemed a good idea, so I went to meet him at his house in the Hollywood hills.
He could not have been more charming and agreed to nominate me. He was
an incredibly civilized elderly gentleman, living in a beautiful, civilized house
full of fine things, which of course has been torn down since then. I met him
again about six years later when he was in poor health.

Long: The Wild Party comes originally from a 1926
blank verse narrative poem by Joseph Moncure March,
about a Greenwich Village party staged by a vaudeville
comic that ends in disaster. In the early 1970s, lyricist
Walter Marks had the idea of turning the story into a
musical set in 1920s Hollywood, and before long you
entered into a collaboration with him. There's one thing
I'm not quite clear about. Was this originally to have
been a Broadway musical, or had Marks envisioned it
from the beginning as a film?

THE WILD PARTY

*A fading 1920s silent film
comedian hopes to stage
his comeback and throws a
lavish party at his Hollywood
mansion that ends in a double
murder. With James Coco,
Raquel Welch, and Perry
King. 1975. Feature. 35 millimeter; color; 100 minutes.*

Ivory: As far as I know, it was always intended to be
a film. However, it was developed by the Broadway pro-
ducers Edgar Lansbury and Joe Beruh. Maybe it did start out as a stage piece.

Long: You've called *The Wild Party* "a drama with music," but this isn't a case
of some incidental music. Production numbers are staged while the action in
the film comes to a halt. At such times I felt that I was seeing a Broadway
musical, and all the more because of the polish that Patricia Birch, a very talented Broadway choreographer, gives to the numbers. *The Wild Party* has a hy-
brid nature: it's something like a straight dramatic film, and it's something
like a musical.

Ivory: Except for Queenie's dance in front of her bedroom mirror in the opening scene, all the musical numbers exist within the story in pretty much a nor-

Raquel Welch (Queenie) dances with Perry King (Dale Sword) in a dance number called "The Herbert Hoover Drag" in *The Wild Party* (1975).

mal way—people dance or sing within the framework of a big Hollywood party, not so much stopping the action as commenting on it or emerging from it. The biggest dance number, called the "Herbert Hoover Drag," takes place on a dance floor, where all the party guests gather to dance to the band music. Queenie is asked by the guests to perform and she obliges them with her song "Singapore Sally."

Long: I understand that Marks's original script was called "highly expressionistic" and "lurid." Was it difficult collaborating with him when his ideas were apparently so much at odds with your own?

Ivory: They weren't all that at odds. But I felt some of his best ideas needed to be developed more, and I also felt the main characters needed to be made more human, more flesh-and-blood. In the original script they were sometimes caricaturish and straight off the pages of March's poem. They were stark, like lurid woodcuts.

Long: You rewrote Marks's script, but the screenplay is credited to Walter Marks alone. Why is that?

Ivory: I can't say I rewrote it. But as the director I needed to flesh it out. Jolly was even more unsympathetic than in the finished film, Queenie lacked any self-awareness; she was a sort of dumb blonde type, a tough floozie. Maybe I went too far in the other direction. Making your characters "more human" can backfire sometimes. You flatten them.

Long: A film about a wild Hollywood party in the 1920s that ends calamitously inevitably makes one think of the Fatty Arbuckle case. Both Arbuckle and your male lead, Jolly Grimm, were fat-man comics who starred in silent films and gave parties that ended tragically. Despite significant differences between them, doesn't the precedent of Arbuckle give credibility to Jolly Grimm?

Ivory: You could not escape comparisons, distasteful though they might be. We were making a musical after all, and who would want to make a musical about Fatty Arbuckle's sad downfall? Actually, these days, I suppose any number of people would.

Long: For Jolly's mansion you used the Mission Inn, at Riverside in Southern California. It was a strange building that might have belonged in Nathanael West's *The Day of the Locust.* Walter Lassally, who photographed it, describes it in this way: "It is a concrete castle, incredibly ornate, complete with gargoyles, a potpourri of rococo architectural styles, inner passages, secret doors, . . . cloisters, chapels, galleries, gardens, a four-room rotunda, bell towers, flying towers and buttresses, stone steps to a dungeon. It's like an entire back lot of wild movie sets scrunched up into one bizarre complex." Why did you choose this building as the almost exclusive setting for the film?

Ivory: You have answered your own question by supplying Lassally's description. It was absolutely an entire back lot, and we could do the whole film there, not just the scenes that took place under Jolly's roof.

Long: Partly because of that big, strange, archaic, and suffocating house, I could not help wondering if you ever thought of *Sunset Boulevard* while you were making *The Wild Party.*

Ivory: Of course.

Long: Jolly's mansion epitomizes . . . is practically a museum of the silent film era, like Norma Desmond's in the Billy Wilder film. Moreover, Jolly and Norma have constant, live-in companions who show them adulation and remind them of their glory days in the silents. But the big connection is the psychological breakdown of Jolly and Norma in their respective, tomblike homes that seem to exist apart from the outer world. Were you fully conscious of these things?

Ivory: Of course, again.

Long: Quite a point is made of Jolly's being sentimental about beautiful and innocent little girls; in fact these young girls were practically a cult in the silents. One of these adorable girls ("America's Sweetheart") was Mary Pickford, whose name comes up a number of times in the course of the film. A big party for the Hollywood crowd is taking place at her estate, the famous Pickfair, at the same time as the one at Jolly's mansion. Did you do much research into the cult of the young girl (Pickford, Dorothy and Lillian Gish, and those innocent little girls in Chaplin's movies)? Oddly enough, that whole curious phenomenon of the sentimentalization of pure little girls coexisted with Hollywood hedonism and wanton sexuality.

Ivory: Yes, that work was done by the screenwriter Walter Marks. I did my own research for the film, but not quite as fully as for later period films perhaps . . . though I don't know. It was a more innocent age, the 1920s. Child abuse as a national nightmare, with witch-hunt connotations, didn't exist yet. In the 1970s, pedophilia could be introduced without starting a riot in the theater.

Long: James Coco was a natural for the part of Jolly Grimm—a heavyset man with a clown's face, oversized and perhaps sad brown eyes. He is a sensitive man who can be broken. But the role of Queenie must have been harder to cast. How did you happen to think of Raquel Welch for the part?

Ivory: I saw Raquel Welch on *The Today Show,* talking about how she was never offered any good scripts or interesting parts. So since we needed a Queenie, we sent her the script, and she said she liked it and would do it.

Long: Wasn't there a potential problem in casting Raquel Welch as Queenie? She's a big presence on the screen—she's in fact tiny—and of course a well-known sex symbol. She might have overwhelmed the others. Seeing her,

Jimmy Coco as the failing movie star Jolly Grimm in *The Wild Party* (1975).

an audience might all the while be thinking "sex goddess," which would be a distraction from the drama.

Ivory: As a matter of fact, the audience obviously didn't want a Raquel who "suffered," who was meant to be thoughtful, sometimes self-aware, and given to recalling her old happier days, as Queenie does. They wanted the slam-bam Raquel Welch of her early movies, a pop heroine. They looked forward to the sex goddess Raquel, which we didn't provide, exactly. So they were disappointed. In the rowdy party scenes she seemed to hold herself apart: always an elegant figure, but in the crowd a bit lonely-looking for the leading lady of a movie. In repose her face communicated very little beyond a sense of wariness.

Raquel Welch in the opening scene of *The Wild Party* (1975).

Long: I suspect that Raquel Welch's singing in the picture may have been dubbed. Was it?

Ivory: People never give these singing actors or actresses the benefit of the doubt, unless they've been on Broadway. Why is that? American actors specialize in being able to sing and dance. Raquel sang the song "Singapore Sally," but then she rerecorded herself later in postproduction in order to improve her vocal performance. But it's certainly her voice.

Long: You've related elsewhere how Raquel Welch threatened to walk off the set unless you apologized publicly for what she construed as a slight on her acting abilities. Were you, in the end, happy with her performance; and in view of the scenes she threw, would you consider using her again?

Ivory: She not only threatened, she did leave the film, but soon returned when faced with a million-dollar lawsuit. Had she not been so paranoid during that film, and concentrated instead on her acting and the part and not spent 50 percent of her psychic energy fighting everybody, she would have been very, very good. But she had her moments nevertheless—many of them. All I said to her on the set was that the first take of her love scene was sort of "dull." I wanted another take. Also the bed fell down in that take: Dale Sword had grabbed her too violently. When I asked her to come back for another take, she refused. What was the reason? she demanded. Then my word "dull" popped out, and all hell broke loose. She jumped up, said "That's it, boys," and walked off the set.

Long: I wonder if there isn't a connection between *The Wild Party* and one of your earlier films, *Bombay Talkie.* To begin with, both deal with film industries (Indian and American) and the personal lives of film stars. In *Bombay Talkie* you have a film idol involved in his personal life in a melodramatic failed romance that mirrors the melodramatic roles he plays on screen. And, similarly, in *The Wild Party* you have a movie clown who becomes a sad movie clown in real life. Was this your intention?

Ivory: It wasn't my concept, it was Walter Marks's. But having tried out something of the same sort before in *Bombay Talkie,* I felt at home with the goings-on in *The Wild Party.* But both films failed to satisfy audiences for the same reason, I'm sure: they couldn't identify with any of the main characters. All were seen in too much of a bad light.

Long: You use a twenty-four-hour time frame for the story, in which everything that could go wrong for Jolly does. His frustration and rage mount through the course of the day. Is one of his woes that he is impotent?

Ivory: Yes, impotence was supposed to be his great sorrow. We treated it as best we could. I always think that dramatically, impotence is something of a cliché, an easy answer. But Jimmy Coco suggested Jolly's affliction—or shame—most delicately. Of course, impotence was also symbolic of Jolly's fading power as a movie star. It wasn't just a gimmick.

Long: The Wild Party has been beautifully mounted and photographed by Walter Lassally and has songs by Larry Rosenthal and Walter Marks that are full of energy and color. Two major stars lead a strong supporting cast. The movie has many things going for it, and yet both audiences and reviewers rejected it. Charles Champlin, in the *Los Angeles Times,* felt that it was hard to know how to respond to the picture. It was too melodramatic to take seriously, he thought, yet too serious and intelligent to take simply as 1920s nostalgia. What do you think?

Ivory: I think its mixed style—part musical, part melodrama, part character piece—would have gone down better if the audience could have entered more into those characters' lives. But they couldn't, or wouldn't. And of course the ending is grim as can be.

Long: You had the misfortune of having Samuel Z. Arkoff's American International Pictures as your distributor. Would you say something about this entanglement?

Ivory: My misfortune was in not having the final cut contractually. It never occurred to me that any distributor would recut one of my movies. That had never happened to me before (and hasn't happened since). Arkoff's company routinely recut all their movies. Vincente Minnelli made a musical with them soon after, starring his daughter Liza no less, and it was cut to shreds by Arkoff and then dumped, like *The Wild Party.* My film in its original form was rehabilitated by the French, who showed it at the Nice Book Fair in 1976. After that it was released for the first time (in France) as I'd made it. But French audiences didn't like it any better than the American ones.

Long: A last question. You haven't spoken about Walter Lassally. He was by this time your cameraman of choice, wasn't he? You'd made three films with him already, I think.

Ivory: Yes. *The Wild Party* was the fourth, and there would be three more. It was Subrata Mitra who first steered us in Walter's direction—laid his hands on him in benediction, I guess you could say. Mitra had pronounced Walter a "world-class" cameraman, which he certainly was—probably the best British cameraman, or at any rate the one with the greatest variety of moods, projects, looks. He was entirely approachable and liked doing all sorts of things, not just big-budget features. He'd received the Academy Award for *Zorba the Greek* and was famous for *Tom Jones*. We got along terribly well, though he was very outspoken, very opinionated—sometimes too outspoken, which would land him in trouble. Our big upheaval with Raquel Welch started with an ill-advised remark he made to her one day on *The Wild Party*. She insisted on doing her own makeup, which meant she had to get up even earlier than she would otherwise. One morning he saw her painting away in front of her mirror, while her makeup lady stood by, handing her the brushes. And he is supposed to have said, "Raquel, why don't you just sit back and let Charlene do it, wouldn't that be much more relaxing for you?" Well, she went absolutely nuts at that and walked off the film. She demanded that he be fired for speaking to her, the leading lady, in such an "impertinent" way. She followed this up by another demand—that Ismail and I also be fired. From our own film! I was to be replaced as director by Ron Talsky, her boyfriend, who was also her personal costume designer.

Long: Then what happened?

Ivory: You know the story. The Directors Guild came in and told Ron Talsky to go away, and Lansbury and Beruh sent Raquel yet another threatening letter. So she came back, but not all that meekly. She still went on making herself up in the morning, and Walter stayed as much out of her way as he could. She never looked better on any film she ever made. In time she realized this, I think, and that it wasn't just a matter of being photographed from her so-called best side (her left).

Long: Two years before you made *Roseland*, the made-for-television movie *Queen of the Stardust Ballroom* was shown on national television. It starred Maureen Stapleton as an aging widow who meets a married mailman played by Charles Durning at a New York dance palace that is something like Roseland. It's a sensitive study of loneliness and the older woman's attempt to recover romance at the threshold of death. Did you ever see *Queen of the Stardust Ballroom*, and if so, did it have any influence on your film?

Ivory: There was no influence that I know of, but I did see it eventually.

Long: There's the shared situation of the New York City dance hall, the frustrated longing of aging women, and the looming sense of death.

Ivory: We were far along in our own movie before we actually saw it.

Long: Your cinematographer was Ernest Vincze, who a few years later collaborated with you again on *Jane Austen in Manhattan. Roseland* was only Vincze's second feature film. Can you tell me something about him?

Ivory: He was a Hungarian refugee who moved to England as a small boy and later on began to work there as a cameraman. He's lived and worked in England ever since. He came to work for us again on Ismail's movie *The Mystic Masseur.*

Long: The first segment of the trilogy, "The Waltz," features Teresa Wright as May, a refined and rather sheltered middle-aged widow, and Lou Jacobi as Stan, an outgoing, somewhat brash type of man, whom she meets at Roseland. There was this business about May's looking into a mirror at Roseland and seeing herself dancing romantically with her late husband when they were both young. I wonder if this is quite believable.

ROSELAND

Three stories by Ruth Jhabvala, set in the Roseland Ballroom in New York City. With Christopher Walken, Geraldine Chaplin, Teresa Wright, Helen Gallagher, and Lilia Skala. 1977. Feature. 35 millimeter; color; 104 minutes.

Ivory: In this hard-nosed city and world, it was perhaps an idea that would be a little difficult for people to accept; could there be such things as magic mirrors? I had just been reading a lot of Hawthorne and became very interested in a wonderful story called "Dr. Heidegger's Experiment," about a magic mirror in which three men and a woman keep seeing their younger selves. That story in some way affected what we were doing. Around that time I had been hired to write a script of another Hawthorne story called "My Kinsman, Major Molineux," for a public television series on the American short story, and I was also to direct it. But it became much too expensive, and the project was dropped. Anyway, I had been reading all of Hawthorne's stories. The one I was most struck by, far more than "My Kinsman, Major Molineux," was the one with the magic mirror. I wish we'd done that story, and I tried to get Channel 13 to agree to do it when they gave up on "Major Molineux."

Long: You know, "My Kinsman, Major Molineux," is considered one of the great American short stories. Robert Lowell adapted it Off-Broadway for the American Place Theater. I went to see it on opening night and reviewed it for a magazine.

Ivory: I can't help it. It could never have been vintage Ivory. And can you imagine public television building the streets of eighteenth-century Boston, which are long gone? Spending that kind of money?

Long: I wonder what . . .

Ivory: The story of "Dr. Heidegger's Experiment," as I say, is about three old friends and a woman they have loved. They drink a magic elixir that Dr. Heidegger has prepared, and all grow young again. And, then, as in the scene in *Lost Horizon* when the beautiful young woman being taken out of Shangri-la shrivels up [*Long laughs*], Hawthorne's characters at the end of the story also shrivel up and become toothless old people again. I loved this story. It suited me perfectly and would have been inexpensive to make. But the producers at Channel 13 wouldn't hear of it. I guess it was too perverse for them, too grotesque or something. But somehow its influence got into *Roseland,* or it got into Ruth's and my thinking. And that's where the magic mirror came from: it's really out of Hawthorne.

Long: Teresa Wright was a big star in the 1940s. Did she have any qualms about appearing in *Roseland* as an older woman?

Ivory: You know, an actress of that age, or the age she was then, is usually *dying* to work. Nobody asks them to do anything anymore. To be offered a role is the most wonderful thing, a gift that comes out of the clouds to them. In no way was she ashamed to appear in it or to be seen as an older woman. She was dying to be seen as an older woman. Or just to be seen!

Long: There is a stereotype of the actress who is asked for the first time to take the part of an older woman, and it is like death. You see this in the movie *The Star,* with Bette Davis as an actress who has to confront the fact that she is now beyond her youth.

Ivory: In fact, we sent the script of *Roseland* to Bette Davis. We wanted her to play Rosa, the part Lilia Skala eventually played. She—Bette Davis—was intrigued enough to agree to talk about it over the phone with us. I made Ismail take her call (or make the call, I can't remember which) while I listened in on the line. He made his pitch, and then she gave her reason why she couldn't, or wouldn't, play the part, while I hovered spellbound by another phone. She wasn't ready for that, she said—which I think meant dying as she spun around on the Roseland floor, a pathetic old woman in a bedraggled gown.

To hear her speak was to be taken back to my adolescence—that voice, its familiar rhythms; I could imagine her puffing away on a cigarette. It was as if we were talking to President Roosevelt, so deeply was that voice embedded in my consciousness, as his is.

Long: I didn't know any of that.

Ivory: The day comes sooner or later when an aging star is offered the part of a mother, the mother of a grown girl. You can be the mother of a boy, but to be the mother of an adolescent girl who may be beautiful and lively and has boys running after her—well that is really bad.

Long: The second segment of *Roseland,* with the double-entendre title of "The Hustle," features Christopher Walken as Russell, a young dance instructor–gigolo, and Geraldine Chaplin as Marilyn, a young woman whose husband walked out on her and who now attaches herself too desperately to Russell. She wants to support him so that he can pursue a "serious" career of some unspecified kind. The trouble is that Russell has competing offers from Cleo (Helen Gallagher), the head of Roseland's dance studio, and Pauline (Joan Copeland), a rich, hypochondriacal, middle-aged woman. Is the cool, ironic, and worldly-wise "Hustle" out of key with the other two stories, which had a sentimental edge to them?

Ivory: Cool and ironic may need to be balanced by sentimental. But, in fact, how sentimental was the segment called "The Peabody"? Its protagonists both die, one of them full of tubes, while the other collapses almost ecstatically on the dance floor. It was her dream to die like that.

Long: The bidding among the women for Russell ends with a big winner and a big loser; but isn't that the conceit of "The Hustle" that love in the world of Roseland is a "game"?

Ivory: Love in Roseland is finding the right partner, meaning the right dance partner. And, if you're really lucky, a life's partner—for what's left of life, anyway.

Long: I liked Christopher Walken as Russell, who never lets his emotions show on his face. He's as smooth as silk and ever so calculating in his moves. We see him dancing with women out on the dance floor only briefly, but it's obvious that he's a very, very good dancer. Walken began as a dancer on Broadway, but I don't imagine you cast him for that reason.

The gallant gigolo Russell (Christopher Walken) and his susceptible partner
Marilyn (Geraldine Chaplin), together in the central story from *Roseland*—
"The Hustle" (1977).

Ivory: That was one of the reasons. But the main reason is that I'd seen him
in smallish parts in other movies and felt he'd be very good as Russell. He had
a kind of sophistication and cool, but he was obviously "street-smart"—the
epitome of the seventies young leading man.

Long: What's impressive in Geraldine Chaplin's performance is how sharply
she suffers. In a striking moment the camera trains on her face and then moves
forward for an even closer view, which it holds for another five or six seconds.
Her needle-sharp wounding is immediately apparent in her eyes. Tell me if I'm
wrong, but don't those dark, glinting eyes remind you a little of her father,
Charlie Chaplin?

Ivory: I felt that they did.

Long: The final segment of the trilogy, "The Peabody," is often satirical in
a dry way. There is a jewel-like comic moment that is, well, preposterous.
Among the couples on the dance floor, for a few fleeting moments, we notice
an old, wrinkled, and tiny woman embraced by a tall, young man with frizzled

hair. There is a look of delight in her eyes as they whirl past. Did you plan this moment, or did it just somehow happen?

Ivory: It was planned, but not as a humorous moment as such. I could tell you who the couple was, but both are now dead. There were many couples like that in Roseland then. Russell's situation wasn't entirely invented by us.

Long: There is also a darkly humorous moment when an elderly couple have just won the Peabody dance prize. Don De Natale, the MC, congratulates the couple, pressed close on either side of him, when the man, who is expressionless, suddenly slumps over dead. There is an Ivory touch to this, if I am not mistaken.

Ivory: Well, it certainly appealed to me, but actually I didn't think it up. That was Ruth.

Long: Really!

Ivory: I liked shooting that bit. We were always playing games in those days, always pretending that someone had just died and stuff, and flopping over "unconscious." We don't do that anymore.

Long: There seem to be a lot of people who die or are said to have died on the dance floor. How realistic is this? Is it usual for elderly people to die on the dance floor from overexertion?

Ivory: Definitely. I was there one day when a man had a heart attack. They laid him on one of the benches downstairs—he was clutching his chest—and a doctor was called. People came in and changed into their dance shoes on the bench next to him and paid no attention to him. And the man, for all they knew, was dying. But, in fact, they say ballroom dancing is good for the heart. It keeps a lot of those old people in shape.

Long: If "The Hustle" is the most intricate of the three segments in the relationships of its characters, "The Peabody" is easily the most charming. It is made so by the performances of the Viennese-born actress Lilia Skala and her aging, easily winded partner David Thomas. They provide much of the touching humor and grace of the piece. What was it like to direct them?

Ivory: They were such perfect embodiments of the kind of persons they had to play that directing them didn't come into it that much. Lilia Skala *was* that character, so she didn't have to spend hours with a voice coach or anything of that sort; and Thomas was a little wispy man, a sort of Mr. Milquetoast type that we found. They were perfection. My work was all but done for me; and the script for that particular story was, I think, especially good—very, very touching and funny.

Long: Did Ruth write the segments all at once or in any particular order?

Ivory: The stories came one by one while Ruth was writing them. She was at that time living upstairs in our building on the floor above, and the stories would come down one by one, and be pushed under my door as she finished them. I remember reading the last one, "The Peabody," and running up to tell her how much I liked it. She wasn't in, so I put a note under the door to tell her how good I thought it was.

Long: Once you had the idea of making this movie at Roseland, you went there fairly often, observing and getting the feel of the place; and Ruth went with you, taking notes, or mental notes, on the people she met there. Had you ever made a film in that way before?

Ivory: Not really. This was early on. Later we concentrated on adapting a number of novels set in the past, so our "research" was of another kind. We read a lot of books instead.

Long: Wasn't it difficult to shoot the film while the Roseland patrons were out on the dance floor—or did you employ them as extras?

Ivory: They were indeed extras, and the very best. But because it was a Screen Actors Guild film, we were also obliged to hire a number of token SAG extras—I think twenty or so—to flesh out the Roseland habitués. Some of the SAG extras said they didn't know how to dance, so they sat on the benches. They charged us, under SAG rules then, for their clothes! But the real Roseland dancers were marvelous.

Long: Did you have any problem lighting the dance sequences?

Ivory: We had the usual studio lamps in various sizes, and we lit the whole dance floor with them, but we couldn't change the ballroom's existing lights around the side, which were mainly pink and supposedly more flattering to the aged couples who trysted there. We were not allowed to change those pink bulbs ever, under pain of instantaneous expulsion. When our huge bank of lights on the floor was turned on, the whole atmosphere of Roseland as you know it disappeared completely. It was gone. Roseland is meant to be dark.

Its inmates don't want some unflattering glare shining into the corners or on to their faces. Illusion is all at Roseland. We tried to respect that, to re-create it, but it was hard going sometimes.

Long: You had trouble with unions while you were making the film, I know. You were picketed.

Ivory: We had a preposterous, no-win situation with the Teamsters Union. Did you know that film set designers are a part of the Teamsters? That is because they are affiliated with the scenic artists of Broadway theaters. We refused to hire a union set designer, since we were unable to make a single change to the Roseland interior, not even to change the pink lightbulbs, as I said. So the Teamsters put a picket line across the Roseland entrance. Many of the dance hall regulars wouldn't dream of crossing a picket line, being old union members of some kind. That was not too bad. But the men bringing in the liquor supplies to the Roseland bar would also not cross the picket line. That was it, and we capitulated and hired a union art director, who spent most of his working hours dusting the leather banquettes. I'm certain he felt as frustrated by all this as we did.

THE EUROPEANS

An early Henry James novel set in New England. A sophisticated European woman and her artist brother unexpectedly descend on their wary American relatives. With Lee Remick, Robin Ellis, and Lisa Eichhorn. 1979. Feature. 35 millimeter; color; 89 minutes.

Long: The Europeans was a pivotal film for you inasmuch as it launched you into filming works of Henry James. It was Ruth who wanted to do it, wasn't it?

Ivory: Well, she gave me the novel to read, which started me out on a program to read all his novels over the next few years. She said, "Read this. Henry James was writing for *you*." This was about 1968 or so. I began fiddling around with *The Europeans* about six years later.

Long: Had you ever attempted making a film from James before *The Europeans?*

Ivory: There *had* been an earlier attempt at James: *The American.* I had an ideal cast for it in my mind, imagining Catherine Deneuve as the beautiful, young French heroine, Madame de Cintré. As we went on sort of half thinking about it for several years, I seem to remember also imagining Christopher Reeve as the American hero, Christopher Newman, though that seems a little unlikely— he would have barely been out of his prep school in those days. Unfortunately, there seemed to be no translation of *The American* to present to Catherine

Deneuve, who I managed to meet. This came about through François Truffaut, and perhaps Richard Roud. She came to New York on a press junket and just called me up, saying, "I'm Catherine Deneuve" and offering to meet. She spoke good English, in a charming way, but felt frustrated at not being able to read the novel. We agreed to meet at the Sherry Netherland Hotel, where she was staying. At that time she was with Marcello Mastroianni. Ismail and I went up in the elevator to her tower suite, where she welcomed us.

Long: Just like that?

Ivory: Just like that. She opened the door, asked us to sit down, and offered us a scotch. At this time she was absolutely at the height of her beauty and had already appeared in *Belle de Jour* and *Tristana*—both big art house favorites. Anyway, there was suddenly a clattering on the stairs that went up to the bedroom, I imagine, and Mastroianni joined us. He, too, was at the peak of his European and American art house fame. A more beautiful couple could not be imagined. We felt we were in the presence of a god and goddess. Deneuve handed me the bottle of scotch, and I poured her drink, but in my haste (or was my hand shaking?), I spilled some on her crossed knee. I whipped a folded, clean white handkerchief out of my pocket, and muttering something idiotic like "Permit me," I dabbed it up. I still have that folded handkerchief, put away carefully, from that day to this.

Long: Then what happened?

Ivory: We had arranged for them to see *Shakespeare Wallah.* Ismail and I accompanied them down to Fifty-ninth Street, passing through the Sherry Netherland kitchen and out a service door in order to avoid the paparazzi. During the screening they held hands. Unfortunately, this meeting didn't lead anywhere, and I think a translation has still not come out in France of *The American.* I doubt that I would have had the experience to bring off such a complicated story at that time, even if we'd found the money. And I suppose that for James, this is one of his more creaky books in terms of plot. It ends with the virtuous heroine, Madame de Cintré, closing herself up in a Carmelite convent. But I bet Ruth would have thrown all that out.

Long: You were able to find funding for *The Europeans* in England but not in America, where it is set. Why was that?

Ivory: The English hold James in esteem; it wasn't unreasonable to them to want to dramatize one of his books. After all, they'd done a huge series of James adaptations for British television, which became very popular. But in the United States we couldn't find anybody financing movies who had any sort of knowledge of James, or any appreciation of the possibilities his books offered.

Long: Visually *The Europeans* is a stunningly beautiful film. The picturesque world of the movie is evoked at the opening when the credits are shown, with watercolor sketches of New England scenes—nature, tidy puritan houses, ships, sailing vessels, a church and its spire. Did you select these scenes yourself?

Ivory: They were painted by Mark Potter Sr. and chosen by him somewhat at random from a lot of still photographs from the film. Some sketches were his own, like the face of the young black boy, who is never seen in the film but in my mind was a sort of oblique reference to the war to come.

Long: *The Europeans* is flooded with beautiful scenery, but the aesthetic richness of the movie isn't confined to exterior shots. Even the interiors of the houses that are supposed, according to the novel, to have a "Dutch simplicity," have been imagined with an eye to pleasing aesthetic effect.

Ivory: But "Dutch" houses do have a pleasing aesthetic effect—look at Vermeer or Pieter de Hooch. What some people didn't like was the profusion of autumn leaves, which conventional critics know must be scorned as being, perhaps, too Norman Rockwell–ish. If they had looked closely (and knew anything about old American houses), they would see the season changing into a wintry look, and the people, too; and would have appreciated the uncluttered, clean, almost childlike, or dollhouse-like 1850s interiors—the kind of interiors and spare furnishings you sometimes glimpse in American daguerreotypes.

Long: I think it's fairly obvious that the beauty of nature in the film isn't there for its own sake but has the thematic purpose of making one aware of the idea of pleasure—of pleasure in life, which contrasts with the idea of life as duty and self-denial. The presence of the artist figure (in Felix) is also related to this pleasure theme, since the artist suggests the idea of the imagination at play—which has been banned in Boston. This makes me wonder about Mr. Wentworth's agreeing to allow his daughter Gertrude to marry Felix, who is not "solid." Would he really have done that, either in James's novel or in your film?

Charlotte Wentworth (Nancy New) knocks on her sister's door in a
scene from *The Europeans* (1979).

Ivory: Could he have stopped it? He wasn't a despot or tyrant. Sooner or
later he would have to submit—or never see his daughter again. Gertrude Wentworth was pretty strong-minded.

Long: Your art director was an American, Jeremiah Rusconi, who had never
before worked on a film. How strange that he should have arrived so suddenly.

Ivory: He was a young friend, a restorer of old houses, with a prodigious amount of information about them and a very good eye, good taste. No English art director knew as much about old American houses, I'm certain. So he accepted the job, his first of this kind. Later he was nominated for the British equivalent of the Academy Award for his work on the movie.

Long: You have said of Rusconi and Judy Moorcroft, your costume designer, that they "laid the foundation, as it were, of Merchant Ivory's 'production values' in the re-creation of the past." Would you expand a bit on that?

Ivory: I meant that up to then, in terms of costumes, makeup, and art direction, everything had been vague, or approximate, in our period films. Well, there had been only two: *Savages* and *The Wild Party.* Judy Moorcroft and her associates, and Jeremiah Rusconi and his, brought a very precise knowledge to *The Europeans.* A kind of scholarship, you could say. And they were artists, bringing an artist's judgment and flair to their work.

Long: The Europeans marks the point at which Richard Robbins began to contribute music for your films. He's provided the musical scores for your pictures for a record number of years and has a following in his own right. You've said that it would be hard to imagine a Merchant Ivory film without the accompaniment of his music. Would you tell me some more about your friendship and longtime collaboration with him?

Ivory: Dick Robbins is another example—Ruth and I are among them, too—of Ismail's determination to train a talented but untried person into a professional in his, Ismail's, own chosen world of moviemaking. I'm sure Dick—a pianist, performer, and teacher—never imagined he was to become a composer of all those absolutely individualistic film scores. Nor did I imagine I would become so dependent on him to write the kind of haunting and sensual music that I first encountered in Satyajit Ray.

Long: The English critic F. R. Leavis wrote of *The Europeans,* the novel, that it was "dramatic" in the word's most obvious sense. "It could readily be adapted for performance. The dialogue is all admirable 'theatre,' and the whole is done in scenes and situations that seem asking to be staged." Yet no film version of *The Europeans* had ever been attempted before you made yours. Why do you suppose this was so?

Ivory: I don't know. It was probably considered too slight a story. Directors want the grander books with the bigger reputations. I know I've heard *The Europeans*, the novel, put down by opinionated people as "not being one of James's best." As for the dialogue, it's delightful to read but too literary to speak, which sometimes is a fault of the film, I feel. We kept a lot of it intact. Too much, maybe. It takes consummate stylists to speak such lines naturally.

Long: In an interview in the *Times* of London, Ruth has talked about the various problems of adapting *The Europeans*. She reveals, for instance, that the final scene was changed a number of times. The first ending was cut, and a longer passage between Charlotte and Mr. Brand that had been cut earlier was tried again as the new ending, but this, too, was considered weak. "Your final exit," she said, "has to sum up or echo what has gone before, but if you don't quite know what that will be when you start out filming, you have to keep your options open. . . . A film takes on a life of its own which is not in the script." Has this been true for you in other films you have made?

Ivory: Pretty much always. We've often just chopped off the ending of a film. Or the opening, choosing to begin the story later. It's a rare film of mine that actually begins with the opening shots described in the script and closes with the final one as originally written. Right off I can't think of even one.

Long: I understand that Lee Remick was an early choice for the lead role of Eugenia, the Baroness Münster, but that at first she turned it down. Who did you consider then?

Ivory: There were a number of candidates. One of these was Lynn Redgrave. She was going to do it, then changed her mind at the last minute, wanting to take a much better-paying TV series, if I remember right, for which I don't blame her.

Long: I read somewhere that Remick called back a month before shooting was to begin and agreed to do the part. I've seen her referred to as a "Jamesian actress" but am not sure what that means. But I do know that she was versatile and had been successful both on the stage and in films. I don't think she had played a character like Eugenia. Was it a difficult role for her to do?

Ivory: I felt she was a bit nervous about it—or about us, maybe. We had decreed unheard-of things like no eye makeup. I felt sometimes as if she was proceeding most delicately, as if afraid of breaking something—breaking a bit of

The Baroness Münster (Lee Remick), pretending to like the simple pleasures of New England country life, as she entertains the hoped-for rich suitor Robert Acton (Robin Ellis) in *The Europeans* (1979).

James, maybe. This gave a tentative quality to her performance. However, that really wouldn't be wrong, since the Baroness Münster did have to tread very carefully, feeling she was constantly being watched and judged by her frightened New England relatives.

Long: Some reviewers felt that Remick's Eugenia was not forceful or European enough, yet she does dominate the film with her presence. She's very attractive, with extraordinary eyes, and very, very sympathetic. How would you yourself characterize her performance?

Ivory: Well, you know, James described a kind of animated, very worldly, *jolie laide* type, with nuanced ideas and sophisticated pronouncements on everything conceivable. Lee was not that. You could imagine Bette Davis in her prime in such a part. But Lee brought a vulnerability to the role. When she gives up at the end and decides to go back to Europe and her awful husband, you do feel for her.

Long: Lisa Eichhorn, who plays Gertrude Wentworth, was praised by most all of the reviewers. What qualities did she bring to the part, do you think, to produce such a favorable response?

Ivory: Here the Jamesian lines were given a really enchanting kind of delivery that undoubtedly came from Eichhorn's own personality—plus the fact that she had been trained at an English drama school, though she is an American. The other two girls sounded far too contemporary to me. Their speech wasn't as believable. It was artless.

Long: The Europeans is essentially a comedy of manners. There is a lot of wit in it, especially dry wit—sometimes at the expense of Mr. Wentworth, who is unimaginative and anxious about his moral grounds. Yet the film has a strikingly poignant quality and in this respect can be compared to *Savages* and *Quartet.* Isn't there, in all three of these films, an edge of sadness about unfulfilled longing?

Ivory: I suppose so, but *The Europeans* also ends like a Mozart opera, happily, with three engaged couples strolling arm in arm, unlike *Savages* or *Quartet.* It was the characters' constant yearning for self-improvement, something better in themselves and their world, which is poignant.

Long: You made *The Europeans* just after you made *Hullabaloo,* a rather Jamesian work having art as a focal concern, and art also enters into the contest of values in *The Europeans.* Am I right in seeing a connection between the two films?

Ivory: I don't know . . . Yes, why not?

Long: I notice that someone wrote that *The Europeans* had been "directed with affection." Is that true?

Ivory: Absolutely! Who would doubt or say otherwise? But it wasn't an entirely happy film, especially for Ismail, who had a great many concerns having to do with unions and disagreements with crew members.

Long: Some of your crew members doubled as extras; you yourself filled in when an additional bit player was needed for a sixty-second or so part of a sharp-eyed New England merchant. Did you enjoy your acting debut?

Ivory dressed up to play a walk-on in *The Europeans* (1979). The part was that of a customs inspector.

Ivory: Yes. But not a merchant . . . a customs inspector. In another film, about Jesse James, I played a banker who rode up on a splendid horse and told a poor widow who was to lose her farm, "I think you know why I've come," a line made up on the spot. But this is the extent of my career of playing heartless money men.

Long: After you completed *The Europeans,* you made an hour-long film for public television's *Great Performances* series, which was one of three "teleplays" adapted from stories by John Cheever. *The Five Forty-eight,* which you directed from a script by Terrence McNally, isn't remotely like anything you'd done before.

Ivory: Deliberately so. A friend of mine told me of the program of three John Cheever stories that Channel 13 was planning. One of them was a "thriller," and as I had never done one before, I thought that it would be fun if I got this chance to direct it. I was able to convince people at Channel 13 to allow me to do it, although I don't think they really wanted me. I think they felt that I had made all those movies in India, so what would I know about life in the American suburbs? I had just made an American film, *The Europeans,* but . . . At any rate, it seemed to me that *The Europeans* and *The Five Forty-eight* were really connected.

Long: How is that?

Ivory: There was a direct link in a downward moral descent between the New England of the Wentworths and the New England of the Blakes of *The Five Forty-eight.* I mean the deterioration of the upright New England middle-class character and morals, sense of personal responsibility, and every other kind of sense. I thought of *The Five Forty-eight* as a kind of pendant to *The Europeans.*

Long: John Blake doesn't want his young son to hang out with the boy next door, perhaps because the boy's father is a carpenter.

Ivory: Is that in Cheever's story or in the film?

Long: It's in the film, but it isn't in Cheever's story.

Ivory: I don't remember that, but if it's not in the short story, it's an invention of Terrence McNally. He must have had his reasons for putting that in; I think it was that Blake didn't like the father. It wasn't that he had any snobbish feelings about carpenters but that the next-door neighbor was a type that was a reproach to him. He seemed to be a counterculture type who gave up conventional nine-to-five jobs in order to "create" something—someone, in fact, more civilized than Blake, and also maybe having more fun.

Long: That's true.

Ivory: The neighbor was a kind of living reproach to men like Blake: to that relentless Madison Avenue, advertising executive, pursuit-of-money sort of American. The neighbor was a happy man doing his own thing in his own way. He was making furniture, or restoring old houses, that sort of thing. He was living a life that he had created, and he wasn't in the rat race like Mr. Blake. That's what Mr. Blake held against him, and it would have been why he wouldn't want his own little boy playing with the neighbor's little boy, who might infect him with similar ideas.

THE FIVE FORTY-EIGHT

One of the John Cheever "Shady Hill" stories. A bad day in the life of an amoral advertising executive. With Laurence Luckinbill and Mary Beth Hurt. 1979. Short feature for television. 16 millimeter; color; 58 minutes.

Long: Blake has a kind of underlying anguish that you see in certain of Jack Lemmon's performances. He doesn't express much in his face. You have to guess what he is . . .

Ivory: It's one of those American male faces that are not meant to express much. It's like a mask. They train themselves, or should I say *we* train ourselves, not to show what we feel. That pitiful Yankee trait. But we are allowed to show that we are feeling *something* by punching a wall and maybe bloodying our knuckles—at least in the movies. Mr. Wentworth in *The Europeans* was very good at not showing anything on his face, and so was Robert Acton, the Baroness Münster's reluctant suitor.

Long: At the end of the film Blake confronts himself through his encounter with his enraged, vengeful secretary, Miss Dent, but there is no indication that he will change his life. We don't see him . . .

Ivory: No, we don't. He's humiliated by her, he's brought up short, but probably the most he would do is to get himself home, clean himself off, and sit down with a drink. But whether he'd be any wiser after all of this . . .

Long: Isn't he the least likable of any of your film characters?

Ivory: Perhaps, but remember that he was just one representative of the mythical John Cheever community of . . .

Long: Shady Hill.

Ivory: He was a particular type shown in those stories, but there were other types, and altogether they made a collective portrait of the citizens of Shady Hill—of American suburbia. So the whole story of Shady Hill isn't told through Blake alone, and there are admirable characters who appear from time to time.

Long: What is Blake's problem? Is it self-revulsion, which turns up in other Shady Hill stories and may be personal to Cheever? Or is the story about Blake's misogyny, the undercurrent of cruelty in his treatment of his wife and Miss Dent? What did you think while you were making the film?

Ivory: I really don't think I struggled with any of those kinds of questions. [*Long laughs*] Blake's weaknesses are common ones. I think I was more interested in the cultural theory I held about New England WASPs, who may discard women once they're through with them. Blake underestimated Miss

Laurence Luckinbill as the advertising executive Blake in John Cheever's *The Five Forty-eight* (1979). At his side, with her gun in his ribs, is his cast-off secretary and lover, Miss Dent, played by Mary Beth Hurt.

Dent's fragility, and then he underestimated her steely determination to avenge herself after she got out of the mental hospital and began stalking him with a gun. The scene at the end where she makes him kneel down in the marshy land by the train track so that she can put the sole of her shoe across Blake's face and press it into the mud, then walk away, is my favorite moment. Rabid feminists should be grateful for that image in one of my films.

Long: Jane Austen in Manhattan, inspired by a childhood play fragment of Jane Austen's, was made expressly for London Weekend Television's *South Bank Show* in 1980. Did it go into theatrical release?

Ivory: No, except when we would have a festival or retrospective. It plays a day or two then.

Long: When you were making *Roseland,* also shot on location in New York City, you were plagued by union problems. Did you have any problems like that with *Jane Austen?*

Ivory: There was a lot of oversight on the set by representatives of various groups. Representatives of the Directors Guild hung around to make sure that none of the prerogatives of their members were in jeopardy. We also had visits from the British film technicians' union, which was angry that London Weekend Television was making a film in New York and not employing any of their members. So a British union representative sort of hung around for a day or two, scowling. Nothing came of it. In addition, the shop steward of the New York crew, all union members, was reporting our infractions of union rules—overtime, short lunch breaks, and so on, to their representative, who also made calls on us. Not a happy atmosphere to work in.

Long: Did you ever consider anyone other than Anne Baxter for the leading role of Lilianna?

Ivory: I think we did. A number of prospective actresses came and went. If I'm not mistaken, we were first hoping to cast Irene Worth. Or at any rate, we offered the part to her.

JANE AUSTEN IN MANHATTAN

Two art groups in Manhattan vie for a foundation grant in order to present their radically different versions of a long-lost Jane Austen playlet. With Anne Baxter, Robert Powell, and Sean Young. 1980. Feature for television. 16 millimeter; color; 111 minutes.

Anne Baxter, the theater star and acting mentor Lilianna Zorska, predicts the future for one of her neophytes in *Jane Austen in Manhattan* (1980).

Long: You would have been using a noted stage actress to play a noted stage actress. Of course Anne Baxter is of the theater, too. In *Jane Austen* she certainly looks like a star, and you light her face at times in a way that gives her a kind of theatrical radiance, as of the footlights. There is a moment in particular when she stands alone on the stage of the empty theater and looks out over the house exultantly. What is implied at this moment?

Ivory: She is reliving triumphs of the past, remembering her great days, which are now pretty much over.

Long: Has she succeeded at this point in outflanking her rival, Pierre, in getting the foundation to finance her staging of the play?

Ivory: I think she has it by then. The scene you mention comes rather late in the film.

Long: Pierre, who is played by Robert Powell, is portrayed as having a hypnotic effect on his group of neophyte actors. His eyes seem to lock onto other people and place them under his influence; his voice, too, is controlling . . .

mellifluous and controlling. Was Pierre inspired by a real person in the avant-garde theater in New York?

Ivory: Yes, sure. He was inspired by André Gregory, to the extent that we knew him. I didn't know him well. The person in that group that we actually knew well was Wallace Shawn, an old friend. Wally told us many things about his life as a performer and his friends' lives as performers with André Gregory's group. Gregory became a kind of theatrical model for the part of Pierre, but I have no idea if he ever saw the film, or what he made of it if he did. As I say, I knew him slightly, had met him through Wally, or perhaps through Larry Pine, another of his favorite leading men and the lead in our own *Hullabaloo over Georgie and Bonnie's Pictures,* made in 1978. But I can't say that Ruth and I knew him well enough to really color the character in our film. But . . . we knew his ways. That was what we needed to know about.

Long: Another André . . . Andrei Serban, was involved in the making of the film.

Ivory: Yes, he staged the scene at Pierre's workshop during which the shocked members of the Midash Foundation discover how Pierre is using the money they've given him. I could never have thought up such a wacky idea as the padded cell and all the rest.

Long: Andrei Serban today is the director of theater studies at Columbia University; before that, I understand, he had quite a reputation in Europe.

Ivory: And still does. He's a Romanian avant-garde theater impresario and director-producer. At the time we made *Jane Austen,* he was a leading figure in the Off-Off-Broadway productions of the classics; he "reexamined" them, turned them on their heads sometimes, emphasized aspects of them that had been overlooked. He had a following not unlike that of André Gregory. His new productions were eagerly looked forward to and appreciated by critics and downtown audiences. On the set of *Jane Austen* the Directors Guild was stirred up that Andrei Serban, who wasn't a member of the guild, was involved in the film. They didn't like it that Andrei Serban was actually directing the actors in the play within the play that he'd concocted at my instruction. Later on the guild thought I should not give Serban any screen credit. Imagine! Such an artist and so well known and so well thought of! His participation in the film added to its value. You have to defy the little apparatchiks that sometimes come out of the woodwork at any of the guilds, in the mood to punish you. Anyway, the credit stayed. Wiser souls at the DGA intervened.

Long: You seem to relish using set pieces, as, for instance, in the recurring moments in the film when a young woman is spirited off in the night by a band of men in black cloaks and masks. They carry torches and next to a rushing torrent imprison her in a sedan chair and make off with her. Are these episodes, which are the play of a child's mind, a reminder perhaps that Jane Austen wrote the play as a child?

Ivory: Well, she did, but what she wrote was based on an eighteenth-century novel by Samuel Richardson in which a young woman is forcibly married to a man she despises. A young woman's abduction is central to the main story of the film: Pierre makes off with Ariadne, steals her away.

Long: Yes, the abduction theme.

Ivory: Jane Austen had taken bits out of Richardson's novel, *Sir Charles Grandison,* and put together this little scenario. It was actually only about seven pages long. That's all there is; the rest of it has been lost, or perhaps she gave up after that. It was a little skit she concocted, no doubt for her family and friends, to be performed at home on a rainy day.

Long: There are other set pieces in the film, too. The performances of both versions of the opera could be considered set pieces, and so could their counterpart, the rehearsal performance of the musical about to open on Broadway, in which Kurt Johnson, as Victor, does the song and dance number "Here We Are Again." Did you stage and direct this number, by the way? It has a strong Broadway look and feel to it.

Ivory: It was thought up by the Broadway choreographer Michael Shawn, and the dancers, too, were from the Broadway musical theater. It's nothing that I could have staged myself.

Long: A reviewer wrote that the choreographer in the Broadway musical dance rehearsal, "Meryl Dante," is an "obvious parody of Bob Fosse," which would seem so to me. Was that your intention?

Ivory: I couldn't do a parody of someone I didn't know, though in fact we lived in the same brownstone on East Eightieth Street when I first moved to

New York in 1958. Gwen Verdon lived there, too, but we were barely even nodding acquaintances. We got a little friendly when the building caught fire.

Long: You've said that the rehearsal scene was "grafted on, like the sequence
of the Sufi dancers." The Sufi dancers appear early in the film in the loft building where Pierre has his theatrical commune, and I imagine they are shown as
a way of emphasizing the quasi-religious or "inspired" aspect of Pierre's approach to theater, with himself as a charismatic leader. Did you happen to come
across the Sufi dancers and then decide to include them in the movie?

Ivory: Downstairs from the location of Pierre's studio on Great Jones Street,
there was a real Sufi center, with Sufi dancing by the people who attended, and
the leaders of the group conducting the proceedings. It was definitely a religious, mystical sort of commune, and absolutely authentic. That footage is
documentary.

Long: Lilianna and Pierre are the central characters in the film, but there is
also Ariadne, the ingenue character played by Sean Young. She is definitely a
beauty, with a surprising facial clarity and big brown eyes. Didn't she make
her film debut in *Jane Austen*?

Ivory: She did, and was chosen over many other young and experienced actresses because of her beauty and for her lively personality. She hardly knew
how to deliver lines; maybe that was a plus, in fact.

Long: Ariadne is torn in different directions. The inner conflict she experiences gives her something in common with Lilianna and Pierre, who seem to
have been lovers but . . .

Ivory: Lilianna is in love with *him*. His feelings for her are more ambiguous.
Was he ever her lover? Probably not.

Long: They seem to dramatize in their different professional allegiances an
ongoing conflict within the theatrical imagination itself—the contradiction
between being faithful to received tradition, on the one hand, and the impulse
to pull away from the past in order to create something new and modern.
Wouldn't this conflict be relevant to your own screen adaptations? You might
want to be faithful to the work you are drawing from, but you might also feel
a need to restage the work to make it something of your own.

Ivory: How scrupulously faithful are we? We're faithful to the *idea* of the book

A Broadway musical actor, Victor (Kurt Johnson), tries to woo his wife Ariadne (Sean Young) away from the mesmeric Pierre, head of an experimental Off-Broadway theater company in *Jane Austen in Manhattan* (1980).

we're filming, and that's about it. We're faithful to the *purpose* of the book, but I think we take liberties where we have to. You do an adaptation because you like the original very much. Presumably, if there were many things you thought wrong with it, you wouldn't do it.

Long: I see both impulses in your production, for instance, of *The Bostonians*. You follow the story line or the plot very closely, at least up to a point, but you also make changes in the way characters are interpreted. Olive Chancellor is a good example. She's presented *very* unsympathetically in the novel, yet compassionately in the film.

Ivory: When we were making *The Bostonians*, hardly anyone gave any thought as to whether we were doing the "right" thing or not with Olive's character or anybody else's. When we adapt something, we just have to take it and make it over into something that we need for the film. I don't feel a conflict, and I don't think Ruth feels a conflict because, finally, we are making something new, for ourselves. It will have its own integrity and make its own demands on us.

Long: As a tale of young people in the arts in New York, *Jane Austen* anticipates another film that you will make eight years later, *Slaves of New York.*

Ivory: They really are linked. Both take place downtown; one is about the world of artists and painters, the other about the Off-Off-Broadway theater. In that way, certainly, they're linked. The localities weren't quite the same. By the time of *Slaves*, the artistic ferment was to be found in Alphabet City and not in and around Greenwich Village and SoHo, where most of *Jane Austen* was shot.

Long: In *Jane Austen* you sketch that Village world—the stages and coffeehouses and the lives of the aspiring young actors. But wherever the scene is set, we encounter a richness of tone and color and texture, which reminds us that we are seeing a Merchant Ivory movie. Some of your critics have claimed that you have presented an aestheticized version of the Village and its inhabitants.

Ivory: It's hard to respond to what these critics have said when you bring them up. I haven't read their pieces, but I can tell you that on such a low-budget film as *Jane Austen in Manhattan*, shot in 16 millimeter, there was neither time nor money to consciously "aestheticize" anything very much.

Long: Of your early films, *Jane Austen* reminds me most of *Hullabaloo over Georgie and Bonnie's Pictures.* Both are concerned with art and its possession, and have a pronounced manipulation theme. In the end, however, the manipulators turn out to be rather likable. And George Midash, the bestower of the grant money, knows that he has been manipulated by both Lilianna and Pierre, but he doesn't seem to mind. Is *Jane Austen* a film without villains after all, a generous-spirited celebration of the artistic enterprise, a comic opera that ends well?

Ivory: Well, that seems to sum it up pretty well. Both films were a problem or a puzzle, to be worked out for London Weekend Television. I think we did work them out. One, *Hullabaloo*, was well liked; the other, *Jane Austen*, was dismissed, the protagonists being described by the British press as "pseuds." But the English, I've seen, tend to like our movies when they're about *them* and to dismiss those that are not about them. Isn't that odd?

Long: Not so very. . . . About *The Bostonians*, you said in 1973 that you were thinking about adapting *The Bostonians* for the screen, but it wasn't until ten years later that you made the film. Why the delay?

THE BOSTONIANS

From a Henry James novel set in Boston and on Cape Cod, involving a duel between an early feminist and champion of women's rights and a reactionary southerner, both of whom love the same young woman. With Vanessa Redgrave, Christopher Reeve, Jessica Tandy, and Madeleine Potter. 1984. Feature. 35 millimeter; color; 122 minutes.

Ivory: Because we didn't seriously try to develop it, and may have felt that it would be difficult to raise the money. In any case, we were pretty busy all through the 1970s making other films.

Long: The Europeans, your first adaptation from a work of Henry James, came out in 1979. Were there things you learned from making *The Europeans* that carried over to your adaptation of *The Bostonians?*

Ivory: I'm sure there were; I'm sure Ruth would say that as regards the script for *The Bostonians*. Perhaps there was less of the original dialogue from the novel than there had been with *The Europeans;* but, then, these were very different kinds of stories, with much more direct dialogue and of course many scenes of confrontation between the two rivals for Verena, and between Olive and Mrs. Burrage and Olive and the Tarrants and Mr. Pardon.

Long: Ruth made certain changes in the novel, including a particularly dramatic one at the end. In the novel, when Olive Chancellor is forced to go to the podium of the Boston Music Hall in Verena's place before a jeering crowd, it is the greatest humiliation of her life, practically a martyrdom. In the film, however, she proves to be moving and persuasive, and one wonders if she may become a public figure in the women's movement. Is this what you were implying?

Ivory: Yes, in a way. We didn't want to leave the story on that note—Olive crushed, Verena in tears as she is led away by Ransom. So we let Olive pick up the torch that Verena had dropped. It made everything more affirmative—and really, to me, more plausible. Olive might well have been able to do that; she had guts and was certainly articulate.

Long: Is it possible, as I have read somewhere, that Ruth once considered having Olive die of a wasting disease? Could that be true?

Ivory: What? I'm sure that's a joke. I'm sure that someone asked Ruth about other possible endings, and as a joke she may have said, "But don't you think our ending is better than having Olive die of a wasting disease?" Something like that. It must have been taken seriously and presented as an alternative ending by somebody who did not realize that Ruth didn't mean it. Many somewhat neurasthenic ladies like Olive did die of a "wasting disease" in the nineteenth century, including Henry James's sister Alice, on whom he most certainly drew for the character of Olive Chancellor.

Long: I don't know if I would put it like that. The inspiration for Olive Chancellor came to James from a literary character, Madame Autheman, in Alphonse Daudet's novel *L'Evangéliste.* James says so himself in his *Notebooks.* But Alice James did suffer from tortured nerves, like Olive, and she had formed a close (I almost said loving) relationship with her friend Katharine Loring that made both James brothers feel distinctly uneasy.

Ivory: Well, James had all sorts of opportunities to draw on women he'd known in Boston to flesh out Olive's part in an American, or high-minded Bostonian, way, beyond the type presented in Daudet's novel. Or so I imagine.

Long: Some of the characters in *The Bostonians* who were a source of brilliant satire have been toned down in the film to the extent that they are no longer really satirical at all. An example would be Miss Birdseye, an elder figure in the women's movement, who has an air of missing the point of things that are going on around her. In the movie she isn't comical at all, is she?

Ivory: There is a kind of comedy in the way Jessica Tandy has played this blinkered old woman, at least to me. I think the actress saw it as a comic part.

Long: There's a splendid tableau of Miss Birdseye seated alone under a large umbrella on the beach at Cape Cod, which makes you wonder what she must be thinking.

Ivory: She's meant to be thinking about death. Or perhaps life, past and present. You know, intimations of mortality. One has seen so many elderly people staring into the distance. Perhaps they're not thinking of anything at all. I do it all the time.

Long: Jessica Tandy is lean as a rake, whereas James's Miss Birdseye was a stout woman. Would you say that she doesn't have to look like her counterpart in the novel?

Ivory: No, she doesn't. Why should she? We were making a movie. All she has to look like is *old.* The problem with Jessica Tandy was that here she was, seventy-two or something, and she felt that she had to *play* being an old woman, to *act* being an old woman. [*Long laughs*] Unfortunately, I couldn't say to her, "You don't have to act this, just *be,* that will be sufficient." Sometimes you have the same thing happening with children. You're making a movie with someone who's eight years old who thinks, having made TV commercials or something, that he or she has to play at being a child when he or she *is* a child. And you want to say, "Don't play at being a child, because you *are* a child." It's the same phenomenon but at the other end of life, you might say, for Jessica's Miss Birdseye. But you can't tell the former Blanche DuBois that she's an old woman now [*Long laughs*] and to let herself go!

Long: Some of the other characters whom you have treated with less satire than James but perhaps with stronger social realism include, I think, Dr. Prance, the little medical lady; Matthias Pardon, the journalist; and Dr. Tarrant, Verena's father, a charlatan faith healer. There is a scalding quality and real exuberance in James's satirical portraits of the Boston reformers, and this has been toned down in your film.

Ivory: You *do* have to tone down strongly satirical parts sometimes; otherwise you may end up with a caricature. I think Wesley Addy's playing of Dr. Tarrant, the humbug faith healer, is absolutely in a satirical vein. I couldn't resurrect Vincent Price, after all, to wave his hands and intone nonsense. Dr. Prance was *not* being satirized by James. She was the lone voice of reason and science in the milieu of the Tarrants. Her dispensary just happened to be in Miss Birdseye's basement. I disagree with your assessment of my supporting cast.

Long: What I'm saying is that all of your supporting characters are plausible and intelligently handled on the level of social realism, but as they appear in James's novel they are treated with a more piercing, or even outrageous, satire. *The Bostonians* is famous for its satire, which includes the robust and exuberant portrait of Dr. Tarrant, who is evoked in vampire imagery, with his "bat-like smile" and "carnivorous teeth." Your Tarrant is quite amusing, but he does not have the lethal edge that he has in the novel. And as far as satire goes, what about Mrs. Luna? The comic opposite of her lean, man-hating sister, she is stout and man-chasing, and is a wonderful comic creation. But I wouldn't say she is satirized in your film. Of course, I suppose you would say, as you have before, that your film characters do not have to match the characters as they appear in James's novel, but have a life of their own.

Ivory: No, I don't say that, but I *do* say that it all boils down to the differences between the written word and the screen image. One involves the reader's imagination—he or she can see the "bat-like smile" and "carnivorous teeth." The other does not require an act of imagination on the part of the viewer. It's right there in front of you to take in. And as I said, when you lay it on too thick, you may end up with a caricaturish performance. Film is always a realistic medium, as a form of photography. Naturalistic filmed storytelling, for that reason, doesn't very often break out of the grip of realism. We see too much on the screen; just as on the stage, illusion can play all sorts of tricks in order to advance the narrative. There we don't really *see*.

Long: Christopher Reeve gives a very strong performance and is a very striking presence as the film's romantic hero, Basil Ransom, a man so charming that he is apt to make one forget that he has a slave owner's mentality. In marrying Verena, it would be part of his sexual politics to keep her in subjection.

Ivory: Well, after all, it was Christopher Reeve keeping Verena in subjection, so it was not *so* bad for her. She was in the arms of Superman. [*Long laughs*]

Long: Still . . .

Ivory: I don't think he quite has a slave owner mentality. He felt himself to be a serious thinker, formulating his ideas about society, however crackpot and antediluvian they might be. He was sufficiently clearheaded and sensible enough to recognize that slavery was not only an abomination but also economically destructive to the South. On the place of women he was, of course, antifeminist.

Basil Ransom (Christopher Reeve), the determined southern lawyer of *The Bostonians* (1984), based on the novel by Henry James.

Long: The feminist response to the film was perhaps summarized by a New York reviewer who wrote that at the end "feminist rowdies in the audience booed Basil Ransom when he carried off Verena, and cheered Olive Chancellor" when she delivered her speech about a new day dawning.

Ivory: No, the feminists weren't happy with the picture then. If you made a film like that now, nobody would say a word about it . . . as far as whether it promoted the cause of women's rights. Nobody would come forward and write anything in defense of women's rights because they are now—and I am speaking of America and Western Europe—mostly taken for granted. It all happened very quickly . . . from 1984, when *The Bostonians* came out, till now.

Long: Madeleine Potter, making her film debut in *The Bostonians* as the inspirational speaker Verena Tarrant, received rather harsh reviews. It was said that she was not convincing as a public speaker who could sway multitudes.

Ivory: I thought that she was very good and that her speaking was sufficiently persuasive. But she was so young then that she looked like a little girl or a pink-cheeked doll who spoke up alarmingly.

Verena Tarrant (Madeleine Potter), champion of
women's rights, in *The Bostonians* (1984).

Long: She does look like a little doll, and even has little doll curls. She looks
something like Bernadette Peters . . . petite and with an innocent face.

Ivory: I think that was part of her attraction for Olive, that out of those rose-
bud lips could come these stirring words. It's interesting, you know, we might
have had a Verena played by Jodie Foster. I went to see her after we had sent
her the script. She was a student at Yale then. We met in a kind of student beer
hall place. She really . . . she did nothing to charm, nothing to attempt to get
the part. Maybe she felt she didn't have to. She was dressed in a shapeless black
sweater and baggy pants and was sprawled in her chair and was very laconic,
not wanting to talk very much. I was disappointed. But I wonder if . . . this
was the time when she was pursued by John Hinckley, the deranged young
man who tried to kill Ronald Reagan.

Long: He became obsessed with Jodie Foster after seeing her in *Taxi Driver.* I think he felt that by killing the president he would impress her and prove his love for her.

Ivory: She had to have guards at Yale and all that sort of thing, and she was probably not in a great state of mind. So I didn't know what to think. I felt she probably didn't want to do the film very much. I came back to town and looked for other actresses. We found Madeleine through James Lapine, who was my tenant up at Claverack.

Long: Is that the James Lapine who did *Sunday in the Park with George* with Stephen Sondheim?

Ivory: Yes. In those days we saw each other quite a bit. I asked him about any young actresses he could think of who might be right for Verena, and he gave me three names. The two I remember were Madeleine and Mary Elizabeth Mastrantonio. Julianne Moore, who might have been considered, was just arriving on the scene at that time, too. She had just graduated from Yale Drama School and had come down to New York to try to get an agent and to meet casting directors. She was desperately trying to contact our casting director, Judy Abbott (George Abbott's daughter), who cast several of our films. Judy couldn't—or wouldn't—see her, so she never got to me.

Long: How did you know this?

Ivory: She told me all this later on when we were doing *Surviving Picasso.*

Long: She played Dora Maar in that, didn't she?

Ivory: She did. And one day she said, "Did you know that when you were trying to cast *The Bostonians,* I was trying to reach you, and no one would ever let me see you?" She could have made a wonderful Verena, I think.

Long: True.

Ivory: So could Jodie Foster, in fact. If Jodie Foster had wanted to play the part, she could have been very good. I had dinner with her in Paris not so long ago and should have asked her if she remembered my Yale visit. Next time I see her, I will.

Long: Can you envision how she or Julianne Moore would have made a different Verena than Madeleine Potter's?

Ivory: Each actress would have tackled the part in a different way, I'm sure, apart from anything I might have suggested. It's always very hard to imagine someone else in a part in a film one has already made. The person you cast makes it her own, and her personality completely takes it over, as Madeleine Potter's did. Jodie Foster had made many films by that time, was a practiced professional film actress, whereas both Madeleine and Julianne were newcomers. Perhaps Julianne is the only one who is a truly charismatic performer, and who you feel can do anything, including swaying crowds with passionate oratory. Whether she had developed these qualities by the time she left the Yale Drama School, I can't say. Jodie would have brought a pluckiness to the role which we associate with her and which would have been absolutely right—the sort of pluckiness the young Shirley MacLaine possessed that was bright and full of charm. All these young ladies have formidable brains, I think, and all of them call up a tremulous intensity, which Verena needed when she wasn't speaking to masses of discontented women and having to deal with her romantic pursuer, Basil Ransom.

Long: Your first choice for Olive Chancellor was Vanessa Redgrave, but when you approached her about it, she turned you down. What other actresses did you turn to after that?

Ivory: Ah—so many. Glenn Close was foremost, having been recommended by Christopher Reeve. But we offered it to Sigourney Weaver, to Blythe Danner, and to Julie Christie, I seem to remember. Finally Glenn said she'd do it and began to do things like have costume fittings and sessions with Ruth. But in the end Glenn didn't do it because of a rival film, *The Natural.*

Long: So when it came out that Glenn Close would not be doing Olive after all, Vanessa Redgrave suddenly agreed to take on the part. You've written about your director-and-star relations with Vanessa Redgrave during the making of *The Bostonians* in an article, "The Trouble with Olive," in the spring 1985 issue of *Sight and Sound.* She was at the center of a storm of controversy then because of her outspoken political views, and she could be stubborn in her interpretation of Olive. But in the end she triumphed in the film. Could you go back over that article?

Ivory: No, that is too much to ask of me. Let an interested reader go to the back issues of *Sight and Sound.* That was in the days of the beleaguered Vanessa

Olive Chancellor (Vanessa Redgrave), Ransom's passionate opponent in the battle over Verena Tarrant in *The
Bostonians* (1984).

Redgrave, set upon by everybody. Now her firebrand days are somewhat behind her, the Vanessa I like to imagine is the Vanessa of Ruth Wilcox and *Howards
End,* an authentic and great English soul playing another great English soul.

Long: I was intrigued by your article because when I did an hour-long interview with her, she spoke in exactly the way you described—with her head
bent downward and her eyes seemingly fixed on some point on a table next
to her while speaking in a rather hoarse, theatrical voice.

Ivory: Yes, later she had Olive look and speak in that way. As I wrote in *Sight and Sound,* it sounded like some sibyl of antiquity, her hollow voice emerging from a cave or a well.

Long: Her comments took the form of a lengthy monologue about James's *The Bostonians* . . . that is, the novel, and the stubborn way she regarded it, as an attack on injustice . . . injustice to women, to New England mill workers, and I don't know what all. She had convinced herself that Olive, rather than being a vampire, was admirable. I didn't agree at all with what she was saying, but it was useless to oppose her; I just relaxed back in my chair while she talked about injustice. To tell you the truth, I really enjoyed my encounter with her; it was like having a great actress perform for you as an audience of one . . . we were only, say, two feet apart. Then when she had finished and had said all she had to say, she became another person—very sweet and unassuming, rather helpless, it almost seemed. We discussed your films for a while and how unique she thought they were, and I found myself liking her. But when I said goodbye, I was left with the feeling that there must be not one but two Vanessa Redgraves. Did you find this to be so?

Ivory: Oh, yes. And more than two, even.

Long: The tight, intense relationship between Olive and Verena has an obvious sexual implication for us today, but how would people in 1875 have been apt to view it?

Ivory: There were what were called "Boston marriages"—two women friends living together and making a sort of cozy domestic life for themselves. One of the reasons for this is supposed to be the high mortality rate for young New England men who fought in the Civil War. There weren't enough to go around afterward. There would not have been the sort of suspicion about this that there would be today—though William James thought long and hard about his sister Alice, who was in one of these ambiguous relationships, and he wasn't pleased. In the late 1880s, overt sexuality between two women was not to be imagined, much less talked about. Today, what was "unnatural" then is everyday and natural; one doesn't bat an eye noticing the smiling faces of same-sex couples while looking over the matrimonial announcements in the *New York Times.*

Olive, Verena, and Dr. Prance (Linda Hunt) at Cape Cod in *The Bostonians* (1984).

Long: The Bostonians was written in a pre-Freudian world, but a new era was fast approaching. In only twenty years Freud was writing about the sexual basis of obsession and phobia in women. The high-strung and neurotic Olive would have made an interesting case for Freud. There was apparently no actual sex between Olive and Verena, but in your film Olive touches the girl in suggestive ways—hugging her, rubbing her feet in one scene, and kissing her on the mouth glancingly. It seems to me that Olive's repression and her desire give the film much of its psychological interest. Another of your films with a strong same-sex psychological interest is *Maurice*.

Ivory: Yes, but there overt sexuality drives the story to the end. Maurice gives up his sterile former existence and empty bed for the joys of sex with a partner and also takes up a new life after quitting his brokerage firm. There is nothing of the sort in *The Bostonians*—not in the film, or the novel, though perhaps in the latter some sort of sexual intimacy between the two women is hinted at, most obliquely.

Long: The earlier part of *The Bostonians* provides the background of time and place, but the later part brings Olive's passion to a point of crisis, as her obsession with Verena turns into desperation and misery. The whole section at Cape Cod, with its tableaux of Olive coming to grief, a figure of an essential isolation and lonely suffering, is very impressive. Walter Lassally's cinematography also makes it the most splendid and visually exciting part of the movie. Wasn't *The Bostonians* a milestone for you? Vincent Canby called it "among the finest adaptations of a classic novel anyone has yet made."

Ivory: I think it was the most emotionally charged film I had made to date, and with the most complex emotions. Perhaps *Quartet* was of a similar complexity, but it was sexually more straightforward, and anything but repressed. Paris in 1927 is not anything like Boston in 1875.

Long: You received worse reviews for *Slaves of New York* than for any other film you've made.

Ivory: Oh, I don't know. There have been worse.

Long: Really?

Ivory: Yes, there were worse . . . well, way back—and more recently, when it comes to that. I think when *Savages* came out over here in 1972, we were all very surprised at how it was attacked by the New York critics. There were only three good reviews . . . goodish. One *very* good review, which was in *Rolling Stone.* There was a pretty good, and very quotable, review in the *New Yorker,* by Penelope Gilliat, and there was a quite good review in the *New York Times.* They—the *Times*—were trying to like *Savages,* and really *did* like a lot of it. But everything else was just . . . I mean we were cut to ribbons.

Long: What were your other bad-luck films?

Ivory: Nobody especially liked *Bombay Talkie* when it came out. It was not well received, but it was not the scathing sort of thing we took with *Savages* or *Slaves of New York.* We were to have two more experiences like that with *Jefferson in Paris* and *Surviving Picasso,* which the critics fell upon with the greatest impatience and almost a kind of rage. In recent times these two films had the most dismissive reviews. Both, coincidentally, were about great men, great heroes, really.

Long: Slaves of New York was received almost as a kind of scandal.

Ivory: Well, you know when something like that happens, it makes you wonder—at least it made *me* wonder—not so much about the film as what the reviews were saying about the people who wrote them. What was it about *Slaves* that made everybody react in more or less the same way? The book had been a great success; Tama Janowitz's collection of short stories was widely read. It wasn't really an all-out best-seller, but it was certainly a very much bought book and had come out in paperback. She was famous.

Long: Didn't the stories first appear in the *New Yorker?*

Ivory: Yes. You might say they had the blessing of the *New Yorker* to begin with. People liked the stories, liked the book, and you would have thought that they might have liked the film, too. I think those people who wrote such awful things about the movie saw it as a kind of *mésalliance,* as one of those terrible marriages that should never have happened. When there are such marriages, the people in them are always punished. [*Long laughs*] And I think we were being punished for making it, as was Tama.

Long: They felt that Tama Janowitz's sensibility and Merchant Ivory's were . . .

Ivory: . . . so widely apart that there was no way for them to mesh. If they did mesh, what would be produced would be a kind of monster . . . a monster child. [*Long laughs*] That, I think, explains the almost unanimous revulsion. [*Long laughs*] The only thing in print in the United States I ever saw that was really nice about the film was a piece in *Premiere* magazine by David Salle, and I never, ever, saw another good review—at least over here. Now, in Europe it was a little different. The French tended to accept it, while the English enjoyed slamming it; the film wasn't about them, for once, so their reaction was utterly dismissive.

Long: Someone who writes on films told me that he couldn't become interested in your characters, those young people who inhabit the New York art world. He thought that they were puerile, self-centered, self-dramatizing wannabes. What would you say to this charge that the characters are so callow that they damage the film?

SLAVES OF
NEW YORK

The 1980s downtown art scene in New York as imagined by Tama Janowitz, in which the slave owner is the party holding the apartment lease. With Bernadette Peters, Madeleine Potter, and Adam Coleman Howard. 1989. Feature. 35 millimeter; color; 124 minutes.

Ivory: Well, sure, they were. Of course they were. They were callow, and perhaps unredeemably so, but I think that some of them were also very likable. The Marley character is an extremely likable guy. I can understand that everyone would think that Stash, Eleanor's boyfriend, was a total creep, but he was meant to be. Eleanor runs away from him when he takes up with another woman, and she loses her place to live because it is *his* apartment. Stash wasn't meant to be anything but the way he was.

Long: That's the way he was in Tama's stories.

Ivory: That's the way he was in the stories, and he wasn't even much of an artist. He was redoing Popeye cartoons and such things as that. When you have a collection of characters that you don't like, and that audiences can't identify with, you still expect that they might get beyond that and be interested in the milieu of these characters as presented. After all, we didn't set out to make a film with a wonderful, comforting story. I mean, there's nothing comforting about Tama's collection of stories, so why should the film ennoble her characters? Perhaps this is a good example of the intimacy of films as opposed to the rather impersonal quality of reading, or I should say, maybe, cerebral. A movie is very much "in your face," as they put it. Not much is left to the imagination.

Long: An interesting thing about the "slave" characters is that they are so inseparable from the special world they live in.

Ivory: I think the film's detractors should at least have been interested in the world of Tama Janowitz's book. Ridiculous worlds, you know, like those Fellini presented and that other directors present, are often made up of the most outrageous characters that you wouldn't want to spend five minutes with but are nevertheless fascinating to watch in action. I would think that the downtown 1980s art scene was also a fascinating world worth putting on film. That is why I wanted to do it. And I never thought for a minute while I was making the film that I was supposed to present these characters in some other way than had been presented by Tama.

Long: How did you direct the actors who were playing these roles?

Ivory: When you cast actors for unattractive roles like those, you try to cast people who are somewhat sympathetic and not too off-putting. There was a very, very good actor who wanted to play the part of Stash, a character who is almost unrelievedly unpleasant. He was somewhat older, however, about thirty-five, and we thought, well, if we give the part to someone about thirty-five, there will be absolute hatred for his character. But if we give it to someone who is twenty-two, the audience will perhaps forgive him a little bit for being such an unpleasant guy. He just had to grow up. Well, it didn't work out that way. Although Adam Coleman Howard was, and looked, twenty-two, he was not forgiven for anything he did in the movie.

Long: Some reviewers said that he didn't have magnetism.

Ivory: They said that, but it wasn't true. He *did* have magnetism. He had a lot of energy and a kind of manic quality which that character had to have. He still has it, as a person, but has now become a director, and the manic energy goes into his manic films, I guess.

Long: Reviews were very spiteful toward him.

Ivory: When a film is disliked, reviewers and audiences tend to lose their objectivity toward the actors and to think that in real life they are like the parts they play. In fact, that can also happen when a film is popular. Madhur Jaffrey played a bitch way back in our *Shakespeare Wallah,* and ladies in New York said about her, "She must be an awful person!"

Long: Wasn't it Ruth who first noticed Tama Janowitz's stories?

Ivory: Yes. She had read the stories in the *New Yorker,* and at that time I was saying, "I wish I could find something I like around here, we've done so much about the English." I felt, and Ismail felt, too, that it would be fun to make a film right here in New York again.

Long: What was it that interested Ruth in the stories?

Ivory: As a writer, she thought that they were good stories, and she said, "Why don't you read these?" I remember that when we were editing *Maurice,* our editor, Katherine Wenning, was reading Tama's *Slaves* stories. She was often reading them in the editing room, and I would see the book on the editing table. But it was only when Ruth told me about the book that it clicked, and I went out and bought a copy.

Long: Could you see it right away as a film, and was it difficult to find studio backing for it?

Ivory: It was a very filmable kind of book. It had so many episodes and incidents and characters and so much color. We already had our three-picture deal with TriStar, and when we approached them about doing *Slaves of New York,* they said "fine." It was the first film they were doing with us, and they wanted to please us, I think, so they didn't have the usual reservations studios almost always have about unconventional properties. They didn't ask if it would be commercial, if the public would like it, that kind of thing. They wanted to get off to a good start with us. They were absolute gentlemen and never gave us any problems. When they first saw the finished film, if they had reservations—and no doubt they did—they didn't share them with us.

Long: The critics weren't so gentlemanly, though.

Ivory: No. And it was a film that needed critics to support it in order to attract the public, since it was so different from anything we had done. They needed to say to the public, "Here's Merchant Ivory in a completely different vein; it's funny and offbeat and if you go to see it, maybe you'll like it." Instead, they were saying, as they had with *Savages,* "I can't imagine why Merchant Ivory took up this stuff."

Long: I liked the film myself, and when I said so in print, I was actually attacked abusively by other critics.

Ivory: I want to tell you a funny story. Even though our hearts were breaking, we couldn't help but laugh, Tama and I: it wasn't only the New York critics who loathed the film, it was apparently every newspaper in the country. She and I were sent on a press junket by TriStar, flying from city to city. Super-first-class, of course—always suites in the best hotels and lavish dinners hosted by the local studio representatives, who probably already had some idea of the bad news that would hit when the papers came out the next day. So we flew from New York to Washington, D.C., then on to Atlanta, then to the West Coast, then, I think, to Chicago. And it was always the same routine: the devastating reviews would appear, we would read them at breakfast, reeling [*Long laughs*], then go down to the lobby and get into our stretch limo to take us to the airport. Then we made our way to the first-class seats that were ours by some kind of Big Studio Divine Right, and on to the next city, where the routine was repeated in exactly the same way—the fancy suite, the fancy welcoming dinner, and of course lots of press interviews, during which we attempted to explain what the hell we had tried to show in the film, what had been in our minds, and so forth.

Long: You know, this has an almost surreal quality.

Ivory: And so it went on, this crazy, frantic trip, which often seemed out of the movie itself in some ways. [*Long laughs*] I remember that neither Tama nor I had seen the Vietnam memorial in Washington. So we were driven to it on the way to the airport in our stretch limo and scrambled out—we had only a few minutes to spare; we might miss our flight—and rushed across the grass to that undulating wall with the almost sixty thousand names, Tama tottering on stiletto heels with her towering hairdo. There we touched some of the names with our fingertips, like everybody else, but only for a second or two, before we had to run back to our limo so we could make it to the airport on time. No doubt we immediately grabbed up the horrible *Washington Post* review yet again to see if we could find *anything*—a single line or even one word— that wasn't a rejection of us.

Long: Tama Janowitz had been enjoying a lot of success at this point, and it may be that it was time for her, and for you, too, perhaps, to be knocked down a peg.

Ivory: Some of these critics were, I am sure, people who had liked Tama's books. But Tama had had such tremendous publicity for so long, had become such a public figure, that it was time maybe to put her in her place. It was time now to deal with Tama Janowitz. As for us, we were "these boys who had come up with a wonderful film, *A Room with a View*"—maybe it was a fluke—and they had mostly loved *Maurice*, which was received rapturously by many critics when it came out. We were everybody's darling just then, but when they let Tama have it, we didn't quite escape; as I said, we were to be punished. When we came out with *Mr. and Mrs. Bridge* next, we were smiled upon again.

Long: When *Slaves* came out, everybody was talking, it seemed, about the "downtown scene." Where exactly was its epicenter?

Ivory: Way downtown, the Lower East Side, really. It was where most of the action happened in the film, as in the stories. The galleries we showed were between Avenues A and B, and from Tenth Street down to Eighth Street and beyond. I can't remember all the various migrations of the galleries over the years since then. They moved from SoHo to the Lower East Side when SoHo became too expensive, and have since moved to Chelsea, or down to Tribeca.

Long: In different films, you've been interested in art. In *Hullabaloo over Georgie and Bonnie's Pictures,* the principal characters are rivals for possession of precious works of "endangered" art. That was before *Surviving Picasso,* which is mainly about the private life of a great painter. *Slaves of New York* is about art, too, very much so, in fact. Are your characters in *Slaves* taken seriously as artists, or are they pseudo-artists?

Ivory: They weren't pseudo-artists. They did take themselves seriously as artists, and some of them really were artists. We didn't want to show any of the art they were producing as being absolutely ridiculous or completely without value, or as being ugly to the eye. There had to be some sort of saving thing about it. A lot of it was pop art, obviously influenced by Andy Warhol. We never presented it in such a way that it seemed to debunk that pop-art world. Stash does versions of cartoon characters. A lot of painters did do that sort of thing, and Andy Warhol himself had been a kind of version of that, or was the fountain of it, you could say. In those days you were taken seriously doing comic strip art.

Long: What about Marley's project, the chapel, which I have to say seemed harebrained to me?

Ivory: It sounds so, but actually it was very much based on the art and thought of an artist Tama knew down there, named Milo Reise. We shot, in fact, in that artist's studio, near Canal Street. The actual paintings of our Marley character, painted by Milo Reise, were really touching in the way that a certain kind of "primitive" painting can sometimes be: simple, hieratic-like Byzantine saints, all in a row.

Long: You don't attempt to create this youthful art scene "downtown" with a gritty realism, or in an almost documentary way that another director might have done had he been an insider to it, but you do capture the scene in essence.

Ivory: There are any number of directors who could certainly have done it in a grittier kind of way. We went in the opposite direction and treated it seriously and as being well worth looking at . . . it could have been the world of Michelangelo or something. Because it was all taking place downtown, with broken sidewalks, it didn't mean to us that the look of the film had to be gritty, although that would certainly have been a legitimate way to do it. It just wasn't the choice we made.

Long: A writer for the *Village Voice*, I think, said that *Slaves* wasn't a realistic depiction of the East Village art scene, since it had only one or two gay characters in it.

Ivory: That must have been Michael Musto. I don't know what he's talking about. There's a whole scene with a gay cop that was the centerpiece of a party. And what about the three transvestites, to me the visual high point of the entire film?

Long: Is the word "transience" especially relevant to this downtown scene?

Ivory: In the sense that everyone's moving from apartment to apartment, desperately trying to find a place to sleep. In that sense it's transient, yes. And there's the transience of the developing relationships, where for a while you're with somebody and then you decide that you don't like that person and they don't like you. Then you're out, and someone else moves in. That's a form of transience also. That was the point of a lot that Tama was writing about. For these characters it was a matter of their holding on to that corner of New York they called home. The precious thing there was the apartment, even if it meant enduring a hellish domestic life with somebody who no longer liked you—or the other way round.

Long: Apartments are scarce and unbelievably expensive, and have been replaced by nightclubs, where the characters crowd together, attempting to make contact with others. I liked the nightclub sequences. Did you have any trouble getting into the spirit of the lunacy of this nightclub world?

Ivory: I think no . . . in fact, I think that my ideas were a little bit more lunatic than Tama's, who was against some of them. For example, there was the performance artist who was sitting in an open icebox that was like a bathtub, sticking a carrot in her ear, which I thought was a really good sequence.

Long: I did, too. Did Tama have a lot to say about the script?

Ivory: She wrote it. I sat with her a lot on it, and it went through several drafts and once had a considerable subplot, which was about Marley—his life as an artist and his relation to Eleanor. But there wasn't room in the film for all of that. There was a violent scene, very well shot by Tony Pierce-Roberts, in which Marley's sister kills herself by jumping out of a window . . . but in the end we cut it.

Long: It's part of the scene you showed, that there is a lot of drinking and use of drugs.

Ivory: All of which you would expect.

Long: Well, that *was* the scene.

Ivory: Sure.

Long: There are a lot of dehumanizing conditions in that particular downtown scene. It's a wonder that the characters manage to remain as sane as they do. Is that one of the things you're saying in the film?

Ivory: As much as anything it's about the pressure of the city on artists, or people who want to be artists. They may want to be artists for different reasons. They may want to be artists just because they want to be artists, or they may want to be artists because they want to make it in the city and become celebrated and rich. But whatever, there is always the relentless pressure of the city on these artists, or would-be artists.

Long: They're marginal people.

Ivory: Perhaps. They don't after all make that much money, and there is the pressure to push them out, to get rid of them because they are taking up valuable room in the city that could be rented out to stockbrokers and so forth, who have more money. Artists, who always used to live happily in downtown New York, in places like the Village and SoHo, or on the West Side, can no longer afford to live in Manhattan.

Long: There's a generational issue here.

Ivory: That young generation of artists we showed in the film couldn't afford to be here anymore, which could only have a bad effect in the long run on the entire art scene in the city, uptown as well as downtown. These young experimental artists (for whatever reason they're experimenting) were forced out, and I feel that the film was showing that process. I think that's an important process to describe in a movie: the flight of poor artists from a great city that preens itself on being the art capital of the world.

Long: I was struck by the fact that the film was *about* something, something pressing and real.

Ivory: Well, that was part of what it was about. It was about young artists who are desperate to be here, and to succeed, pitting themselves against the relentless changing conditions of the city, and mostly being unable to survive extinction.

Long: Tell me more about the three drag queens in the brilliant red dresses who suddenly appear in the deserted street at dawn, lip-synching a song by the Supremes.

Ivory: Well, ah . . .

Long: Do they appear there for some reason?

Ivory: Just say they're there for their beauty. [*Long laughs*] Yes. For their beauty. They are like a strange and unearthly orchid that might grow out of some crack in their building. That's why they're there—three drag queens in their stunning red dresses singing a Diana Ross song.

Long: A startling moment.

Ivory: Both visually and orally. Like an apparition. If it is not seen in that way, there is something wrong with the beholder.

Long: I'm not sure that the humor in the film always works. Chuck Dade Dolger, the art patron from Texas who heaps Marley with a breakfast large enough to feed a dozen people, seems to me a conception that is forced.

Ivory: Probably . . . he was a version of a kind of omnivorous collector type. Yes, it was way too . . .

Long: He works better somehow in Tama's fiction.

Ivory: I agree. No, there are too many things like that . . . if I did it over, I suppose some of it would be done in a different way.

Long: On the other hand, Stash is always amusing, and one loves to see him deflated.

Ivory: Yes, he deserves to be deflated every five minutes.

Long: As a kind of extreme male chauvinist.

Ivory: Yes.

Long: And Bernadette Peters is beguiling, and is always great fun. Did you have her in mind for the role from the very beginning?

Ivory: No, I didn't. Eleanor was almost the last role to be cast. You'd think she would have been the first. We met every conceivable young actress for that

Eleanor (Bernadette Peters), the hat-designing heroine of *Slaves of New York* (1989), and her boyfriend Stash (Adam Coleman Howard).

part. It was the only film when the writer sat in with me during casting sessions. Tama was there for all of them, and she saw every actor that I saw. In a
way that was very useful because, as you know, I'm not of that world. Actors
would come from every possible agent and from every possible background . . .
from the stage, from TV talk shows, from the movies. They all came. So it was
useful to have Tama there evaluating them with me. The last big part that was
cast was Bernadette as Eleanor. She wasn't someone we had thought of early
on and kept in reserve.

Long: Had you seen her previously on the stage?

Ivory: Oh, yes. And in a couple of films.

Long: In *Slaves* she plays an ingenue type that she's often played in the musical theater.

Ivory: I had her in mind as my original choice for Queenie in *The Wild Party.*
That's who I most wanted, and she would have been perfection, but at the time
she hadn't done that much. She was a rising young Broadway star, and this
was in 1974, so she was probably in her midtwenties then. Apparently she
wanted to do it. She was intrigued by the thought of doing the part that was
finally given to Raquel Welch.

Long: What was chiefly the problem then?

Ivory: Her agent and managers thought it would be a bad thing for her, as
a nice young Catholic girl, to be playing the part of a kept woman in some Hollywood mansion, and supposedly they influenced her to turn it down. That
was the story we heard. It was such an obviously good thing, why was she turning it down? She was being told, I guess, that she would be making what is
called a wrong career move. And in a way that was right, considering what happened to the film. It would have been a wrong career move.

Long: The world of *Slaves of New York* involves kinds of exploitation of people
by other people, including sexual exploitation sometimes, infidelities, and
meanness, and yet one thing I liked about it was that the spirit of the film was
very generous. One feels an affection for the characters.

Ivory: Tama did have an affection for her characters, and still has, and an understanding of them. I think she got them down very well. And if you know
her, I think you recognize Eleanor as a kind of projection of herself. Bernadette
Peters plays Tama to perfection.

Long: When I spoke of the generous spirit of the film, it was you I really had in mind.

Ivory: Well, I don't believe that I made fun of, or was judgmental about, or coldly reproving toward, any of the characters.

Long: About the ending where Eleanor is riding off on the back of a motorcycle with her newfound boyfriend, crossing one of New York's bridges at night . . .

Ivory: It was the Williamsburg Bridge.

Long: It seems a very romantic ending: the couple riding off together in the night toward a new life. But then we hear the curious sound of the whinnying of a horse.

Ivory: There was a reason for that.

Long: It left me wondering if it could be a send-up of certain westerns in which the young couple ride off together into the sunset. But I don't know . . .

Ivory: No, it wasn't that. Now he, the boy she rides off with, was someone who extracted sperm from horses for breeding purposes. That was his job, to work in and around stud farms and extract sperm from horses. That's where all that came from . . . where they were going to, in fact. They were leaving New York to go to a stud farm.

Long: There are some night shots that evoke the mystery and romance of the city and are reminiscent sometimes of the cityscapes in Woody Allen movies, which are valentines to Manhattan. But I wouldn't call *Slaves of New York* a valentine. It is too knowing and detached. How do you feel about the movie today?

Ivory: I like it very much. Very, very much. I know we're supposed to hang our heads because of it, that it's supposed to be kept right down at the bottom of all our work, out of sight and never referred to, like a monster child, in fact. But I think *Slaves of New York* belongs well up toward the top. It's sandwiched between *A Room with a View* and *Maurice,* on one hand, and *Mr. and Mrs. Bridge* and *Howards End,* on the other—I couldn't have lost it as much as everybody said, do you think? I saw it again the other day (Sony is preparing a DVD), and I found myself laughing and enjoying it. Enjoying Bernadette, the dialogue, the visual look: the crazy clothes and sets, the club scenes. Tony Pierce-Roberts never shot a better-looking film, including *A Room with a View.* And the music. Especially the music.

I met someone the other day, a very intelligent young writer-photographer who often writes on art, and he was saying, "Oh, that's one of my favorite movies. I love that movie." And recently the *New York Times Magazine* did a piece on fashion in movies, saying that the fashion show in *Slaves* was the greatest fashion show ever seen in a film. This surprised me, because I had never been to a fashion show till then, and I knew nothing about that world.

Long: Slaves is an absolutely unpredictable Ivory film.

Ivory: I have a feeling that, as with *Surviving Picasso*, it needed a kind of treatment which was not your normal narrative treatment. For instance, the whole split screen thing. We did a lot of that in the movie. But instead of being praised, it was, as far as the critics were concerned, just a further proliferation of bad scenes: instead of having just one bad scene on the screen, you had two, which was even worse. I think we were experimenting there in the movie, rather expensively, because of the optics that were difficult and costly and took an incredibly long time to make; but this was just all dismissed with contempt.

Long: I remember reading a review that said the use of a split screen was tacky.

Ivory: Oh, that was the least that was said. But don't forget that the Andy Warhol movies used a lot of split screens.

Long: He did that back in the 1960s in movies like *The Chelsea Girls* . . .

Ivory: . . . He would combine two utterly different scenes on the same piece of film, running the camera with the lens half covered, I believe, then wind the film back, cover the other side, and reshoot the same footage—rather the way you do a double exposure in the camera, or anyway as Walter Lassally did it in *Savages.* When the film is finally developed, you have two separate images side by side. But ours was done the more precise way, as opticals.

Long: Slaves has a kind of freakish vitality and uniqueness. How has it done in the long run? It's often been shown, I know, on TV.

Ivory: I get residuals all the time from *Slaves of New York.* Not very big ones, but it's certainly being shown somewhere. And it didn't cost that much to make. I think it cost five million dollars, which is nothing as films go.

Long: It's a cult film with unexpected shades of Andy Warhol in it. Did you ever know Warhol, by the way?

Ivory: I met him many times over the last twenty years of his life, but I can't say I knew him, which is what most people say, even those who were his intimates.

Long: It's curious you should say that. In 1968 or so, when Warhol's movies were very much in vogue, I was living on New York's Upper West Side, and because I knew people who knew him, I invited Andy Warhol to a party I was giving. David Bourdon, an art critic for the *Village Voice* and Andy Warhol's best friend, sent word that Andy was coming. He arrived, his wig-hair bright with silver sparklers, accompanied by eight or nine others belonging to the Velvet Underground. I had a long talk with him that night, and what I couldn't get over was how bland he was. There were no edges to his personality, nothing to get hold of. Like those people you just mentioned, I had no idea who he was. What was your experience of knowing Warhol like?

Ivory: Once he came to dinner with a group of his Factory friends at my apartment on East Fifty-second Street; he spent the whole evening talking about precious stones, famous jewelry, and so on. He wasn't talking to me; I don't know anything about diamonds. He'd found someone else at the party who had an interest in such things. I remember that he or someone else left a dirty plate, with chicken bones and knife and fork, in my bathroom wash-basin. It seemed a symbolic gesture, to be a matter of style, and not just bad manners.

Once Ismail and I went downtown to Warhol's headquarters on Union Square to see him; it was a building where Saul Steinberg also had a studio on a floor above. Steinberg said of it that whenever he got into the elevator, it was always full of people trying to be something they were not, like young black boys trying to be blond girls. Anyway, when we got to Warhol's floor and got off, he immediately thrust a microphone on a long cord in front of us and led us around, recording everything we said. He himself said almost nothing.

I possess the towering mahogany wardrobe that was in his bedroom in his magnificent townhouse on the Upper East Side. When it was sold at the famous Sotheby's auction of all his things in 1988, no one wanted such a giant piece of furniture, and I was able to buy it quite reasonably. In one of its drawers I found a woman's hairpin. Was that the way he kept his famous white wig in place?

Long: Mr. and Mrs. Bridge takes us into another world entirely—the American heartland of the Midwest. Mr. Bridge is like a latter-day Puritan; he is all work, as if to prove his worthiness. He's not at ease with simple pleasure or the sensual relaxations of art. Coming into contact with artists during the trip that he and his wife take to Paris, he asks Mrs. Bridge, "Why don't they get jobs? Then they could do their art on weekends." Isn't it part of Mr. Bridge's interest that he is so recognizably an American husband of his time and place? I've heard people say that ... "Why doesn't someone or other have a regular job and do his artwork on weekends?"

Ivory: Well, that is what people who aren't artists say. I guess they think that creating art is rather simple, and you don't need as much time for it as you need to create money [*Long laughs*] or whatever. Yes, one has heard that.

Long: You've said that your father, at least in certain respects, was like Mr. Bridge. But your father ...

Ivory: Not in those respects. He never said those kinds of dumb things.

Long: From what you say, your father was far more cosmopolitan than Mr. Bridge. He was a Francophile, while Mr. Bridge feels uncomfortable and out of his element in Paris. So how did your father resemble Mr. Bridge at all, and what would he have made of him?

Ivory: He would have known him in their overlapping business worlds and understood him, but ... My father had very few close male friends, almost none at all. He was affable and friendly with everybody—a popular, sought-after person—but he had no intimate male friends, or female ones, for that matter. I don't think he would have especially liked Mr. Bridge in the sense that he would have felt Mr. Bridge was a little too uptight and not outgoing enough. He might also have seemed too self-righteous.

Long: But he wouldn't have disliked him?

Paul Newman and Joanne Woodward in the title roles of *Mr. and Mrs. Bridge* (1990).

Ivory: He would have admired him for his honesty and his absolutely cor-rect way of dealing with moral issues. I think Mr. Bridge never got muddled on the real moral issues, just as Mr. Wentworth didn't in *The Europeans.* He got muddled on other kinds of issues, but not in matters of right and wrong, in a kind of commonsense morality. The kind of things you would want to teach your children, the distinctions between right and wrong that you would want to inculcate in them. I always thought that Mr. Bridge was a good man. My father was like that, too. So I think in those ways he would have admired him. But I don't think he would have wanted to spend much time with him. Mr. Bridge wasn't that much fun.

Long: In the Bridge novels, Mr. Bridge reveals a certain amount of anti-Semi-tism that isn't in the movie. Did you feel that if his anti-Semitism were shown, it would withdraw sympathy for him?

Ivory: No. If that had been useful to us, helped tell the story, we would certainly have included it. But there were other ways of showing Mr. Bridge's intolerance.

Long: In the film he does make a revealing remark about their black maid's bright young nephew who wants to go to Harvard. "Why the devil doesn't he go to a colored school?" he exclaims, out of patience. "Harvard!" There is no give to his mind. Isn't he a man who is closed off from life, just as his wife is in the end?

Ivory: I don't think he was closed off from life. He's a lawyer, and when we see him in the opening scene, he's representing a poor boy who's been hurt in some kind of accident, and he's hoping that the people responsible, against whom the suit has been brought, are going to be willing to assume their responsibility for the boy's being crippled. He's hoping that the judge will award a larger amount of money because the boy is now going to be in a wheelchair all his life. Mr. Bridge took that case in a pro bono way. So, no, I don't think he was cut off. He was less cut off than the judge who awarded the crippled boy a very small amount of money. Mr. Bridge was arguing for more but lost. To me, this is not someone who is cut off from life.

Long: He may on this occasion have been trying to help the boy, but that doesn't mean he isn't held in the grip of his own rigid nature. This is more obvious in the novel *Mr. Bridge* than in the film. In the novel at the end, he even mocks the idea of experiencing joy, which certainly sounds to me like someone who is closed off from life, or who has at least a very restricted response to life. The reason that Evan Connell gave the couple the name Bridge, I suspect, is that they are not able to bridge the gulf between themselves and the world beyond themselves. In the film you have made Mr. Bridge seem more attractive, more empathetic, less cut off than in the novel.

Ivory: He deliberately cut himself off from the types that he didn't care for, that he had met along the way. He did not like Grace Baron. He thought that she was self-indulgent and difficult and perverse and a trial to her husband and all that sort of thing. He really didn't like her. He did not like Dr. Sauer. And really, for one evening in his life anyway, he certainly did not like his secretary, Julia, who wants to celebrate the twenty years she's worked for him.

Mr. Bridge, about to call the security guard, and his long-suffering secretary, Julia (Diane Kagan), in *Mr. and Mrs. Bridge* (1990).

He's completely obtuse about it and refuses to unbend at all, and even to toast her on their shared years. . . . I think he is seen at his worst there. I think his scene with her in the bar is worse than any other thing he does in the movie . . . in terms of his being a cold and unfeeling character. There was the added strain that in reality Paul Newman did not get on well with the actress, Diane Kagan, whom I'd cast as Julia. She felt . . . I felt . . . that he was freezing her out on the set. So later, in the scene in the car outside her house, when she flings down her purse in the rainstorm, the ferocity of her character, which finally snaps, was probably unfeigned.

Long: The scene at the country club when a tornado is approaching and Mr. Bridge will not go down with the others to the cellar reveals how unyielding he can be . . .

Ivory: That was admirable.

Long: Admirable?

Ivory: My father would have done exactly the same, exactly. . . . He would never have gone to the cellar. And my mother would have sat there clutching her pearls. [*Long laughs*]

Long: He must have been very sure of himself.

Ivory: My father was someone who would never change his plans because of the weather. If, for instance, we were to go on a picnic or take a trip, and there was suddenly a wild blizzard or a virtual hurricane, we still set out. He never stopped. Ismail's been like that. Ismail never changes his plans because of the weather.

Long: When I was on the set of *Mr. and Mrs. Bridge,* I had a chance to talk to Evan Connell about how he wrote the Bridge novels. He was there as a script adviser to Ruth. What was it chiefly that he advised her about?

Ivory: Small things that Ruth, with her European background, couldn't really be expected to know about Kansas City, and prewar people of that milieu. But you are wrong about Evan's role as a "script adviser" to Ruth. When we had a first draft, we sent it to him. This is a customary courtesy. And she was grateful for his comments about it.

Long: He said that Ruth's second draft of her screenplay was *much* better than her first. Was there any particular problem that Ruth had with the first version?

Ivory: First drafts of screenplays are often absolute messes. In fact, you don't want to show them to anyone. I don't think Evan advised Ruth on structural things—he would never have done that—but on those little details, as I said. People who want to know what he told Ruth can go to the Knight Library at the University of Oregon and read his notes to us in my papers there.

Long: Although the Bridge novels are set in a large city, they remind me of Sinclair Lewis's *Main Street,* about the small midwestern town called Gopher Prairie, where the heroine's circumstances do not permit her to move into some larger, outer world. *Main Street* contains a prototypical American couple—a professional man, a doctor, Will Kennicott, and his wife, Carol, who feels her life going numb in a place that is quite satisfactory to her hardworking husband. These prototypes of the American couple in Lewis's novel and in the Bridge novels have many things in common, don't you think?

Ivory: Yes. It's a recurring kind of situation . . . twenty years on. Not a different part of the world even. I'm sure you could find the same sort of couples now. I'm sure there are today's equivalents of the Bridges and the Kennicotts. In fact, I know some.

Long: Joanne Woodward in an interview had something very insightful to say about Mrs. Bridge and her situation. "There was a time in my generation," she remarked, "when you formed your home life around your boyfriend or your father or a husband. It had always been that way, and it was very hard for women of my generation to get out of that. In Mrs. Bridge's situation, there was simply no hope at all."

Ivory: I found, when the film came out, that younger members of the audience could not imagine such a situation. It was simply beyond their comprehension. A life of service to one's family seemed a doom, apparently, to them. For that reason they could not empathize with Mrs. Bridge. I said, "Ask your grandmothers about Mrs. Bridge."

Long: In the novel *Mrs. Bridge,* Mrs. Bridge is unable to communicate with her children, who will in any case grow up and leave her, and it is made clear that Mr. Bridge will die, making her isolation absolute. In the film it isn't quite so bad, with a rescue of Mrs. Bridge at the end. Didn't you have a different ending for the film originally?

Ivory: Different from what? You must remember that the film is made up out of two novels, each with different endings. In one we suppose the widowed Mrs. Bridge will freeze to death trapped in her garage; in the other Mr. Bridge contemplates the meaning of the word "joy" while at church. The final image of our film was of Mrs. Bridge tapping on the glass of her stalled automobile and saying, "Is there anyone there?" But an earlier version of the final image was of Mr. Bridge driving toward his house in a snowstorm singing "Stout-Hearted Men." We changed it because it seemed too open-ended. It wasn't perhaps clear to audiences what happened next; they after all *were* concerned with our heroine as it turned out. Her fate *did* matter to them.

Long: Did that earlier version confuse the audience?

Ivory: It was not satisfactory somehow. Either to viewers or to us. So we left her knocking on the glass, calling out, "Is there anyone there?"—knowing,

Mrs. Bridge leaves a pamphlet about the facts of life on the desk of her son, Douglas (Robert Sean Leonard), in *Mr. and Mrs. Bridge* (1990).

with the audience, that Mr. Bridge was on his way. But would he in fact get there before she froze to death? We had to underline what happened. Otherwise the audience might troop out feeling depressed, thinking that poor Mrs. Bridge had frozen to death, even though it is highly unlikely that she would have.

Long: Yes, but . . .

Ivory: Because you don't freeze to death so fast. So then it was decided (I concocted this and wrote the whole thing up as a sort of joke, which was then taken seriously) that we would use the home movie footage we had shot and, with titles, say that Mr. Bridge had come in time to save her, and then what happened to the children afterward and so on. After having done that, which people seemed to like and accept, we decided to go further and do a bookend thing, with some more home movie footage at the beginning to set up the story better. I'm glad we did that because otherwise you would not have known the film was set in Kansas City until something like the fourth reel of the movie.

Long: I heard that you worked eighteen-hour days on *Mr. and Mrs. Bridge* for eleven weeks and that shooting might continue until 3:00 A.M. Was the making of the movie grueling, or was it fairly normal for shooting a film?

Ivory: Who told you *that* story? We had a regular schedule, not at all rushed, worked regular hours, and had regular two-day weekends, during which the crew shopped in the excellent malls of Kansas City, Paul Newman raced his cars somewhere, unknown to us and the insurance company, and I lay on a couch reading *The Remains of the Day.*

Long: An article has this to say about the making of the movie: "Because it is cheaper to film all the scenes in one location at the same time, little is shot in sequence. . . . Mr. Newman leap-frogged half a decade in every scene. Furniture, make-up and clothes had to be changed every hour at the office of Walter Bridge, Kansas City lawyer, in the spring of 1932, the fall of 1938, the winter of 1945, the summer of 1938." Isn't it more awkward to shoot a film in this way than it would be if a chronological sequence were possible?

Ivory: Yes, all that happened, but it will only sound frantic to people who know nothing about how movies are shot. You try to shoot all the scenes at one location, in one go, despite the different epochs of the story, the weather, or whatever. You still pack up by 7:30 P.M. and take two-day weekends. At least we do.

Long: Writing on the film at some length in the *New Yorker,* Terrence Rafferty remarked that as its director you shared quite a few of Evan Connell's prose fiction qualities—"the meticulous, sometimes fussy, attention to physical detail; the flat, clean, neutral style; the air of cultured nonconformity; the dry, ironic tone that verges on haughtiness." Is this a fair characterization?

Ivory: Of me? Of the film? What is the difference, I would ask him, between a meticulous attention to physical detail in a movie, or novel, and a fussy one? What does Rafferty mean by "cultured nonconformity" exactly? I would always feel complimented if my work were in any way to be compared to Evan Connell's prose fiction qualities. A director could hardly do better than that, in my eyes.

Long: About Paul Newman and Joanne Woodward as the film's stars, was elaborate direction of them required, or did they rehearse together privately and in a certain sense direct themselves?

Ivory: They certainly didn't direct themselves. Not at all. But I imagine they ran their lines together many times. And we rehearsed for two weeks with the main actors in New York before heading to Kansas City—not a luxury most Merchant Ivory films enjoy.

Long: Paul Newman directed Joanne Woodward in a splendid television production of *The Glass Menagerie,* and they had also acted together on different occasions before doing *Mr. and Mrs. Bridge.* They knew each other's moves, you might say.

Ivory: They acted together on several occasions. . . . I'll tell you the sense in which they directed themselves. Each of them was calling up, summoning up, people that I had never met, that I never knew, who were their models. Paul Newman was remembering his father.

Long: Ah!

Ivory: I was aware that he was "doing" his father, but I was also checking his father against my father, using my own father as a way of judging the whole thing; and Joanne was "doing" an aunt of hers. She was born and raised in Georgia, I believe, so Joanne's very southern. She had been very close to her aunt; had watched, had observed her, all her life. They were creating their characters out of people they knew; but Paul was also creating his along lines that I understood because it involved my own father. It was a matter of charting it along as we worked from day to day, according to those ideas we had of these long-vanished people, two of whom were unknown to me. But there were still a lot of things I had to do.

Long: Such as what?

Ivory: There was a slight tendency sometimes for Paul to go a little bit out of character. I'll give you an example of that. When the young man played by Paul Giamatti, who is determined to marry one of the Bridges' daughters, comes barging into Mr. Bridge's office and confronts him boldly, Paul Newman's first instinct was to show his impatience with the boy by slamming a desk drawer, to do something noisy in the American male sort of way. I thought that this was the *last* thing Mr. Bridge would have done. I felt that he would have been absolutely gritting his teeth, but absolutely hanging on to his composure. I had to tell Paul to do only that, and at first he didn't want to do it; but in the end he agreed that slamming the drawer shut would be wrong. There were things of this kind all the way through.

Long: Did you always have the last word?

Ivory: There were times when I would lose an argument. For instance, in the Eagle Scout scene, when the scoutmaster says to the boys, "Now you must turn to your closest friend and give her that token that she likes best, which is a kiss," Douglas won't kiss his mother. Mr. Bridge, watching from the bleachers, is supposed to have then said under his breath, "Kiss her, dammit, kiss her." Paul Newman wouldn't say that because he felt there would not be enough time for him to say it, since the camera would have to be on them, rather than on him. But certainly there would have been time, and I told him, "You *must* say it, it's so important." But he just would not speak the line, and I did not have the last word. He probably felt, as a director himself who has spent a good deal of time in the editing room, that there wasn't room for that extra line. But he was wrong. I think not speaking the line weakened the scene, and after all, it was Joanne's scene really, and Bobby Sean Leonard's.

Long: Joanne Woodward's Mrs. Bridge isn't merely a pathetic character at whom one sometimes smiles; there is a simplicity about her, of course, but you also accord her a certain respect. There are things about her that one likes. She has some complexity, after all.

Ivory: More than some. She is quite complex, like many women I've known from that generation. Or thought I knew. She is sensitive and to some extent self-aware. She thought she could be more so through psychoanalysis with Dr. Sauer, but Mr. Bridge snorted at such an idea. Finally she was an old-fashioned, very decent but uneducated woman. Someone my age can look back on fifty years of reading popular psychology articles and books that in some measure do increase one's self-knowledge. But such articles in the 1930s and '40s were rare; and whatever books there were hadn't been written with the layman—or Mrs. Bridge—in mind.

Long: A critic wrote that on the printed page Mrs. Bridge is a conceit, and we experience her humiliations in a fairly abstract way. Woodward, however, embodies her so vividly (and unpatronizingly) that she eliminates our sense of distance from the character. Would you agree with me that this is one of the finest achievements of the film?

Ivory: Of course! But the qualities that Joanne Woodward exhibits on the screen are there first on the printed page for any imaginative and sympathetic reader to see. Mrs. Bridge a "conceit"! What a total fool that critic must have been to describe Mrs. Bridge that way! He only exhibits his own shortcomings, not hers or the book's—which has been described by other critics as one of the greatest American novels of the last century and has been compared, as a portrait of American life, with *Huckleberry Finn!*

ENGLAND

Robert Emmet Long: A Room with a View was nominated for eight Academy Awards, including Best Picture and Best Director, and enjoyed a phenomenal run in both America and abroad. Would you say that it was your most famous film?

James Ivory: It was—once. But now I suspect that *The Remains of the Day* is better known. *A Room with a View* came out sixteen years ago. A whole generation has grown up that doesn't know it, as it hasn't been rereleased very often.

Long: It was a picture of exceptional visual beauty, and as it happened, it was the first film you made with Tony Pierce-Roberts as your cameraman. What would you say are some of his special qualities as a cinematographer?

Ivory: Well, his energy and good humor—a cameraman needs a large supply of both. And then he has a superlative technical grasp of everything; he's an impeccable perfectionist, but at the same time, as I say, he has such high spirits, such energy. Nothing is too much for him, nothing is impossible. He will try anything you want, and I've worked with cameramen who would not—who had a fixed idea beforehand that something would not work or would not be worth the effort, and therefore didn't try it.

Long: You've collaborated with him now for quite a number of films . . .

Ivory: We've done seven together: *A Room with a View, Slaves of New York, Mr. and Mrs. Bridge, Howards End, The Remains of the Day, Surviving Picasso,* and *The Golden Bowl.* That's nearly a third of my features.

Long: Is there a particular look he gives to a picture that makes you know you are seeing Tony Pierce-Roberts's cinematography?

Ivory: The best cinematographers don't have an individual look, I think. They are there to serve the director, who sets the tone and look. That tone and look really come from the various stories you are telling. Each one is different. Lately I've spent a lot of time watching *Mr. and Mrs. Bridge,* and there the cinematography was so perfect for that particular world that it shone, like something very pure. The style is quite spare, even minimalist—though very, very evocative. And it's not like any of the others: there's a wonderful sense of what *ought* to be there. I suppose it's what is meant by painterly: you can't add anything, neither can you take anything away.

Long: In composing scenes to be shot, have you sometimes found yourself influenced by artists of the past? Someone has written of *A Room with a View* that the "Italian picnic scenes have a touch of Renoir (père et fils)."

A ROOM WITH
A VIEW

E. M. Forster's early novel about a muddled young English girl who discovers love in Florence and then almost loses it when she goes back home to Surrey. With Helena Bonham Carter, Julian Sands, Simon Callow, Maggie Smith, and Daniel Day-Lewis. 1985. Feature. 35 millimeter; color; 117 minutes.

Ivory: Well, I was certainly not much influenced by either Renoir in that film. But if you put some good-looking women in long white dresses in a field dotted with red poppies, and they're holding parasols, then people will say "Renoir." I think any artist who works in a visual way—any painter, photographer, or filmmaker—unconsciously (and sometimes consciously) refers to works of art that have given him, or her, pleasure. However, I have definitely tried to evoke Sargent in *The Golden Bowl* and Pahari miniatures in *Hullabaloo over Georgie and Bonnie's Pictures.*

Long: Appearing with *A Room with a View*'s credits are those wonderful designs that are works of art in themselves . . .

Ivory: They are called grotesques.

Long: Who selected them?

Ivory: I did. For the most part they came from the walls of the villa where we were shooting. There were a lot of them there, part of the decoration of the rooms in the villa at Maiano that was used as the film's *pensione.* We then asked a painter to do a whole series of them . . . enough for titles . . . and for titles between sections of the film, like chapter headings. That idea caused arguments.

Long: Why was that?

Ivory: Some people said they stopped the story dead each time they appeared. But such people were far outnumbered by the others who enjoyed them. These chapter headings had, after all, been placed by Forster in his novel, and they were witty and lighthearted and quite unusual for a modern film.

Long: Was it you or Ruth who initiated *A Room with a View?*

Ivory: It was my idea. Forster's estate thought we ought to make *A Passage to India* instead. But for all sorts of reasons we didn't want to. We had, after all, just done a British Raj film, *Heat and Dust.* Anyway, I wanted to revisit Italy after a twenty-year absence.

Long: But when the time came to do it, you had begun to change your mind. You told Ruth and Ismail that you couldn't do another period picture, another literary adaptation. What brought you round?

Ivory: We didn't have anything else in the works that was ready. As I've said elsewhere, our plan to make a film based on the ideas that later became Ruth's novel *Three Continents* wasn't concrete enough to embark on anything so ambitious. She'd already written the screenplay of *A Room with a View,* and we decided to go ahead with it. Ismail went to Sam Goldwyn with the project and was told that the characters should be made into Americans, and that the older characters such as Charlotte Bartlett should be dropped entirely, not being of any interest to young audiences. The two Emersons, old Mr. Emerson and his son George, were to be combined into one character. I was present at this meeting, so I know what was said. We said "thank you" and left, and Sam Goldwyn has been kicking himself ever since. Somehow this meeting galvanized Ismail, and he went out and found the financing we needed almost at once, though it became something of a cliffhanger at the last minute. We were ready to start shooting in Florence, and the financiers were still trying to better their deals. Anyway, they finally all came through and were very glad afterward!

Long: Did you run into any problems once you got under way making the film? Weren't you over length in your shooting schedule?

Ivory: No. We had ten weeks, and we shot ten weeks, to the day: four in Florence, six in England.

Long: Didn't you find that modern-day Florence didn't exactly match the turn-of-the-century city described by Forster?

Ivory: Really only in that the famous view described by Forster no longer exists. Lucy looked out across the Arno toward the church of San Miniato on one side and the Ponte Vecchio on the other. But now, the south side of the Arno has a motorway along it, and all the old houses next to the Ponte Vecchio were blown up by the Germans in World War II. They've been replaced by some ugly modern apartments. So the view of the novel is mostly gone. We had to concoct a substitute, which we did by shooting *from* those modern apartments toward the intact old center of Florence, with its domes and striped towers. That is the view everybody remembers from the film's poster and its final shot.

Long: You've said that *A Room with a View* was "enormously enjoyable to make." Why was that?

Ivory: Well, it was a comedy, full of bright and vivacious young people, being made in Florence in the spring. Naturally, that was fun—and the fun carried over to England, luckily.

Long: Vincent Canby wrote in the *New York Times* that you and Ruth had "somehow found a voice for the film not unlike that of Forster." Were you working consciously for this effect?

Ivory: Yes and no. His was a very pleasing voice, and it was easy to follow. Why turn his books into films unless you want to do that? But I suppose my voice was there, too. It was a kind of duet, you could say, and he provided the melody.

Long: Pauline Kael, your bête noire, actually wrote a very favorable review of the film.

Ivory: She *quite* liked it, as the British say—which means it was tolerable.

Long: But she did like it, very much so.

Ivory: I've recently read the review, so I know pretty much what she said. She praised many things about the film, had obviously enjoyed it, but could not bring herself to praise *me*, my work. She would rather have eaten poison than do that. [*Long laughs*] It was as if the things she liked about the movie—its playful tone, the acting, and so on—had all happened on their own, independent of me. I felt there was a basic insincerity, or dishonesty, in her attitude. Yes, she liked the film, but couldn't bring herself to write that she liked me, that is, my contribution to it. The next film of mine she reviewed (and, luckily, the last) was

Maurice, and she had no use for it whatsoever. And that was the end of our professional relationship, you might say. But she was very prompt about venting her spleen on *Maurice,* was in a rush to, because when I came down from *The Today Show* in Rockefeller Center, where I had been asked to talk about the film with Jane Pauley on its opening day, there was the new issue of the *New Yorker* on the newsstand with Kael's bad review in it: she was already in print on the opening day of the film's run at the Paris theater (a long and successful run, I might add). I felt Merchant Ivory had somehow become part of her emotional life, you could say, and her haste to get her negative review of *Maurice* and other films of mine into print seemed to prove it. I came to believe that to have a powerful enemy like Pauline Kael only made me stronger. You know, like a kind of voodoo. I wonder if it worked that way in those days for any of her other victims—Woody Allen, for instance, or Stanley Kubrick.

But, after a time, she too became a firm fixture of *our* emotional lives. You know, she was exceptionally foulmouthed, using every four-letter word you ever heard, and in her trembling little overeducated girl-of-good-family voice the effect was sometimes comic. We used to see bag ladies on street corners in New York, Ruth and I, hurling filth and abuse at the world, and we'd say, "Oh, there's Pauline Kael again." I had a fantasy of offering her a glass of water if ever her car broke down on the road in front of my house upstate when she was on the way from the Hudson railway station to Great Barrington, where she lived. I used to imagine that I'd send the butler down my long drive with a glass of cold water on a little silver tray, which she would accept gratefully as she sat on the grass waiting for AAA to come. I don't have a butler; that, too, was part of the fantasy. Or a silver tray, for that matter.

Long: Did you never imagine asking her into the house, say, if it was a very hot day?

Ivory: No. That might be taking things too far. [*Long laughs*] To be fair, even when she was attacking you, she was very entertaining to read—like her spiritual descendant at the *New Yorker,* Anthony Lane. I remember reading her review of *Roseland*—her first big blast at me—standing in an air terminal line. My knees were shaking in fury, but I was laughing out loud at the same time. Her jokes were mostly at the expense of overblown studio movies and overblown studio egos, but sometimes they were directed at true artists in the profession that she admired, after all, more than any other. Did she imagine—was she vain enough to think—that any of them were going to change their ways because of something she wrote?

Long: In her review of *A Room with a View,* however, Kael did make a nice point: that the clash of manners and viewpoints is swifter, more direct, and closer to theatrical farce in Forster than in James. All of Forster's characters are unmistakable social types, and they interact at times in rather theatrical situations. Cecil Vyse as played by Daniel Day-Lewis seems to belong most of all to theatrical farce. About your director-and-actor relationship with Day-Lewis, did you encourage him to go all the way in his performance, or did you try to tone him down?

Ivory: I never tried to tone him down. Not at all. I felt he was perfect; he was a pleasure to watch, always.

Long: In his novels Forster allows "unlikely" things to happen. After Lucy leaves Italy with Charlotte Bartlett, we next see them at the Honeychurch home in England with the rather creepy Cecil Vyse as a constant visitor and Lucy's prospective fiancé. Did you have any problem with the improbability of Lucy's willingness to marry someone like Cecil Vyse?

Ivory: No, he was a charming person when he wanted to be, and you could imagine someone who was a great talker like that charming and beguiling a younger person, flattering her. . . . I never for a moment thought of Cecil Vyse as being "creepy," and in fact Daniel Day-Lewis made him delightful, like some snobs in Wilde or in earlier English plays, like those of Goldsmith.

Long: Day-Lewis's Cecil Vyse is delightful, yes; he's one of the great things in the film. What's interesting, too, is that in the same year he played Cecil, an excessively bookish young man from a well-to-do background, he also played a gay Cockney punk in *My Beautiful Laundrette.* He went on to play other roles that were very different from each other, including the grotesquely handicapped writer-painter in *My Left Foot,* which won him an Academy Award. When you cast him for Cecil Vyse, were you aware that he possessed this great versatility?

Ivory: Not really. I'd heard about his acting abilities from both my casting agent, Celestia Fox, and a young friend who worked backstage on *Another Coun-*

The snob and aesthete Cecil Vyse (Daniel Day-Lewis) in *A Room with a View*
(1986).

try. I signed him up on the basis of our meeting. I liked his personality. I liked
him. It was as simple as that.

Long: When you were casting *A Room with a View,* you considered not only
Day-Lewis but also Rupert Everett for Cecil Vyse, both of whom a few years
earlier had played the lead in the London stage production of *Another Country.* Was Rupert Everett your first choice?

Ivory: He was. But when we met to talk about it, he said he'd rather play
George Emerson. I felt that would be inappropriate but didn't say so, and he
went away. Later on I think he felt he'd made a mistake, but by that time the
film had come out.

Long: Helena Bonham Carter was only nineteen and had almost no dramatic
training when you cast her for the leading role of Lucy Honeychurch. What
made you feel that she was up to it?

Ivory: There was something artless about her which seemed right; she sat scowling on our sofa with her short legs stuck out in front, and her outlandish shoes. But she was very quick, very smart, and very beautiful. Though coming from a grand aristocratic family, she had a terrible modern London accent and needed a lot of coaching to get rid of it.

Long: The film careers of Day-Lewis and Bonham Carter were both launched with *A Room with a View,* but this was also true of others in the cast. Rupert Graves, who plays Lucy's brother Freddy, had even less film experience than Helena Bonham Carter, was virtually unknown. He had been a circus clown and performed on the stage. How did you happen to discover him?

Ivory: Again, through Celestia Fox. I think he, too, had been a graduate of *Another Country,* playing one of the schoolboys. Again, I just liked his natural, unpretentious charm. I knew he'd be good.

Long: In addition there was Simon Callow, who had the role of Mr. Beebe and would thereafter turn up in other Merchant Ivory films. Callow had already established himself on the London stage for creating the role of Mozart in Peter Shaffer's *Amadeus,* but his first significant film role was in *A Room with a View.* How did you first cross paths, and why do you like working with him?

Ivory: We actually wanted him for *Heat and Dust*—for the role of Harry, the Nawab's tormented friend, played by Nickolas Grace eventually. But Simon, though interested in the part of Harry, and happy enough to go off to India with us, was contracted to stay for a long, long time in a West End play. He was a great friend of Felicity Kendal, and that is how we met him.

Long: And there was Julian Sands, who played the English photographer in *The Killing Fields* a year earlier, but whose first important role was as *A Room with a View*'s romantic lead, George Emerson. *A Room* proved the making of all five of these newcomers. That's quite remarkable. Do you consciously look for performers who are about to emerge as stars?

Ivory: Now how could I have known that, any more than I could have known in advance that *A Room* would be a hit?

Long: Do you have any favorite scenes in the movie?

Ivory: Plenty. I like the big scene in the Piazza Signoria where Lucy sees a young man get stabbed to death. I also like its counterpart in England very much—the "Sacred Lake" scene.

The murder in the Piazza Signoria, Florence, the sight of which caused Lucy Honeychurch to faint in *A Room with a View* (1986).

Long: Many people are fond of that scene in which Freddy gets George Emerson and Mr. Beebe to join him for a swim and frolic in the nude in the woods
adjoining the Honeychurch house. A critic called the episode "an explosion of
movement and light and physical joy that is one of the great things in recent
movies." Was this scene difficult to bring off?

Ivory: No, it was easy. We were only worried about whether or not we would
have good weather for it. That was our only fear. And on the day that we were
scheduled to do it, we had perfect weather. It was also one of the longest days
of the year, so we were able to shoot from early in the morning right on through
until it got quite late and we lost the sun. The "Sacred Lake," as a pond, did
not exist, by the way. We had to create it in a glade in the woods. Under all the

ferns and water plants was a sort of swimming pool inside a giant black tarpaulin. We even heated the water.

Long: There are two really major actresses in the picture that we haven't talked about, Maggie Smith and Judi Dench. There is some comedy in the picture at the expense of Charlotte Bartlett, played by Maggie Smith, who is prim, tense, and afraid of making a mistake but is at heart a secret romantic. A year after *A Room*, Maggie Smith had the title role in *The Lonely Passion of Judith Hearne*, about the desolation of an Irish lady who drinks, and it is as if the vulnerability in Charlotte Bartlett had now turned tragic. She can evoke and suggest so many things that I'd be surprised if Maggie Smith wasn't one of your favorite actresses.

Ivory: Of course she's a great, great actress. I've always liked her. She's very funny but also very, very touching. Remember how she was in *Quartet* as Lois Heidler, five years before *A Room with a View.*

Long: What about Judi Dench, another formidable English actress who has become a household word in America?

Ivory: She was certainly there, all right. But afterward, when we were all done with each other, I had the feeling she wished she'd never agreed to play Miss Lavish after all.

Long: Why is that?

Ivory: Because it wasn't a very big part, and then we ended up cutting it down even further. It wasn't that she wasn't good, but because one of her "big" scenes, where she paces out with a measuring tape the murder that Lucy Honeychurch witnessed in the Piazza Signoria, in order to put it in her novel, just wasn't needed to tell the story. But, as with many actors, the scene that you cut is always the one that they seize on, arguing that it "delineates" the character best or is their "best work" in the film, or whatever. She never forgave me. It's too bad, because audiences enjoyed what remained of her performance very much. She got an *Evening Standard* Best Supporting Actress award for the part in 1987. To make amends, I sent her a beautiful little drawing that an artist in Florence had made of her, but she never acknowledged it.

Long: The expression on your face seems to say, "I could tell you a lot more." *Is* there more?

Ivory: Well, there was a bit more. During postproduction we—I mean Ruth and I—weren't so happy with Judi's accent for Miss Lavish. Ruth grew up in England and has a very good ear for English accents. This one was, well, a bit too brightly aggressive, even for a sharp-eyed lady novelist; she seemed always to be too much "on." So I asked Judi at her post-sync session to tone it down, and even asked her to consider making Miss Lavish into a Scotswoman. You know, they can do any sort of accent you want, all these English actors—Royal, Yorkshire, Cockney, Birmingham, whatever. It's like choosing a salad dressing for them. But she refused. A Scotswoman would be all wrong, she said, looking displeased. Maybe for a mere American to question her accent was too much.

Long: What was there about *A Room with a View* that made such a great impact when it came out, do you know?

Ivory: I think people hadn't seen that kind of a funny, lighthearted English period film in many, many years. Not since *Tom Jones.* It was in the tradition of British films such as *Kind Hearts and Coronets* and *The Importance of Being Earnest.* Wonderful acting, wonderful locations, and meant to be enjoyed—you know, "sophisticated entertainment." It's a very rare thing in the movies. It attracted all kinds of people, including teenage girls all over the world, as well as intellectuals, nostalgia buffs, and people who were crazy about Italy—like me.

Long: There is a freshness about it and a great richness in the music, the visualization of the story, the high caliber of the acting, the robustness of the comedy. It has a magnanimous spirit and is witty, clever, and engaging. *A Room with a View* immediately raised your status, but did it also change your life?

Ivory: Well, it made it easier to . . . it proved that you could make a lot of money with a small investment, and in any business, let alone art, it's a wonderful thing if that can happen. We must obviously have the touch, must know how to do that, and for that reason we were able to get financing for other low-budget movies. This last is the main difference between our careers and those of a lot of other people who have a low-budget hit and immediately are given masses of money to do a big-budget film, which may of course flop. Or may not, but too often they do. We've gone on doing low-budget films, and we all have to hope these low-budget films will make half the money *A Room with a View* did.

Long: Did this ever happen for you again?

Ivory: Actually, it did happen when we came to do *Howards End*. *Howards End* was also quite a low-budget film, and again it was a hit and made a lot of money. So because of that, people were (and still are) willing to finance our movies, provided that they are not too expensive. We made three bigger-budget movies for studios after *Howards End*—*The Remains of the Day, Jefferson in Paris*, and *Surviving Picasso*. But they, too, were relatively modest compared to the big Hollywood movies.

Long: Did you have any qualms about making *Maurice*, in which a young man in Edwardian England awakens to his homosexuality, and in the end defies the taboos of his time and place by going off to live with his male lover?

Ivory: Absolutely not at all. Nor did anybody warn us, or threaten to withdraw finances for such a film, with such an ending.

MAURICE

From another Forster novel, a long-suppressed story of homosexual love in Edwardian England. With James Wilby, Hugh Grant, and Rupert Graves. 1987. Feature. 35 millimeter; color; 135 minutes.

Long: Maurice was written by Forster in 1913 but only published posthumously in 1971. How would you compare it with novels published in the 1950s—such as Fritz Peters's *Finistère*, Gore Vidal's *The City and the Pillar*, and James Baldwin's *Giovanni's Room*—in which young men also confronted their homosexuality?

Ivory: If I remember rightly (and I have read all three), their protagonists were every bit as tortured and full of self-loathing as the hero of *Maurice*. The prospects for homosexuals must have seemed almost as bleak in the 1950s as in Edwardian England. *Maurice*, however, holds out more hope— perhaps because of the sunnier disposition of the novelist compared to the other authors. No one walks into the sea with a broken heart or is sent to the guillotine.

Long: What is different about *Maurice*, too, is that in that novel Forster dreams of a classless society in England. Maurice, of good family, goes off with a butcher's son into some kind of undefined life. Isn't there a quality of fantasy, including erotic fantasy, in the ending? You know . . . Scudder, the handsome young under-gamekeeper, coming through the window to awaken Maurice to life?

Ivory: Fantasy? Or wish fulfillment? Forster was writing a novel with a happy

Maurice Hall (James Wilby, left) and his platonic lover Clive Durham (Hugh Grant), in a scene from *Maurice* (1987).

ending, so somewhere along the way he had to prepare for that, and he chose the magical appearance of Alec, the gamekeeper, at Maurice's window. It was a scene audiences like very much; it doesn't seem to matter whether they're gay or straight, male or female. It's a kind of universal dream of surprising or unexpected love, and I think everybody working on the film responded to that, too. None more so than Richard Robbins, who really surpassed himself—at that moment especially.

Long: How far back does your interest in Forster go?

Ivory: Well, I started with *A Passage to India* like most people—that would have been in the late fifties—and moved on in time through *The Hill of Devi*, which was also about India, and then finally through the English novels, ending with *Maurice*. There weren't that many of them, unfortunately. As with Fitzgerald, I reread them from time to time, and they always seem new, fresh.

Long: Forster was still living when you began making films; he lived in some rooms at Cambridge, dying there in 1970, I think, at the age of ninety-one. Did you, or did Ismail, ever attempt to meet with him about possible film adaptations of his novels?

Ivory: No. But there was to have been a meeting between him and me in 1961. I had an Indian friend in New York named Natwar Singh, who was a diplomat at the UN. (He's now the foreign secretary in the present Indian government.) Somehow he had come to know Forster, who he always referred to as "Morgan." I was making my second trip to India, and Singh wrote to Forster telling him about me—a young American filmmaker, passing through London, great interest in India and all things Indian, has read all your books (not true), et cetera. Forster and I made a date; I was to go up to see him in Cambridge. But on the morning I was to visit him, I got a letter from him saying he wasn't feeling very well, could he be excused, et cetera. When, later on, as I was reading the two-volume life by Philip Furbank that described Forster as a very old man dozing in a lawn chair outside King's College, with various adoring undergraduates sitting around him at his feet, I felt it was just as well I'd never gone to see him. What would we have talked about? I would have felt too shy and been dull, tiring him out.

However, in the last ten years of his life there was an attempt to persuade him to allow *A Passage to India* to be made into a film. The attempt was made by Satyajit Ray, not me. Ray went to Cambridge to meet him and showed him *Pather Panchali.* But Forster held out. He said that after he had died people could do whatever they liked with his novels, but not while he lived. This is odd because he allowed *A Passage to India* to be adapted for television by Santha Rama Rau; it had already been a successful stage play. Ismail offered to produce Ray's film of *A Passage to India,* and that offer was enthusiastically accepted. He suggested that Ray might like to meet Vanessa Redgrave for the part of Adela Quested. But then—I don't know quite what happened, but one must not forget that Ray was a very proud man and not much used to being turned down by authors—then Ray had a change of heart about the project. He had come to feel that there was something not quite right about *A Passage to India,* something false and something out-of-kilter about the main character of Dr. Aziz. Or let me put it another way: Forster's point of view, and main interest, was in Muslim India. Hindu India hardly existed in the story, either as a milieu or as principal characters. Ray felt, I think, that Forster's view of India was unbalanced, one-sided. So he dropped the idea. And then Forster died and Ray got busy with other films.

But by the mid-1980s Forster's executor at King's College, who had inherited the film rights, decided to put the novels onto the market. They invited Ismail and me to lunch at King's, imagining, I think, to open up a dialogue about *A Passage to India*. We drank our sherry and waited for the executors to speak, but when they did, we surprised them by asking for *A Room with a View* instead. What! That little, inconsequential early novel? Yes, we said, that's the book we want to option.

A few years later, when we asked for *Maurice* (this was after the success of *A Room with a View*), they were also hesitant, calling *Maurice* a flawed work, and probably nervous at the prospect of what might be done with such a story. But in the end, they came around.

Long: Because Ruth was writing a novel at the time and was unavailable to do the screenplay, you wrote *Maurice* with a young Englishman, Kit Hesketh-Harvey, a former pupil at Tonbridge, Forster's old school. What sort of professional background did he have, and how did he contribute to the screenplay?

Ivory: He was my collaborator from Day One, writing the scenes with me, or off on his own. His background in terms of class was the same as Maurice's and Clive's—upper middle. He, too, attended Cambridge (Clare College). He is a gifted musician and songwriter, performing all over England in a nightclub act called "Kit and the Widow." He's extremely witty, and very, very knowledgeable about the life described in Forster's novels. He's full of odd information no American could possibly possess. That information also sometimes helped to prepare me for *The Remains of the Day,* and he was an absolute gold mine of social gossip when we were at Belvoir Castle during the shooting of *The Golden Bowl.*

Long: You've been quoted as saying, "I thought that I could make *Maurice* quickly. . . . As it turned out, the writing and casting and filming were more complex than I had thought. It took us 54 days to shoot—our longest shoot-

ing schedule ever." What was it chiefly that took more time than you
expected?

Ivory: For one thing, I was embarking on a film without Ruth. Luckily she
read the script and made some very good suggestions, one of which was having Lord Risley get arrested and tried on charges of indecency, which would
have a cautionary effect on Clive. In the novel, Clive's sudden "conversion" to
heterosexuality while on a trip to Greece was not something we could really
show, and for most people who read the book was something that rang false.
Then, during the shooting we were plagued with labor problems. One day all
of the camera crew, except for Pierre Lhomme, quit. It was on a day when the
young actors had a big scene to play, and they were just left flat. I thought it
was an appallingly selfish and stupid thing for the crew members to do, and
I'll never forgive them, or the particularly bloody-minded attitude that brought
everything to a halt. Part of that attitude, I'm sorry to say, came from the fact
that as Englishmen they were working under a Frenchman, with very definite
ideas about what he wanted.

Long: There were some important casting changes. You first wanted Julian
Sands to play the title role of Maurice, but at the last moment he backed out.
I wonder how Julian Sands would have been as Maurice.

Ivory: I don't know. Physically he was interesting, a big athletic type. But I
wonder if he would have brought the vulnerability and sensitiveness to the
part that James Wilby supplied. I suspect not. The two actors were exactly the
same age, but in a way Julian had lived more. Could he have played an undergraduate? Again—perhaps not.

Long: There was a story that John Malkovich, a friend of Julian Sands (they
were in *The Killing Fields* together), was considered for the role of Lasker-Jones.
Is that true?

Ivory: Yes, I asked him to do it, and he more or less said "OK." But when
Julian backed out at the last minute, it may be that John Malkovich felt less
interested in doing the film. Julian Sands was going through quite a personal
upheaval just then; he left his wife and little son, his agent, and for a time his
country, when he fled to New York. He also told me that he felt he wasn't that
interested in acting. Perhaps the responsibility for doing the big lead role in

Maurice was just too much. He may even have been protecting me by bolting like that. We were awfully close friends at that time; he may have felt that his performance wouldn't have done either of us any good.

Long: For Lasker-Jones, Ben Kingsley turned out to be an inspired choice. He brings a sharpness and intensity to the role. The night I saw *Maurice* the house erupted into wild cheering when Kingsley delivered Forster's line "The English have always been disinclined to accept human nature." I didn't realize when he starred in *Gandhi* that he was born Krishna Banji and was the son of an Indian physician and a British actress. Had you ever considered using him in one of your earlier films?

Ivory: No, in fact. But we would certainly like to give him a big role sometime—perhaps again as an Indian. I know he was disappointed that I didn't offer him Picasso. But he's too wiry physically to play that role.

Long: In casting *Maurice*, weren't you taking a chance with James Wilby, who had only a walk-on in *A Room with a View* and was by and large unknown?

Ivory: You should be working for a Hollywood film company! That's the sort of question they ask there: "Are you very, very sure?" Haven't we, Ismail and I, been taking chances from our very first film on young unknowns? And doesn't it always work out, sometimes triumphantly, for the young unknown?

Long: Didn't James Wilby audition for the small part of Clive Durham's brother-in-law?

Ivory: Yes, along with another very good actor, Julian Wadham. I remembered these two from our casting sessions, and for a day or so it was a toss-up which one I would choose to replace Sands. But as I'd already cast the dark-haired Hugh Grant as Clive, I decided on the blond James Wilby. When he reads this he'll yell, "What! The only reason Jim cast me was that I'm blond! Bloody hell!" The dark-haired Julian Wadham took a tiny role as one of Maurice's stockbroker friends just for fun. Later on he was cast as the icy and determined Pitt in the stage and film versions of *The Madness of King George.*

Long: Wasn't *Maurice* also the screen debut of Hugh Grant, who at that time was also pretty much unknown?

Ivory: Yes, more or less. He'd worked in a sort of semiprofessional student film with James Wilby, made at Oxford. Celestia Fox sent Hugh to me, as well as James Wilby, and I cast him on the spot.

Long: Rupert Graves was a sparkling presence in your Forster films—as the wholesome, squeaky-clean brother of Lucy Honeychurch in *A Room with a View*, and then as Maurice's secret working-class lover. The pairing of them, particularly in scenes that involved their lovemaking, must have required some finesse. I mean, audiences at the time the film was made were not accustomed to that and might have responded with embarrassment or even cringing. The interesting thing is that they didn't.

Ivory: "Cringing"? How could that be, unless one subscribes to English ideas about class? Hugh Grant is acceptable, but the equally handsome and magnetic Rupert Graves is not? In fact, Rupert thanked me for giving him this working-class part. Usually, he said, he was doomed to play young upper-class "twits."

Long: I think you may have misunderstood the question. I wasn't asking about differences in class but about all that same-sex lovemaking and how you were able to make it acceptable to the audience, which wasn't used to seeing it on the screen.

Ivory: There was actually very little lovemaking; it was more suggested than graphic. The proximity of two naked young men in bed, obviously affectionate, but in a joking rather than an amorous mood, may have made these scenes more acceptable. There is only one passionate kiss, at the very end when Maurice comes to the boathouse and finds Scudder waiting for him.

Long: Times have changed very, very fast since *Maurice* was made; today there is more openness about what can be shown. Look at the raciness of the British and American versions of *Queer as Folk*. Yet *Maurice* doesn't seem dated. Why do you suppose that is?

Ivory: Because the problem of living honestly with one's emotions will be with us, I guess, as long as people make films, write plays, or write novels. Wouldn't that be it? Trying to live honestly with one's emotions could end tragically, or in farce maybe. Maurice contemplated suicide in the novel because of his "unspeakable" lusts. Or look at poor Blanche DuBois; she's never dated as a figure, any more than Lucy Honeychurch has in *A Room with a View*, with all her muddled ideas.

Maurice on the way to meet Alec Scudder in the Durhams' boathouse in *Maurice* (1987).

Long: Maurice is a film concerned largely with men, women being more in the background or off to the side. I liked Helena Michell as Maurice's sister Ada, and Billie Whitelaw as his mother, but they have very small parts. I was puzzled that Billie Whitelaw, who is after all a celebrated actress, would have taken such a small role. Did you perhaps have to cut some scenes in which she appeared?

Ivory: I think one or two were dropped from the flashback section of the film we later cut out. But she's a strong presence in the film. You talk about celebrated actresses taking small roles—or hesitating over taking them. But my experience has always been that actors, and actresses, want to work, to be seen, once they are no longer young.

Long: You had the advantage in making *Maurice* of being able to film splendid views of Cambridge, including the King's College dining hall and chapel, and aristocratic country houses like Wilbury Park, the setting of Clive Durham's Pendersleigh estate. Were there restrictions on your ability to shoot on these premises?

Ivory: Well, there are off-limits signs everywhere on a location like these, but it's almost as if they provoke the desire to penetrate to the innermost parts of certain places. I know of one very stately house in England that charged proportionally for the off-limits areas that the film crew eventually came to shoot in; for greater access the charges were doubled and even tripled. An aristocratic woman told me that she was able to reroof her house this way, once she'd turned over her bedroom to be a set for a whole month.

Long: It was said when *Maurice* was published posthumously that it was a thin book, and perhaps even an embarrassment compared to Forster's other works, and a number of reviewers also said that your movie version of *Maurice* was better than the book. What did you think about that?

Ivory: I'm no critic of novels. But if a great author like Forster writes a book that isn't, say, up to his masterpieces, it is still sure to be interesting in all sorts of ways and perhaps lend itself very well to being filmed. Perhaps the film will strengthen what was only passing good in a flawed novel; or what was not so very good may not be taken up in the filmed version, or will end up being camouflaged somehow.

Long: The American writer Ethan Mordden has written a story called "The Woggle," which has to do with *Maurice,* but which you may not have read or ever heard of. "The Woggle" is set in Australia, where *Maurice* is being shown at an art house theater. Several gay young men stay on after the screening to talk about the movie with the sympathetic usher. One of them asks the question, did Maurice and the gamekeeper stay together despite the demands of an intolerant society? "I'm very certain," the Cockney usher replies, "that they lived together 'appily ever after." Do you yourself have any sense of what their future life together will be like?

Ivory: Yes. My idea is that it might have gone like this: the film ends a year or two before World War I breaks out. Clive, by this time a young father and with a budding political career, volunteers when hostilities begin in 1914, becomes an officer, and is sent to France, where he is killed. Maurice, also officer class, decides to become a conscientious objector instead. But Alec Scudder, full of patriotism, enlists and in time also is sent to the trenches to fight the "Hun." Maurice then has an about-face and, perhaps shamed by Alec's decision, goes into the army, too—not, however, as an officer but as an enlisted man, in order to share Alec's trench life. The pair of lovers survive and eventually return to England. I should add that Forster wrote a little coda to their story—other than anything I have just proposed—but didn't include it in his novel. More or less it goes like this: the two men go to live in the woods together, doing some sort of rough work. Maurice's sister Kitty gets up the courage to go and see them and rides her bicycle to where she's been told they live. But at the last minute, almost when their camp is in sight, she loses her nerve and rides away.

Long: Seeing *Maurice* again recently, I was particularly struck by the visual beauty of the film. I don't mean that it's a series of pretty pictures; its cinematography is continually imaginative and engaged. *Maurice* had a warm reception (John Simon called it your best film to date), and you yourself were quoted at the time as saying that you were "even more pleased with the result than with *A Room with a View.* It has more psychological interest for me." Do you feel the same way about it today?

Ivory: I don't know if I think that now. It's been a while since I saw either

film. But for me, the psychological interest of *Maurice* lay more in the character of Clive Durham than in the simpler, maybe more direct, Maurice. It is also
what I felt sometimes in relation to Cecil Vyse in *A Room with a View*. Vyse,
though often unpleasant, like Clive Durham, is more fascinating to watch, more
unpredictable, I think, than the two young male protagonists of both of those
stories. Vyse and Durham are more interesting to me than Maurice and
George Emerson, the nominal heroes of these two films.

Long: Howards End is an unusually handsome film, both in its photography
and in its costuming by Jenny Bevan and John Bright. You collaborated with
them not only on *Howards End* but also on a series of other major films that
include *The Bostonians, A Room with a View, Maurice,* and *The Remains of the Day.*
I am curious about how this collaboration works. In making *Howards End,* did
you work closely with them or not?

Ivory: It isn't like directing actors or working with my
cameramen, for instance. I don't have a very precise idea
about styles or how things—that is, clothes from another period—should actually look. How could I know?
I have a vague idea, of course, from having seen count-
less photographs and paintings going back centuries of
how people were dressed at a particular time, but it's
still very imprecise. If you're doing a film, you really have
to turn things of this kind over to experts to reconstruct
all that exactly. I'll give you an example of the expert
knowledge that our English designers possess: I own
a life-size painting of an elegantly dressed woman, sitting in an elegant interior from the first half of the nineteenth century. I have no idea who she is; she's what
French antiquaries refer to as "une dame de qualité." I asked John Bright, who
was visiting me, what he could tell me about her, and he and the late Judy Moorcroft, another designer of ours, stood in front of the picture debating that question. From the dress the unknown woman wore, they dated her to 1837 or possibly 1838! But they went further. They pointed out that she was not wearing
a petticoat, or crinoline, under her skirt, so that her knees showed through the

HOWARDS END

*The third Forster novel to be
filmed by Merchant Ivory.
The intertwined stories of the
Schlegel sisters, the Wilcox
clan, and the downtrodden
Basts. With Emma Thompson,
Anthony Hopkins, Vanessa
Redgrave, Samuel West, and
Helena Bonham Carter. 1982.
Feature. 35 millimeter; color;
143 minutes.*

heavy fabric of the dress. This was very odd, they agreed. Why was this rich, unknown woman not wearing the appropriate undergarments while she sat for her portrait?

Long: You've done many period films, so the costumes and the styles and the atmosphere of each period would be particularly important for you.

Ivory: Yes. But it's not just reconstructing what is right for a given period. It's not only that. It's what suits the actor or actress. Some things look good on some people and bad on others. Some dresses are wonderful on one figure and may be terrible on another because of the cut or the colors or whatever. I can't possibly know the reasons for such things or have much input into it beyond simply saying "very nice" or "not so good." I imagine, however, that part of one's reaction isn't that different from seeing actors, or anyone, including myself, in new clothes today. The same rule applies: "very nice, not so good, awful!"

Long: There must be an immense amount of detail work involved.

Ivory: Yes, there is, and it's what I don't know much about, not being a costume designer. I don't know how Jenny Bevan and John Bright achieve their effects. When they have done all the detail work and decided among themselves—Jenny and John *and* the actress involved, or sometimes actor—what it is they like, or what ought to look good, they then put together a kind of collection of costumes for different scenes. They've already tried them on the actor and feel optimistic. But they may have some doubts. They may seek confirmation from the director of their choices.

Long: So they show them to you.

Ivory: Yes. They want to ask, do I like this better or that? And so forth. Usually I go to the costume house, to Cosprop if we are in London, to see what they have to show me. All this stuff is laid out. Sometimes the actress involved is there, and she models the costumes, and then what can I say? Usually it's "That's very nice" or "I like this one more than that." Once in a while I'll see something I really, really like, that I think looks great, and that I want to include, no matter what. And once in a while they'll put something out that I think is a wrong note, and I'll scratch that one. For the most part I leave it to them, give them my consent, you might say.

Long: You've been compared to the late David Lean as a director who excels at capturing very striking scenic backgrounds in your films, someone with an uncanny eye for visual beauty. Is this an apt comparison?

Ivory: Scenic backgrounds? It's part of my work, of course. It's something that I have to do. Every director has that as a job, and if you're doing period films, then you have to work harder at that. It helps to have an eye for it. But it's not only what's *in* the background in terms of costumes and objects and cars or carriages or whatever. It's also how the people move around, whether they move in an interesting way, whether, for instance, if you see a couple crossing the street, they could in fact *be* a couple.

Long: How is that?

Ivory: I've worked on sets where assistants were extremely insensitive to pairing the extras off. Here you had everybody dressed up in costumes and you would have the grand lady being put arm in arm with the man who pushes the wheelbarrow. That kind of thing. The assistants actually don't know what they're doing sometimes. I've seen that in many movies. You don't believe in the crowd because the people in the crowd are made up of disparate types that don't go together. So it's very important to have someone to do all that extremely well for you. The crowd has to be cast as carefully as the main actors, especially if it's that part of the crowd that's up close to the camera. Sometimes I get desperate and wade in, pull this extra out, pull someone else forward, turn someone in profile, make someone else stand with his or her back to the camera. How they look daggers at me then! Assistants *and* the extras.

Long: Anthony Hopkins and Emma Thompson seem exactly right for the leads in *Howards End.* Did you pursue them aggressively for the picture?

Ivory: I didn't do it aggressively. Anthony Hopkins was suggested. It was James Wilby who suggested him, because I didn't really know his work that well. I hadn't seen that many pictures of his. So I brushed up a bit on him, and we sent him the script. He was interested right away. We met in London at Browns Hotel and had breakfast, as I remember. He liked the script and wanted to do it. He was free, and the money was right. This was before he became a big, big star. He was about to become world famous as Hannibal Lecter. That film had not been finished and released yet.

Ivory in Devon with Helena Bonham Carter, Emma Thompson, and Anthony Hopkins in 1991, during the shooting of *Howards End* (1992).

Long: What about your casting of Emma Thompson?

Ivory: Her name was put forward by Simon Callow; at that time I didn't know *her* work. I met a lot of actresses for the part of Margaret, lots of good people who came to read. And then Emma came to read, and she didn't read the script but instead read directly from the novel; and from that moment on there was no question. She was exactly right, and she knew it was the part of a lifetime. There was no pressure put on me to find someone with a bigger name. In fact, at that point Helena Bonham Carter outranked her in terms of being a star. Helena was a better-known actress because she had been in *A Room with a View* and a few other films. Emma didn't really have a name except in England.

Long: She certainly came to have a name. She's been called "the most brilliantly talented young actress out of England since the young Vanessa Redgrave." Rather ironic, since she and Vanessa appear together in this film, which earned her an Academy Award for Best Actress.

Ivory: She did. And though I usually don't think much about such things when I'm working on set, I felt, watching her as we went along, that she was creating an Oscar-winning role. I didn't say anything to her of this kind, but I couldn't help being very impressed. What she was doing seemed somehow to be unique. How often do we really see a very intelligent and articulate woman on the screen? Intelligent in an imaginative way? You could see her mind clicking along, formulating some subtle theory that Margaret Schlegel comes up with in her scenes again and again.

Long: She was the warm center of the film.

Ivory: Yes. I don't think one could ever say that Henry Wilcox was the warm center of anything in that story.

Long: It was considered her film. Not that Anthony Hopkins wasn't . . .

Ivory: It's her film, and to me her part is like an extension of Forster himself, I think. His compassion and good sense . . . Margaret is really a female version of Forster, and that's why she speaks so much more directly about everything that takes place in the story. She expresses the author's point of view and imagination.

Long: Henry Wilcox in the film is a softened version, it seems to me, of Henry Wilcox in the novel. In the novel he is not a very attractive figure, and you wonder why Margaret would have married him. In the film Anthony Hopkins's Wilcox is complacent and so on, but also more sensitive and more vulnerable. He dances a jig with Margaret at his office at one point, and it's a humanizing touch. You can see more clearly why it could have been that despite their different backgrounds and ways of thinking they could still have married.

Ivory: Well, in the book you have plenty of explanation of what Margaret's thoughts were. She justifies her actions for everything she does at great length, and the author justifies them as well. It was never a puzzle to me why she married Wilcox. It was the most basic kind of thing. She was getting on, and she would rather be married than not married, rather have a man with her than not have a man. I didn't have to be convinced. And then, in the film Anthony Hopkins *is* a very attractive figure, full of vigor. One could, I think, believe that she could be attracted to him. There is a kind of magnetism about him that is convincing, the "man of action" and all that.

Henry Wilcox (Anthony Hopkins), about to propose to Margaret Schlegel in *Howards End* (1992).

Long: Vanessa Redgrave is as good as anyone could be as the first Mrs. Wilcox. But isn't it a difficult role in the sense that in the novel she's a kind of mythic conception, or at least partly a kind of living ghost of the past?

Ivory: That's why we have Vanessa Redgrave. [*Long laughs*] It was easy to see her embodying this figure. Vanessa, on the one hand, is very real as a flesh-and-blood person; she herself is very solid. But, on the other hand, her manner and her acting style have an evanescence that suggested the idea of this semimythic person. In my mind there was no one else who could have played that part. I never thought of anybody else. I hoped that she would accept it. As I remember, I kept badgering her and sending her copies of the script because she is notorious for forgetting that she has been sent scripts, and also notorious for forgetting that she has accepted them.

Long: Did you ever have that experience with her prior to *Howards End?*

Ivory: We offered her many parts, and long after a film we wanted her for was made, she would get back to us and say, "I think I've decided that I will play that part after all." By that time the film may even have come out. This happened three different times. So all I could do was hope she would actually get and read the script. I was told that when she arrived for the first day's work on *Howards End,* there was some question as to whether she *had* read the script. This was told to me by the hair and makeup people, who said that she seemed a bit . . . not quite to have pinned it down. They weren't quite sure which character she was talking about. [*Long laughs*] Was she talking about Ruth Wilcox, or could she have been talking about Margaret, who was another Mrs. Wilcox? But I must say that from the first instant you saw her in the film, she was *it.* It was a great, great lucky thing that she agreed. That everyone agreed, in fact, and were all my first choice for their parts.

Long: Does Vanessa Redgrave often approach her roles like that?

Ivory: I think it's probably like that with a lot of her roles. I don't believe she thinks about them in some laborious way that much. I think it's all the inspiration of the moment with her. She doesn't really improvise, but she has to be inspired. She may go wildly off the lines that you thought were so right, but what she does with those lines is so wonderful, so interesting, that

Helen Schlegel (Helena Bonham Carter) hears all about the nocturnal hike out of London taken by Leonard Bast (Samuel West) in *Howards End* (1992). On the wall behind is the sword that later will be used to kill him.

you wouldn't dream of trying to pull her back and force her into some kind of mold.

Long: Jemma Redgrave, Vanessa's niece, is wonderful as Evie.

Ivory: She is. Physically you see a family resemblance to the other Redgraves, and her manner of playing sometimes reminds you of one or the other of them.

Long: James Wilby plays Charles Wilcox, in a way, as a fool.

Ivory: Charles is not a fool, but he's not very bright.

Long: I know what you mean, but there's something foolish about him.

Ivory: He has a foolish ending, assaulting Leonard Bast with a sword and in effect killing him; and then snobbishly thinking that he can get away with it and not go to prison.

Long: Did you know or suspect when he starred in *Maurice* that he was capable of playing comedy?

Ivory: I always thought that he would make a very good villain.

Long: What about comedy? Did you see his potential for that?

Ivory: Sure. You sort of take it for granted that an English actor will be up to doing comedy. And he's quite a humorous person.

Long: Oh, is he? You mean personally?

Ivory: Yes, in life. I think he a little bit fought the notion of playing someone who was very unsympathetic. Charles was a sort of middle-class English snob, of a certain dangerous kind that Forster always had it in for. In one book after another a person like Charles Wilcox is always there to be beaten with a stick by Forster—someone who represented a side of the British character that Forster hated. I think James Wilby was a little reluctant to embody that, but then he really got into it. There were moments when he went too far, I thought, and you don't see them in the movie because I cut them out. But, in fact, Maurice and Charles were not all that different. Maurice was missing something; he felt "different" from all the Charles Wilcoxes he knew at Cambridge and in the City. But he'd been born with all the same snobberies.

THE REMAINS
OF THE DAY

Stevens, the perfect butler, gives his life to a fuzzy-minded English aristocrat hobnobbing with Nazis in pre–World War II Britain as the compassionate housekeeper, Miss Kenton, looks on. From the novel by Kazuo Ishiguro. With Anthony Hopkins, Emma Thompson, and James Fox. Feature. 35 millimeter; color; 134 minutes.

Long: Your film *The Remains of the Day* comes from a distinguished novel by Kazuo Ishiguro, which won the Booker Prize in 1989. How did you happen to discover the book?

Ivory: An actor, Remak Ramsey, gave it to me to read while we were shooting *Mr. and Mrs. Bridge.* I will be forever grateful to him.

Long: Harold Pinter had an early involvement with *The Remains of the Day.* What happened? He's not listed in the credits.

Ivory: By his request. It's a very interesting chapter in the film's history. Pinter became involved before the novel was ever published, having read it in manuscript. Liking it very much, he is supposed to have told Mike Nichols about it, and the two made a development deal with Columbia. The script was written by Pinter and turned in, there were meetings with actors, and so on. But then Nichols decided not to make the film after all, and Columbia began to shop around for another director. I knew of the project and by then had read Ishiguro's novel, as I said; I offered my services, which eventually were accepted. The whole production was to be handed over to Merchant Ivory; at that moment we were having an enormous success with *Howards End.*

Long: And Pinter's script? What happened to that?

Ivory: It was as Ruth said in some interview: Pinter had written his script for a Mike Nichols film, and she had now to write one for a James Ivory film. She nevertheless admired and incorporated some of Pinter's dialogue scenes, which were sharp and well paced. Contractually, both writers were to be credited, but Pinter, in a sort of everything-or-nothing mood, I guess, asked not to have his name on the film. He had been an executive producer as well, and that role also he didn't care to acknowledge.

Long: And the tone of his script compared to Ruth's? Could you call it Pinteresque?

Ivory: Only to the extent that Ishiguro's original might be called that. It was terse perhaps, but not especially gnomic or stylized in a way that people associate with Pinter plays, rightly or wrongly. There was certainly more warmth in Ruth's version, which Columbia had hoped for when they signed us all on.

Long: The most important change from the novel in Ruth's version was the expansion of the role of Miss Kenton. In the novel she was a shadowy figure whom Stevens the butler scarcely admits he might once have been attracted to.

Ivory: No, I feel, on the contrary, that Miss Kenton was always very much there. Of course, what she said and did was observed by Stevens—but in a pretty detailed way, down to his exact recall of many of their conversations.

Long: Did you do research into the political life in England in the late 1930s? Lord Darlington wasn't an anomaly. There was the "Cliveden set" of English Tories who wanted to accommodate Hitler as far as possible; there was Sir Oswald Moseley, whose views and those of other members of the British aristocracy, were eerily close to Hitler's.

Ivory: No, I didn't read up on all that as I might have. Actually, the film made me interested later on in that period of English politics. I had no idea when we started out that there were people like the "Cliveden set" and the really unspeakable Moseley.

Anthony Hopkins and Emma Thompson, paired once more in *The Remains of the Day* (1993), playing the butler Stevens and Darlington Hall's housekeeper, Miss Kenton.

Long: Emma Thompson did background research for the film on her own—histories of the period and books on domestic management of the great country houses. In addition, she had a grandmother who had been a domestic and filled her in on many matters. Did you find yourself becoming fascinated by the life of the country houses?

Ivory: Yes, it was yet another complete social system, with its own rituals, rules, and so on—not unlike that of the British Raj in India, on which I did a lot of research for *Heat and Dust.* I was lucky also to have been exposed to the life of an aristocratic English country house. Henry Herbert, the Earl of Pembroke and the owner of Wilton, was on the board of directors of Merchant Ivory in England. I had gone to Wilton on weekends and to parties there. But I had no idea of its backstairs life; I picked that up a little when we made *Maurice.* There may have been another influence, further back—from my college years: the novels of Evelyn Waugh and Nancy Mitford. They were full of country house

Lord Darlington (James Fox), the tragically befuddled and tricked aristocrat of *The Remains of the Day* (1993).

episodes and characters, in which "staff" figured prominently. And beyond that, or before that, I should say, there was Hitchcock's *Rebecca*, though the influence may be more that of Daphne du Maurier's novel, which I read as a teenager, than the film itself. Certainly Stevens the butler and Mrs. Danvers the housekeeper resembled each other in their mad infatuations for their employers, which allowed them to look away from, or cover up, anything criminal, like persecution of the Jews, or possible murder.

Long: I know that you brought in Cyril Dickman, the retired butler to Queen Elizabeth II, as a technical adviser, and that even *he* had to call on other specialists for their expertise. This was all very thorough and meticulous, but would audiences have noticed if you had some small detail wrong?

Ivory: Audiences of butlers and footmen would have noticed, and I suppose audiences made up of old earls and their guests from the 1930s. But they don't go to the movies much.

Long: You are reported as having inspected some twenty great houses be-

fore deciding that Darlington Hall should be a composite of four houses in
the west of England, Badminton Hall being the principal one. What was it exactly that you were looking for as Darlington Hall?

Ivory: I don't know who came up with the number twenty. It was more than
that and included houses in Ireland as well. Mainly, I decided that Darlington
Hall should be some huge classical pile from the eighteenth century. They're
more spacious, better suited to filming, less cramped than earlier houses, and
less fragile. Mind you, an American like Lewis would not have bought a house
like Darlington Hall, which was actually a house called Dyrham Park. A rich
American would have gone for something more romantic, with spires and gargoyles and Tudor windows; that's much more the American aesthetic, you know,
like the Yale colleges. And Lewis, being practical and modern-minded, wouldn't
have encumbered himself with some vast pile. We set this right in *The Golden
Bowl;* there the American millionaire Adam Verver sets up housekeeping in an
Elizabethan house, with miles of stone crockets on the roof.

Long: Your supporting actors always seem to be skillfully chosen. I'm thinking in the case of *The Remains of the Day* of Peter Vaughan, who plays Stevens's
butler father. He's comic in a way but also rather tragic; he's a big, powerful,
odd-looking man who compels the audience's attention. What made you see
Peter Vaughan as Stevens's father?

Ivory: Partly it was his size: he towered over Anthony Hopkins as a forbidding father should. And he was a very good actor; I saw other films he'd done,
and he seemed to be the one.

Long: In one episode Stevens travels through the west country, and his automobile runs out of gas. He stays overnight at a nearby inn, where the bar-
man-proprietor encourages him to talk about himself. He seems confused about
his place in life with Lord Darlington now in disgrace. Would you comment?

Ivory: I think it was more the case of attempting to pass himself off as a gentleman and not as a servant. He was unmasked at once, in the midst of his
story about knowing famous people, by the village doctor coming in to the
pub. Stevens knew the game was up as soon as the doctor began asking him
questions. Later, when the doctor gives Stevens a lift back to his car, he asks
more questions, and the disgraced pro-Nazi Lord Darlington comes up.

The demoted underbutler, Mr. Stevens, Sr. (Peter Vaughan), gets some instruction on mopping up and polishing the brass from his son (Anthony Hopkins, right), in *The Remains of the Day* (1993). The palatial location was Badminton House, Avon.

Stevens must fall back weakly on the explanation "I was only a servant; what else could I do?"—like Germans after World War II being asked about the concentration camps, who said, "We were just technicians; we knew nothing."

Long: There is a very dramatic moment at the end of a Satyajit Ray movie, *Charulata,* or *The Lonely Wife,* in which a husband and his unfaithful but repentant wife reach their hands out hesitantly to one another. The image of their clasped hands fills the entire screen as music surges. I was reminded of this moment in a passage in *The Remains of the Day* when Stevens and Miss Kenton, now Mrs. Benn, are saying good-bye for the last time. They shake hands at night in a rainstorm, and their clasped hands reluctantly break apart as Miss Kenton's bus pulls away. Their hands fill the entire screen like the hands in Ray's film. Could you have had Ray's image in mind in this late scene in *The Remains of the Day?*

Ivory: Who knows? Not consciously, but some memory of that moment in *Charulata* may have inspired me to do that as I planned the scene. One could

Stevens says farewell to Miss Kenton: their "unromantic" final scene, in which the Columbia Studio chief executive supposedly saw fifty million dollars melting away in the rain, in *The Remains of the Day* (1993).

say that it's a natural, the image that would come to most directors. Suppos-edly it is that image that caused the head of Columbia Pictures to jump up at the first screening and say, as the bus pulled away, "There goes fifty million dollars!" He would have preferred to see Stevens run after Miss Kenton and hop on the back of the bus, to live happily ever after with her.

Long: The film focuses sharply upon two men, Lord Darlington and Stevens, who are each devoted to an illusion. At the end Darlington's reputation is ru-ined, and Stevens is forced to see that he has wasted his life. What do the re-mains of Stevens's life appear to hold for him?

Ivory: Carrying on, upholding his own and his father's tradition of being the perfect butler—but now for a new master, the American Lewis, played by Christopher Reeve. Not an ignoble ambition for a man who has been forced to recognize his mistakes, which include his failure to encourage Miss Ken-ton, and who goes soldiering on until he topples over with a heavy tea tray, like his father.

Long: Critics have tended to regard *The Remains of the Day* as one of your finest films. Do you feel that this is so?

Ivory: But more than critics, it's the public that has decided that.

Long: A reviewer wrote that *The Remains of the Day* is "the deepest, most heart-breakingly real" of your films.

Ivory: It's curious, you know, that this should be so, because if you think of what it's about . . . the stories at the center of it—there are several stories—and the nonheroic sort of hero at the heart of it, it's curious that the film should have been so . . . that there was such a response to it.

Long: You've said that there were some very good scenes in *Remains of the Day* that ended up on the cutting room floor. Do you recall any of those scenes that you sacrificed?

Ivory: I didn't sacrifice anything. I've seen all those scenes recently, and any-one buying the DVD edition of the film can look at the best of the outtakes. But they didn't deserve to be in the film. That's why they were cut. Had they really deserved to be in the film, they would have been in it. But they also didn't de-serve to be thrown away. They gave further information about the estate, Dar-lington Hall, and the way it was run. They told us more about Lord Darlington.

Long: Are they interesting in any other respect?

Ivory: They're interesting also in that they contain an abortive scene that was very dear to Anthony Hopkins's heart. He really felt that it was a wonderful scene, a scene that comes at the end—it's in the novel—when he sits out on the pier where he meets another retired butler. He breaks down and weeps with the recognition that his whole life has been in vain, that he has placed his trust and affection in the wrong person, Lord Darlington, and has come to grief. This scene was in the Harold Pinter script. It was a scene that Anthony Hopkins liked a lot. All actors love to cry [*Long laughs*] . . . and if they get a crying scene they're really happy. [*Long laughs again*]

Long: No actor would want to lose what he believes is one of his big scenes.

Ivory: Anthony Hopkins certainly didn't want to lose that scene. But in the new script that was written by Ruth it was removed because I didn't like it very much, and she felt it was a very sentimental sort of thing, which undercut everything that was in, or would be in, the film. Anthony Hopkins had already agreed to do the film, but when he saw Ruth's new script minus that scene, he got very upset. He said, as actors often do about some deleted scene, that the scene defined *everything,* defined his character, was the movie's most important scene . . . and on and on. He told us that he wasn't sure he wanted to make the film if he didn't have that scene.

Long: How did you handle that?

Ivory: I said, "All right, we'll shoot the scene, and we'll leave it to me to decide later on whether we really want to have it," and he agreed to that. We did shoot the scene, but nature was against him that night because just as we were trying to shoot, there was a wild storm out on the pier . . . like a hurricane blowing. We were lashed by the rain, and pieces of the equipment blew into the water, the wind howled, and it was a disaster. It was as if nature was rebuking us for trying to do that scene. But once it had been cut out, Anthony Hopkins never seemed to miss it. He never once asked me where it was, or said that he would like to look at it. I think, after all, that he didn't like it either— that he came to feel that it was not quite up to the rest, wasn't as good as the rest, which it wasn't. Watch the DVD.

Long: You always wanted Anthony Hopkins and Emma Thompson in *The Remains of the Day,* didn't you?

Ivory: Actually, Anthony Hopkins sort of belonged to the project already in that he'd heard about or read the book and the fact that Mike Nichols was going to film it for Columbia. He sent a message to Nichols through his agent, saying that when it came time to really prepare the project for filming, he wanted to be considered for the part of Stevens the butler. By the time we were asked to do the film, he was a big star. He'd already gotten his Oscar for *The Silence of the Lambs* and could be seen in theaters all over the country playing Henry Wilcox in *Howards End.* Everybody liked him very, very much, and he was tremendously visible at this point and so was a very acceptable star for *Remains of the Day.*

Long: There was no one else you ever had in mind?

Ivory: Hopkins wasn't the only one who actually asked Mike Nichols to consider him for the part. It's funny, because both Kenneth Branagh and Emma had been out in California working on a film of theirs, *Dead Again,* and they had also heard that Columbia was going to make *Remains of the Day,* with Mike Nichols to direct. They approached Nichols, and I think they even read for it. There was also Jeremy Irons, who had just gotten an Oscar. The day after he got the Oscar he trudged to Columbia, so people say, and I think also read for Mike Nichols. So all these people were being thought about, but I think Columbia liked Anthony Hopkins the most. I know they felt that Kenneth Branagh was just too young, as I did.

Long: So when Columbia asked you to direct, Anthony Hopkins was already the front-runner.

Ivory: When I came into the project, they asked whether I would like to work with Anthony Hopkins again, and I said, "Absolutely, that would be wonderful, great." Already in the back of my mind, or in the front of my mind, I had decided that he was the very best person to play Stevens. I had also decided that the very best person to play Miss Kenton would be Emma. But immediately there was a campaign against her in Hollywood, a campaign that came from outside the Columbia studio, that came from the big agencies. Whoever I wanted for Miss Kenton was fine with Columbia, it seemed, because they knew they had Anthony Hopkins as their star, and that was sufficient.

Long: Can you tell me something more about the campaign against Emma Thompson?

Ivory: What happened was that all these meddling Hollywood agents had clients that *they* thought should be playing Miss Kenton—American clients, it should be noted, like Meryl Streep. They brought a lot of pressure, and particularly Anthony Hopkins's agent, Ed Limato at ICM, brought pressure on us to cast this lady or that. Limato had gotten the idea that Anthony didn't want to work with Emma. He told that to the people at Columbia, who told me. But when I asked Anthony, "Is this true? Did you ever say that?" he said, "No, I never said it. I love her, I'd love working with her again. She'd make a perfect Miss Kenton."

Long: That clinched it.

Ivory: That was the end of that. But I had to hear an awful lot about why Emma wouldn't do. . . . When I'd answer that she was wonderful in *Howards End* and was just the right person, I'd have to hear all this stuff: "Oh, yes, but that's just a little English film, you know; this is a big Hollywood production, and you need more of a name." This was before Emma had won *her* Academy Award. Anyway, I got my dream cast. The third member of the dream cast was James Fox.

Long: He's good.

Ivory: He's more than good. He's fabulous. He's just exactly right. The reason that I cast him was that I had seen him in one of the two British television films, together called *Single Spies,* that Alan Bennett wrote and that John Schlesinger had directed. These had already been very well received on the stage in London. You know, Burgess, Maclean, and Anthony Blunt. Fox plays Anthony Blunt in the film called *A Matter of Attribution.* He was the spy ("Keeper of the Queen's Pictures," he was called), and Prunella Scales, who was Aunt Julie in *Howards End,* played the Queen. That's a marvelous pair.

Long: I agree. I remember seeing it.

Ivory: The other film, *An Englishman Abroad,* starred Alan Bates and Coral Browne. That was the Burgess one.

Long: How is it that Anthony Hopkins and Emma Thompson haven't appeared together in a film since *The Remains of the Day,* do you know?

Ivory: I have no idea. I'm sure lots of scripts were sent to Emma with letters saying, "We'd like you to play so-and-so, and we'd like Anthony Hopkins to

play such-and-such." He, too, would have received offers pairing him up with
Emma.

Long: Anthony Hopkins has been quoted as saying "Stevens is a dead man, a
walking dead man. Roles like that are a trap. . . . I can't play dead men anymore."

Ivory: Perhaps you can do it once and then you don't want to do it again.
It's true that after that he played an awful lot of men of action, one after the
other.

Long: In the novel Miss Kenton remarks to Stevens that his narrow room
reveals him painfully. "Really, Mr. Stevens," she says, "this room resembles a
prison cell. . . . I could well imagine condemned men spending their last
hours here." One of the finest things about Hopkins's performance is the sense
of solitude and isolation that always surrounds him and defines his life. What
is behind his inability to come out of himself, to express the feelings he has
for Miss Kenton? Is it sexual fear?

Ivory: Remember the things his father tells him on his deathbed.

Long: Something like "Beware of women"?

Ivory: He tells him a story about his mother.

Long: The father's unfaithful wife . . .

Ivory: The unfaithful wife, the kind of thing, according to psychiatrists, that
can get passed on and color a son's later life. The experience for Stevens was
so painful—the experience of watching his parents suffer—that presumably
he decided to dispense with that side of things and not get himself in such a
mess. There's that. You could also say that there's the priestly function he's
assumed.

Long: That's true.

Ivory: That kind of celibate life serving the Lord, who actually *is* a lord. And,
you know, there could be sexual fear there also, but none of us cared to go into
that. Who knows? Presumably there was also something of that sort.

Long: He's a very curious, a very odd figure.

Ivory: Well, he's less odd if you think of men's devotion to the military—or
the priesthood. There are people who give their whole lives to the military, to
serving others above them, carrying out orders without question, being the
best master sergeant there is kind of thing. Being a butler is a similar kind of

devotion, giving up one's life to this kind of unquestioning service. It's quite understandable. And very English. Emma once told me that an enormously high proportion of the English population was made up of people descended from individuals who had been "in service"—meaning domestic service, not the military.

Long: A writer remarked that the picture "offers riveting, almost documentary-like sequences, showing how such houses once functioned, how dozens of guests were accommodated, how elaborate meals were prepared, how servants preserved order among themselves through their own hierarchies." What is it that makes these downstairs scenes of such interest to the viewer?

Ivory: Nobody knows very much about any of that outside of England. It *is* intrinsically interesting, I think. And our two main characters are from that world, the downstairs, or below stairs, life of servants. Showing them hard at work is at the heart of the story, and it's much more concretely shown than the goings-on upstairs. You never see the upstairs except through the eyes of the servants. We never go upstairs without a servant. You never see the life of Lord Darlington unless it is connected to either Miss Kenton or Stevens. It's not there to be shown for its own sake.

Long: The Remains of the Day is wonderfully absorbing. There was a story floating around at one point that you hoped to make another film from a book that Ishiguro is writing. Is there anything to that?

Ivory: Not from one of his books, actually, but from a book that the Japanese author Tanazaki wrote called *Diary of a Mad Old Man.* I had an idea it might be the basis of a story taking place in America and Japan, but largely about an elderly American. Ishiguro took it on, and as is often the way with original writers, ended in throwing Tanazaki's book out the window. The result is a script called *The White Countess,* set in Shanghai just before the Japanese invaded in the 1930s. God knows how this happened, but I have to say it's a very unusual script.

Long: How so?

Ivory: The story mainly takes place in a bar called "The White Countess," owned by a disillusioned American ex-diplomat, who is also blind. He is one of Ishiguro's obsessive antiheroes—like Stevens the butler or the lunatic detective nicknamed Puffin from his last novel, *When We Were Orphans*, who thinks his mission is to save the world from criminals. That story, like ours, is set in wartime Shanghai.

Long: The Golden Bowl completes the trilogy of films that you have adapted for the screen from novels by Henry James. You've become associated in the public mind with James, and I've even seen you referred to in reviews as a "Jamesian director." Do you think this description is appropriate? Are you a Jamesian director?

Ivory: What does that mean? There were no film directors in James's day, so I don't really know what that means. Am I a Jamesian person . . . ?

Long: I'd say they were using the term very loosely. If a novelist is described as being Jamesian, it might imply that he has certain qualities that James had. He might be a detached observer of manners; he might have moral sensibility, possess wit and psychological acuteness. You *do* seem like a detached observer at home in a world of manners, though of course you're not a carbon copy of James. You're someone else.

Ivory: As long as I can remember, writers and critics have said that our films had a Jamesian side to them, starting with *Shakespeare Wallah* and continuing with a great many of our other films. You know, if I get to talking on that subject, it will sound so vague and imprecise . . . not to mention conceited.

Long: But your films have a strong social-psychological element. It was what attracted me to your films in the first place.

Ivory: From very early on, from the time I was in college, I have been interested in psychological motivation and its taking some sort of artistic form, or of being put into some sort of dramatic context. Those are the kind of books and plays I like, as well as other people's films of course. I have always been interested in that, but such an interest was encouraged to expand really only after I went to work with Ruth Jhabvala. She is a modern writer, and her contemporary screenplays for us are sometimes called Jamesian. She admires James a great deal, in the same way that she admires the great Russian writers. It's only because . . . you know, it is through her . . . that I think I may have developed that side of myself.

Long: Perhaps we could talk about how you came to do *The Golden Bowl.* I understand that it wasn't *The Golden Bowl* at the beginning but *The Portrait of a Lady* that Ruth wanted to adapt as a movie, except that *The Portrait of a Lady* was preempted by Jane Campion's film.

Ivory: It didn't happen quite like that. It's an interesting story. After doing *Howards End* and signing a production deal with Disney to make other films, we talked to Jeffrey Katzenberg, then the head of Disney, when he was in New York, and he said, "Well, what else would you like to do?" At that point we had not yet made *Jefferson in Paris* and were still, I think, completing *The Remains of the Day.* When he said, "What would you like to do?" Ruth spoke up and said, "Well, we'd love to do *Portrait of a Lady.* We've always wanted to do that." I seconded this, Ismail did too, and Katzenberg made a little notation in a book he took out of his breast pocket. He seemed to think it was a good idea, and shortly after that it was announced in *Time* magazine that Disney was going to do *Portrait of a Lady* with us.

Long: I remember seeing it.

Ivory: The write-up in *Time* was a rather jokey affair, a "lowbrow meets highbrow" kind of thing, which was ridiculous, since Disney, as far as I am concerned, is probably the most highbrow of studios because of the kind of films that they sometimes choose to make. . . . But at any rate, we decided then that we would start work on *Portrait of a Lady.* A script, of course, had to be written, and Disney was going to develop it for us. But we were still finishing *The Remains of the Day,* and after that we started making *Jefferson in Paris.* So a lot of time was passing, and meanwhile Jane Campion decided, along with Nicole Kidman, that they, too, would like to make *Portrait of a Lady.* They came up with the idea independently, and then the story goes that Jane Campion, on hearing that we were going to do it, told Nicole Kidman, "Well, if they're going to do it, I won't do it." But we had also heard that Jane Campion was going to do it, and we said, "Well, if Jane Campion is going to do it, *we* can't do it," for, as Ruth pointed out, there wouldn't be room for two versions of *The Portrait of a Lady* in the same decade. So both sides gave it up, although not before making certain inquiries about casting and so forth. I presented the novel to Glenn Close, for example, having her in mind for the part of Madame Merle. I hoped that she would accept it, and she did accept it at once. It would have been a marvelous part for her. . . . Time passed, and neither side did anything. We thought that Jane Campion was making it, and she thought that we were making it.

Long: What happened then?

Ivory: Strangest of all is that all of us were at the same agency in Hollywood, Creative Artists. At Creative Artists every day they have staff meetings at which various projects of their star actresses and star directors are discussed. . . . So here you have Jane Campion and Nicole Kidman, and Merchant Ivory Jhabvala and Glenn Close, all at Creative Artists at the same time, in two rival versions of the *Portrait.* And in all the time that this was going on, nobody at Creative Artists caught on that there were *two* rival films involving *two* different groups of their clients. Nobody ever spoke up or said anything apparently.

Long: It's hard to imagine such a thing.

Ivory: Well, yes. However, at one point Jane Campion decided that she couldn't make *Portrait of a Lady* because she had had a miscarriage and didn't feel like doing anything for a while. But when she recovered, Nicole Kidman is supposed to have gone to her and said, "Well, look, they're not going to make it; why don't we make it after all?" Jane Campion supposedly said, "OK, let's make it." And so they did.

Long: How did you get from there to *The Golden Bowl?*

Ivory: After that we thought we would try another of James's big European novels. We turned to *The Wings of the Dove.* We began to discuss the project both at Disney, because we still had our deal with them at that time, and at Paramount, which already had some sort of an involvement with *Wings of the Dove*— as did a producer friend of ours, Annie Wingate, who had worked with us on *Howards End.* She was planning to produce *Wings of the Dove* with someone else, and it seemed to be a viable production. They wanted to cast Uma Thurman in the film, with shooting to take place in England and Italy. For the second time we backed away. It was then that we decided to go for *The Golden Bowl.*

Long: Were you enthusiastic about doing it?

Ivory: We felt that *The Golden Bowl* as material was perhaps actually more interesting than the other two. Its ending was less inconclusive, less a dying fall into sadness than either *Portrait of a Lady* or *Wings of the Dove.* The ending of

The Golden Bowl is not quite that, it's something better than that. It's not quite a happy ending, but it's more positive. And it's a very, very good story.

Long: Did you have any trouble finding backing for the picture?

Ivory: For a while the project was at Disney. We tried to make a deal with them so that the script could be written; if they didn't like the script and didn't want to go forward, we would buy back the rights to the script, or someone else would. But a lot of things were going on then at Disney. People were coming and going there. By this time Jeffrey Katzenberg had long since gone to set up Dreamworks. The next film we made after *Jefferson in Paris* was *Surviving Picasso* at Warner Brothers. We made friends with people there during *Pi-*

THE GOLDEN BOWL

Henry James's late, complex novel about a London-based American tycoon and his devoted daughter, who marries a penniless Italian prince. The prince has had a secret affair with her best friend, and then the friend, in turn, marries the father. With Nick Nolte, Uma Thurman, Kate Beckinsale, Anjelica Huston, and Jeremy Northam. 2001. Feature. 35 millimeter; color; 130 minutes.

casso who later switched studios and who were now interested in developing *The Golden Bowl* at Paramount. *The Golden Bowl* script was ultimately developed by Paramount, and it luckily was one of those situations where we could buy the script back, which happens all the time in the movies. Finally it was made independently, you could say, by Miramax and TF-1 in France.

Long: I find it surprising, frankly, that the big studios were as receptive to the idea of adapting James as they seem to have been.

Ivory: It *was* surprising that throughout this whole period of the nineties there was so much interest in turning these very complicated James novels into movies— that there was that kind of eagerness among filmmakers, and that kind of commitment among big Hollywood studios to do Henry James. Twenty years before, when we went to them first with *The Europeans* and then with *The Bostonians,* there had been absolutely none.

Long: But in the end you had trouble with Miramax, which wanted cuts in the film that you weren't willing to make. Could you elaborate on that?

Ivory: Although as usual I had final cut, provided the film didn't exceed 130 minutes, I was expected to listen to their suggestions in good faith. This I did, documenting every step of the way so that later on no one could say I'd failed to do that. Basically Harvey Weinstein, the head of Miramax, wanted a shorter film, shorn of some of the additions we'd made and liked, such as the flash-

backs to a violent Italian family feud centuries earlier, and the sequences showing "American City" and New York harbor that we'd created out of old archive
footage. Also, it appears, Harvey wasn't happy with Uma Thurman. I kept getting strange, unexplained notes to cut this or that bit out of Uma's performance.

Long: During all this hullabaloo with Miramax and Harvey Weinstein, did
he end up actually making you change the film in ways you didn't like or cut
out material that you wanted to keep?

Ivory: Not one frame or bar of music. The only change we made—or cut—
was to remove his name from the credits. [*Long laughs*]

Long: Before that occurred, I take it that he continued to complain about
things both large and small.

Ivory: For instance, the moment when Charlotte yells "No!" to her husband's
suggestion that they leave at once for America. Weinstein kept hitting on that
moment; there almost seemed to be something visceral in this repeated demand of his. I resisted all these suggestions, turned in a film under 130 minutes in length, as was my right, and waited for events to occur, or, as my agent
Rand Holston said, for the other shoe to drop. It soon did.

Long: *The Golden Bowl* didn't achieve the box office success that your other
James adaptations did. How do you account for that?

Ivory: I feel that I can truthfully say: Harvey Weinstein willed it to be so.
When, with all his messing about with it—experimentally shortening, staging a sneak preview in a New Jersey mall, stomping and threatening, affronting
Uma, trying to frighten the French co-financiers with dire predictions of failure (the French stood firm), and so forth—we still refused to go along with
his suggested changes, as was our contractual right. He then said that he would
take the movie straight to television and not give it a theatrical release in the
United States at all. This was the other shoe dropping. But then he surprised
us by offering to sell the film back to Merchant Ivory, and we immediately took
up his "offer." It nearly broke us, but we did it. How much better it would have
been for us if we'd told Harvey what Julie Taymor is supposed to have said to
him when he used the same threat about her *Frida:* "Fine. I don't care. At least
it will be my cut of the movie on TV, not yours." After she'd called his bluff,
he backed down. Months and months now passed while we searched for an
American distributor, some of whom said, "Oh, *The Golden Bowl* is damaged

goods." There was a lot of talk, speculation. This is always bad for a new movie. Eventually we landed ourselves with Lion's Gate, who agreed to buy it. But by the time they could bring it out, prepare properly for its release, the man there who liked and bought it, Mark Furman, had left the company to become a producer. The new head of the company—I don't even want to say his name— had little feeling for it. When it finally opened at the Paris theater in New York in April 2001, its day had passed. We had to look to its overseas release for any satisfaction—which we got, surprisingly, in England and then in Japan, where it appealed very much to audiences and to the press.

Long: I would like to hear more about Harvey Weinstein. What is he like?

Ivory: I can describe how he's been with us; there are hundreds of stories about him and other directors with whom he's fought that have come out in the press. Such stories might make you think directors and distributors automatically become natural enemies. But in a day when film directors are supposed to be *the* supreme artists of the age, ousting novelists, composers, and painters as awe-inspiring figures—how to put this?—Weinstein's relationship to directors—or *with* them—must be full of tension. Here is a large, restless, and ambitious man, unlovely in manner and speech, possessing no artistic talent of any kind. All he has is his money and the power that gives him. It must be irresistible, if you're feeling left out and always an onlooker, and if you are also a bully, to try to humiliate and break artists financially beholden to you. I think these kinds of complicated personal feelings are the reasons behind Harvey's antics, causing him to behave as he does. That he is emotionally about twelve years old doesn't help matters: he is the overlarge and physically powerful bully in the school yard who twists the boys' and girls' arms behind their backs until they scream and kneel down in the dirt at his feet. To be in a room with him for five minutes is to be back in the school yard. You know, he has a wonderful speaking voice—deep and resonant like some great actor's—a voice made for cajoling. Maybe that's why so many of us felt reassured in the beginning and let ourselves be persuaded that everything would turn out fine.

Long: Ruth, who wrote the *Golden Bowl* screenplay, called it "a very difficult script . . . the only other one that has been equally difficult and equally rewarding was *Mr. and Mrs. Bridge* . . . those two were the hardest." What was it that gave her, and you, the most trouble?

Ivory: The fact that there were so few scenes in the novel depicting action; all was hidden, or hinted at, or spoken of at two removes by the Assingham couple. We had to show our characters interacting, working out their destinies. Something of the same sort occurred on *Mr. and Mrs. Bridge.*

Long: Your adaptation of *The Golden Bowl* was interestingly different from an earlier one made for British television in 1972 in six parts—for *Masterpiece Theatre,* in fact. It starred Gayle Hunnicutt, Barry Morse, Daniel Massey, and Cyril Cusack. How would you compare your production of *The Golden Bowl* with the *Masterpiece Theatre* version?

Ivory: Well, you know, mine is a film made with a great deal more money presumably than the TV series had at its disposal. It was probably a more than usually expensive series, yet there was something threadbare about it visually. The BBC version suffered from being done in a studio. Everything was done on a BBC stage, and that's a very hard way of working; the sets looked like the minimalist TV kind of thing. Also, you never saw any of Adam Verver's art; you had no idea that he was a great collector, was passionately involved in buying art, and so on. You never get any sense of that at all. You never had wonderful views of the kinds of houses that such people lived in, or any of the countryside, or of London, let alone Italy. It was all very, very studio centered.

Long: What about the acting and direction?

Ivory: They cast unusually good actors, though I felt a bit shortchanged in that they chose mostly English actors for the parts of the American characters, and I thought that was a pity. There was an exception in Gayle Hunnicutt, who played the part of Charlotte Stant. I didn't think the women were made to look especially beautiful, and I didn't think the prince was that good-looking. But it was a strong cast, and they did a good job, I thought, all of them. I particularly liked Kathleen Byron, who played Fanny Assingham, and Cyril Cusack as the colonel. He was excellent, and he was really, in a sense, a kind of author's voice, a chorus throughout those six programs. Anyway, our film was a great deal different from a TV production.

Long: Their version was much longer than yours. Did that make a difference?

Ivory: The movie was to be approximately two hours long and not six hours. It's there to be seen in one viewing, and you have to take the total impression away with you then. It doesn't have the buildup that you can get in the best kind of television of this type. So we had to do everything we could in the comparatively short time we had of two hours. I don't count the additional ten minutes' grace. That mostly went to titles, as usual.

Long: It seems to me that the movie overwhelms the television production in practically every respect, but there is one dimension of the novel that the television production brings out more fully—the dense, oblique, psychological atmosphere that was peculiar to the late James. Cyril Cusack as Bob Assingham steps out of his role as a minor character in the novel to become a central one as narrator, whose very tangled tale creates suspense and drama. He's splendid in that role. You and Ruth have obviously rejected this approach. The characters' motives and relationships are all perfectly clear, and what you concentrate on is strong plotting, dramatic confrontations, and an extremely powerful visualization of the material. Is this a fair description of your approach?

Ivory: I suppose. Or a fair description of our aim. There would not have been time to savor the colonel's running commentary on the characters' possible motives. We had to provide the action of the story through invented scenes, which we had to think up for ourselves, as well as the dialogue, a lot of which James didn't provide in the novel. The film became less layered as a result; there was little time to savor the characters' predicament or to appreciate the Ververs' eventual handling of it. That's the problem with turning a great and subtle novel into a film; one is forced to take out so much that gives pleasure in the reading.

Long: Adam Verver's having been a millionaire art collector abroad certainly gave you an opportunity to put the world of great art on display. How did you go about putting together Verver's art collection? Where did these paintings and other artworks come from?

Ivory: We worked in English country houses that had a lot of art on the walls, choosing our angles very carefully so that there weren't too many dingy family portraits. If a house was strong in some area of collecting, as, for instance, the Burleigh House sculpture collection, then we made something of it. Verver's paintings were actually at Belvoir Castle in a picture gallery with five

large Poussins in it as well as Gainsboroughs, Flemish pictures, and rare Elizabethan goldwork. We don't accentuate the gold, but it's there in the background, glinting away. Burleigh and Belvoir Castle were meshed together to
become one house, the Fawns of James's novel.

Long: Another artist, John Singer Sargent, enters into the making of *The Golden
Bowl.* There was a moment when it seemed to me that Kate Beckinsale had the
look and the styling of a young woman in one of Sargent's turn-of-the-century
paintings. In fact, in an interview you discussed your having been to two Sargent exhibitions just before making the film, and about Sargent's and certain
other artists' influence on the look of the film. Would you talk about that?

Ivory: Well, that *was* an obvious influence, Sargent; it couldn't help but be.
He painted all those transplanted American millionaires hobnobbing with English aristocrats, who also sat for him. The costume designer, John Bright, was
much influenced by those portraits, and now and then we found ourselves in
rooms that had "Sargent" written all over them, especially when filled up with
costumed actors. Sometimes these portraits affected the actors' playing of their
roles. I think the Sargent painting called *Doctor Pozzi at Home,* showing the handsome Parisian society doctor in a red dressing gown like some Veronese prince,
affected Jeremy Northam's somewhat feline presentation of Prince Amerigo.

Long: The film also suggests that your interest in architecture continues un-
abated. Where in Italy were the scenes and views involving Prince Amerigo's
palace, the Palazzo Ugolino, actually shot ?

Ivory: The Palazzo Ugolino was made up of rooms and views from a castle
at Arsoli belonging to the ancient Massimo family, and at the Palazzo Bor-
ghese in Artena, belonging to the Borgheses, who still live in it and use it as a
country retreat. These small towns are south of Rome.

Long: Someone I know asked me about a visually dramatic moment when
Adam Verver walks alone on the great lawn of his rented castle at dusk. She
wondered if the castle, looking at that moment almost like a cardboard cutout,
was a digitally produced image. I told her that I was sure it wasn't, but I do
wonder if digital technology was used anywhere in the film.

Ivory: About that view of the castle, we were shooting on location at Burleigh
and wouldn't have needed any digitally produced effect. We did, however,

As close to a portrait by John Singer Sargent as the Merchant Ivory team could make it in *The Golden Bowl* (2001). Perhaps only the shiny metal stand for a light flag behind Kate Beckinsale gives it away.

employ digitally *enhanced* shots when we cleaned up the old archive footage to make it more presentable—taking out scratches, blemishes, and so on. In one case we turned a hat of 1918 into one of 1910 on one of the shipboard ladies. This is the use, or is one use, of the digital technology that we had in the film. It wasn't the first time in our career. We changed the actual pictures on the wall in *Surviving Picasso*—and of course the owl attacking and flying off with a cat in that film was digitally produced, the same as in any horror movie.

Long: Did you have any difficulty in getting Nick Nolte to take the part of Adam Verver?

Ivory: None. Previous to his accepting the role, I'd gone to several fiftyish top American actors proposing the part. They all refused. Did they feel they had not reached the point where they could have a twenty-five-year-old daughter *and* a grandson?

Long: I thought Jeremy Northam's Prince Amerigo is the best performance he's given. I also liked Kate Beckinsale as Maggie Verver—and a number of the supporting actors, including Peter Eyre, Madeleine Potter, James Fox, and most particularly Anjelica Huston. But I had a problem with Uma Thurman, who doesn't seem to me to be a Jamesian actress and whose performance lacks subtlety. Stephen Holden, in the *New York Times*, wrote a strongly favorable review of *The Golden Bowl* in general, but he did not care for Uma Thurman. He speaks of her "flailing emotional abandon" and her outbursts that are like a teenager's tantrums.

Ivory: I don't at all agree. I can't imagine another young American actress who more exhibits the qualities Charlotte must have: great beauty, high spirits, intelligence, striking physical presence (she is six feet tall), and a decent way of speaking English. She is a talented actress, but perhaps a somewhat inexperienced one where roles of this kind are concerned: "classical" roles, I suppose you'd say. For much of her performance she seemed exactly right, fulfilling the demands of a very difficult role. Remember that she was meant to be something of a trophy wife: beautiful, clever, sexy. Can the *New York Times* come up with a better choice?

Long: In an interview she gave to the *Guardian* newspaper in London, Ruth was asked about Gore Vidal's essay on *The Golden Bowl*, in which he views Adam

Verver and Maggie as members of the superrich class who bend the prince and Charlotte, more economically helpless characters, to their will. He views them, in fact, as vampires who drain the prince and Charlotte of life. Ruth replied that she felt, on the contrary, that the Ververs "are all goodness, and Henry James painted them as goodness, in a way that the earlier Bostonian knows goodness." Do you believe that the Ververs are all goodness?

Ivory: Well, only in contrast to Charlotte and the prince, who might represent wickedness, I suppose, though not *all* wickedness. The Ververs were principally motivated to shield each other from a terrible hurt, a terrible knowledge. All their actions vis-à-vis the other couple derive from that. It is absurd of Gore Vidal to call them vampires, crushing the life out of people. Perhaps Vidal took more of the professional hedonist's viewpoint, seeing the virtuous Ververs as the evil couple, and the duplicitous prince and Charlotte as sterling characters thwarted by them from fulfilling their sensual destinies.

Long: Well, you know, James scholars have tended to view Adam Verver as an almost sinister controlling figure who brings Charlotte back with him to American City as one of his museum pieces. There is a famous image in *The Golden Bowl* of Verver's imposing an invisible silken cord or halter around Charlotte's neck, to every twitch of which she must respond. The cruelty implicit in this image is pitched in the same key as the ominous fate awaiting her at the end of the novel—of being "buried alive" by Verver in American City, a suffocating world.

Ivory: I don't feel that Adam Verver will be burying Charlotte alive in American City. We went out of our way to suggest the opposite. To me, and I've said this many times before, at the end of the film the more interesting couple, the couple whose story you want to follow, is the Ververs. We deliberately tilted away from the more conventional and predictable story of the younger couple. (What would that have been, anyway?) Instead, in the concluding scene, you see the Ververs arrive in New York, being treated as celebrities, almost as world figures. In the open car in which they drive away from the pier, they laugh together at some joke. They are obviously enjoying themselves. New York, after the inconvenience of the First World War, will soon be getting ready to enjoy the 1920s. American City can be borne by Charlotte on her presum-

The Ververs (Nick Nolte and Uma Thurman) ride off into their American future at the end of *The Golden Bowl* (2001).

ably infrequent visits. The two will travel the world, like royalty. Charlotte will become the great figure predicted by the prince. And when Verver dies, she will be rich beyond belief. She will marry again, perhaps find another agreeable young Latin man to have fun with. They will dance the Charleston and go to speakeasies and live in some palace in Florida.

Long: Charlotte's future, as you speculate about it, seems garish, and I don't know what it would have to do with the morally serious novel James wrote. You are faithful to the plot of *The Golden Bowl* and to the world of the Ververs; the ending, however, becomes something of your own. But you've made adaptations in this way before.

Ivory: A film somehow takes its own course, assumes its own form, and delivers its own message.

Long: The Golden Bowl is such an extremely difficult novel that I'm surprised you chose to adapt it as a film. Was a reason for your interest in doing it that it seemed almost to defy translation to the screen, that it would be the ultimate challenge for you?

Ivory: The ultimate challenge was really more Ruth's, I think. Ultimate, too, in that this novel represented the pinnacle of James's art and was Ruth's favorite of all his novels. I didn't have those feelings to frighten me—just another example, I suppose, of the rather mindless optimism I have that carries me along.

Long: You usually have at least one very striking set piece in your pictures, but in *The Golden Bowl* you have many of them. Among them is the modern dance entertainment at a great London house that is like a Ballets Russes performance of an *Arabian Nights* tale. Who, by the way, devised this bravura interlude?

Ivory: Karole Armitage, our choreographer, and I thought it up in about five minutes. Like the play in *Hamlet*, the ballet's action was to mirror the story of the Ververs, the prince, Charlotte, and the principino, but in a broad way. You had a harem intrigue, ending in murder and suicide—like the Renaissance flashback at the beginning of the film.

Long: What special visual quality did you have Tony Pierce-Roberts give to the film?

Ivory: We shot with anamorphic lenses this time. One of the reasons for that decision was that with those lenses it is possible to slightly blur the background, make it softer in focus than the foreground. I felt that our sets, being so overwhelmingly ornate, might be a distraction and take away from the foreground action. And I prefer to print directly from the original negative if I can, which is possible when you shoot with anamorphic lenses. We could never do that during *Howards End* and *The Remains of the Day* for our 70-millimeter show prints because of the several intervening steps in that process. Apart from this change, Tony's approach followed his normal procedure.

Long: While the English and European parts of the film are in color, the scenes set in America are in black and white, or black and a kind of rust or sepia color. How did you get that effect for the American part that looks as if you were photographing a negative?

Ivory: Your question is based maybe on a slight misapprehension, but I know what you are referring to: you thought you saw a negative image of a bridge with trams and people (a scene actually shot in Pittsburgh around 1900). In fact the image was "solarized" digitally to obtain a more abstract effect, suitable for Charlotte's dream of hell. Charlotte's vision of America is meant to suggest a nightmare of rude and violent ugliness, heightened at the point in the story when she fears not only having to go there but also, and even more important, of having to part with her lover, the prince. So the sulfurous colors and clanging sounds—the impression of being in a steel mill or coal mine (where we briefly were, in fact)—seemed appropriate to her imaginings. But the sea voyage and arrival in New York harbor was a more straightforward sequence, and if anything—because of the swelling, almost melodic music—was meant to convey a different effect: one of promise. I think it mostly worked out in this way for the audience. They felt exhilarated by the early New York images—even thrilled, as I was. So I think you can understand my outrage when Harvey Weinstein wanted to do away with all of this, as well as Charlotte's vision of hell.

Long: A final question. *The Golden Bowl* is the last novel completed by James. Is your screen version perhaps also your hail and farewell to him?

Ivory: Yes, I feel I've gone as far as *I* can with James. Other directors may very well take him much farther; there are a lot of novels, or even the same ones we took up. For me to go on might be a little dangerous. What if I fell back on what I knew to be successful ways of presenting James, or got in some kind of rut—that sort of thing? Or failed to take up the challenges James presents to all directors?

FRANCE

Robert Emmet Long: Most people who know and enjoy your films may not realize how many of them have been made in France. In fact, there are as many as those you've shot in England. It can't be all that easy to work in France if you're not French.

James Ivory: Yes and no. The failure to have an exact understanding of the language is a drawback for me sometimes; my French ought by now to be more fluent, seeing that I've been going to France for half a century. I have a good ear, but I'm lazy; a pretty good accent, but a bad memory. On the other hand, it's a real pleasure to work with a French crew—perhaps the greatest. In a very democratic way—not usual in England or the United States—they become one's artistic collaborators, every last man and woman, no matter how small their role. I found this to be true in 1980 when we made our first film in Paris—*Quartet*—and it's still true today.

Long: You must have found some very good assistants.

Ivory: Some tremendous ones, articulate and bilingual. They've saved me from making some terrible mistakes. So has Humbert Balsan—Ismail calls him the "Maharaja of Paris"—who started out with us on *Quartet* and has become one of the biggest French producers. He's made all the right doors swing open for more than twenty years. Where would we have been without him, I wonder?

Long: Speaking of *Quartet*, I understand that Ruth wrote three different versions of its ending, is that correct?

Ivory: There was an earlier version, and, yes, she did rewrite it during shooting. The new ending had Marya being not only abandoned by her husband but also taken over by a friend of his from prison named Schlamovitz.

Long: According to what I've read, Ruth's first ending had Stefan going off with another woman. Then she decided against it because she thought the emphasis at the end should fall not on Stefan but on Marya. In a second, also discarded, version Marya commits suicide. Is that right?

Ivory: Yes, that's what we were planning to do, but later we felt that was too grim. We actually shot the scene of her body being pulled out of the Seine. We did use those shots for a sort of vision that Marya has of herself when she's alone in the hotel room waiting for Heidler and feeling depressed.

Long: The third version and the one that was used had Stefan going off with another woman while Marya takes up with another man, a pattern that carries out the idea of the "quartet." I notice that in the novel Stefan's prison friend Schlamovitz is referred to only by name, but that in the movie he appears at the end as a character.

Ivory: Yes, that's right. He was played by Daniel Mesguich, the French actor and theater director.

Long: What sort of life would you foresee for Marya and Schlamovitz?

Ivory: The same sort of life that you saw with Schlamovitz and the other woman he was living with and mistreating, the woman whose arm he was twisting. We had just seen that. That woman doesn't want to take any more, and she leaves him. And I would think that the very same thing will happen to Marya in a day or two. [*Long laughs*] No wonder people didn't like the movie. It's such a grim prognosis.

Long: The film is set in Paris in the 1920s. You've said that when you were in Paris in 1950, people were still there who could remember what it was like in the twenties.

Ivory: There were, of course.

QUARTET

Life in bohemian Paris, 1927, as seen by Jean Rhys. A corrupt English couple befriends a beautiful young woman whose husband is thrown into prison for dealing in stolen antiquities. With Isabelle Adjani, Alan Bates, Maggie Smith, and Anthony Higgins. 1981. Feature. 35 millimeter; color; 101 minutes.

Long: Wasn't there a personal pleasure for you in re-creating that legendary Parisian world of the 1920s?

Ivory: Naturally there was. I wouldn't have taken it up as a project unless I felt I would have had that kind of pleasure.

Long: A number of your films have shown a consciousness of art, and this is present, too, in *Quartet.* Paris, after all, is where art is being produced, where everyone seems to have an association of some kind with it. Heidler and his wife are both associated with the arts.

Ivory: Mrs. Heidler is a lady painter, with an elaborate studio where she does portraits influenced by Marie Laurencin.

Long: And Heidler himself is . . .

Ivory: He's a sort of dealer, or middleman, between artists and buyers.

Long: They are both afflicted with a sense of inner emptiness. Marya Zelli isn't an exceptional or isolated case of lonely suffering but a barometer of the desperate mood of Montparnasse.

Ivory: It was shown as being desperate by Jean Rhys; it was a projection of her unhappiness. The whole thing was also shown as being a sort of hedonistic world of fun that Marya, once she lost Stefan, felt cut off from. All she wanted was to be happy, and she couldn't be any more. She had been happy up till then. She and her husband had been poor, but it was the two of them together in an uncertain world where it was possible to have fun and be in love.

Long: Unlike Marya, the Heidlers seem born to this world, and they cast their shadow over everything, don't they? They "play the game" and would have everyone think that they have a fulfilling marriage, but inwardly they are miserable. The discrepancy between the surface glamour of that stylish Parisian world and a gnawing inner malaise runs throughout the film. There is a nice sequence when a man at a sidewalk café approaches Marya as if he were a legitimate artist in need of a model, but he turns out to be a pornographer. Didn't you write that scene, by the way?

Ivory: Yes, I wrote that.

Long: The "nun" who greets Marya at the door of the photographer's studio seems to be wearing a conventional nun's habit, but then we suddenly see from the rear that she is naked within the backless garment. Inside the studio several

On the set of *Quartet* (1981), as Ivory indicates a camera position for his cameraman, Pierre Lhomme (left).

naked models, two women and a man who have been striking a pose for a sado-masochistic scene, engage in a sordid dispute over money with the photographer.

Ivory: I wrote that scene, but it was suggested to me by a scene in a book by John Glassco called *Memoirs of Montparnasse.* The nun business was either from a porno movie or a pornographic photograph I saw somewhere.

Long: Was this the first time there had been nudity and sexual scenes in your films?

Ivory: Pretty much. There was a lot of, if not total, nudity in *Savages* as well as sexual scenes. Remember Ultra Violet and Asha Puthli in the back of the Pierce-Arrow? And in *The Wild Party* there was a glimpse through a suddenly opened door of a heap of nude bodies writhing about on a bed. *Quartet,* in a way, was about sex, and Isabelle Adjani was fearless in undressing. Oddly, the pornographic couples, or threesome, were not. They were very prim. We couldn't find a French actor who would strip, and the actresses, who had been

recruited from French X-rated movies, now seemed equally reluctant to be photographed in the nude. Finally we found a young Englishman who was willing to bare all; the English don't have this kind of inhibition. But the girls insisted on wearing bits and pieces of material in strategic places, little aprons
and so on. This was explained to me as being necessary because we were a *foreign* production, with English movie stars. It was a respectable film that lots
of people would go to see, so the nudity of the pornographic actors might cause
them embarrassment.

Long: About Alan Bates, as Heidler, hadn't he played previous roles as a rot-
ter and a cad?

Ivory: Oh, yes, he had.

Long: Making him a natural for the role.

Ivory: Well, he wasn't a natural for it because he had played these kinds of
roles, but because he was one of the greatest English actors of that time, someone who took up every sort of part. In 1980 he was at the end of his young
leading man days and had just turned fifty.

Long: Why did you particularly want Maggie Smith as Lois Heidler?

Ivory: I'll tell you one thing: *nobody* wanted to play that part. It went around
to many actresses, both English and American, and they all turned it down.
They said things like "Oh, it's so sick," "I wouldn't want to play a part like
that," "It's creepy," and this kind of thing . . . a judgmental, moralistic thing.
I remember that Julie Christie didn't want to do it; she made it sound unhealthy
somehow. No doubt she was right. But it was still a very good part, which Maggie saw at once.

Long: Lois is a kind of slave to Heidler. She knows the worst about him, but
she can't leave him, and then Marya becomes another victim.

Ivory: Both women love him and are tied to him. Both of the women are attracted to this man, Marya partly because he is protecting her. He gives her a
place to live while her husband is in jail. So that's on a basic level. She has no
money, she has no job. She really has to go to Heidler. That's not the case with
Lois. Lois can leave any time she wants, except that, you know, she is in one
of those marriages that one sees sometimes . . .

Long: Is she masochistic?

Makeup artist Kenneth Lintott touches up Maggie Smith for the night-club sequence in *Quartet* (1981).

Ivory: To some extent she is, sure. But her husband depends on her, needs her. She gets him through these things, these destructive love affairs. She is a good companion, and they probably together have the best jokes, share all kinds of ideas; they are two people linked together for better or worse. There are plenty of marriages like that.

Long: Lois blames Heidler, at least partly, for the suicide of another girl, a waif he brought in to live with them. How do you explain his effect on these girls who are so wretched and despondent?

Ivory: Lois says that the other girl came for the same reason as Marya. She had no place to go. She was a poor, unfortunate girl who was down on her luck, and he gave her a place to stay and was providing her with sustenance, a roof over her head, and taking sexual favors from her. She couldn't bear it and killed herself.

Long: Heidler needs these women, but he treats them all very badly.

Ivory: He treats them badly if badly means selfishly and self-indulgently. That's true, he does. But I don't think he's a thoroughly bad man . . . he's just weak.

Long: Isabelle Adjani is an astonishingly beautiful girl. Wasn't she at the beginning of her career when you cast her in the leading role?

Ivory: She was well into her career by then. She had done a number of things that had brought her a lot of attention.

Long: Some reviewers said that she seemed too strong a person to be playing such a helpless waif. And with her stunning looks, they thought, she ought to have had many men ready to help her.

Ivory: You know, the sort of person who really looks like a helpless waif is sometimes not very interesting. And perhaps not very beautiful either. You need a bit of fire.

Long: Adjani won the best actress award at the Cannes Film Festival for her part in *Quartet,* so she obviously made an impact. But *Quartet* wasn't a popular film. What did feminists feel about it, do you know?

Ivory: I don't know. They probably didn't like it. They probably wouldn't like to see women put in the position Heidler put them in.

Long: I'm not sure of that; it would be something to protest against. Certainly they liked Jean Rhys. Rhys was taken up by the feminists in a big way at that time and had quite a following. She showed women being taken advantage of and exploited by men, but her heroines always saw through these men, were somehow superior to them.

Ivory: As a storyteller she's very compelling, very sharp.

Long: I don't know if *Quartet* could in any sense be called a "study," but it *is* an observation of this young girl's being adrift in Paris that is so scrupulous as to make one feel almost like a voyeur.

Ivory: I never thought of it in those terms at all. *Quartet* is a somewhat squalid retelling of one of Jean Rhys's many misadventures with a man. Not a study to *her,* I think.

Long: *Quartet* is an autobiographical novel in which Jean Rhys and Marya are intertwined. Rhys, as you say, had great sharpness as a writer, but she also felt sorry for herself. I think that she uses Marya as a way of pitying herself . . . the whole world is against her. As a "crushed petal type," Marya is hard to identify oneself with. Or do I sound like a heartless monster?

Ivory: Marya is self-destructive, passive, masochistic in her obsessions,

The obnoxious H. J. Heidler (Alan Bates) with the apprehensive Marya Zelli (Isabelle Adjani), heroine of the Jean Rhys novel on which the film *Quartet* (1981) is based.

but that does not foreclose compassion on the part of the viewer, or should not. She is a beautiful, charming girl who becomes a victim and is broken to bits. Some kind of imaginative pity might be expected from even the most hard-hearted.

Long: At the beginning of the film Stefan stands by an open window, through which come the noises, some of them quarrelsome, from a narrow street below. We seem to be hearing the voices of men picking up women. Are they prostitutes? Is this a kind of prostitute lane?

Ivory: Yes.

Long: The question is relevant because Marya is later abandoned in the street at night—it may even be the same street—as Stefan drives off with another woman.

Ivory: Not on that same street. She is abandoned in the apartment house

on the respectable rue du Faubourg Saint Antoine that Stefan had been allowed
to stay in briefly after he got out of prison. But from then on her life will be
only one step away from actual prostitution—unless she throws herself in the
Seine as in our first screenplay.

Long: I am sure it would be folly to dispute details with the man who made
the film, but I do recall that although she is abandoned by Stefan in that apartment building, she does pursue him into the street. She is in the street at night
alone and abandoned at the end. Then in the uncertain lamplight the dark
figure of a man approaches who turns out to be Schlamovitz, who leads her
up the steps of the building. She could as well be a prostitute in his picking
her up in this street. Doesn't the Parisian world as depicted in the film constitute a whole culture of the abuse of women and their harsh treatment by
men?

Ivory: It can be seen as that, I suppose; however, people do forget that in
those days women couldn't really get jobs in a man's world. There were no legitimate moneymaking careers for young women like Marya. You could maybe
go on the stage, but more likely you ended up as a lady's paid companion or
fighting thousands of others for a position as a shop girl.

Long: Quartet seems to have had special importance for you. You've said that
"the experience of making it marked us forever and no doubt led to our being
in Paris so much later on." Could you elaborate on that?

Ivory: Making *Quartet* turned out to be one of our most enjoyable shooting
experiences. I had visited Paris and the rest of France all my adult life, but now
I was to live there and be in close contact with French people of all different
kinds. Especially my crew members, who as film technicians seemed to be a
breed apart from their colleagues in America. They were passionately involved
with their work . . . their jobs, whatever those were. They believed we had all
come together to make a work of film art, I guess I'd say. So the atmosphere
on the set was quite special, quite serious. After we'd finished, Ismail and I
wanted to get back there as soon as we could, but that didn't happen until *Mr.
and Mrs. Bridge* in 1989—almost ten years later, and then we waited another
four years before we could go back and make *Jefferson in Paris.*

Long: How do you feel about *Quartet* now?

Ivory: I've always liked it. I think it was the first film in which I really hit my stride—where there was a general harmony of theme, and of structure, as well as of photography and acting. I was very lucky with those four actors who made up the quartet, Anthony Higgins being the last. He played Marya's Polish husband, Stefan. None of the four were weak or failed to make the hoped-for impression. I think if one had to divide up my work into periods, *Quartet* might be the first in phase 2. Up to that film I took a more tentative and less disciplined approach, sometimes too hit-or-miss.

Long: And where would your phase 3 begin? Or is there one?

Ivory: Oh, yes. With *Jefferson in Paris,* I think, and going on to the present. Depending on who you're talking to, the phase 3 films might be films of experimentation, maybe in a way more personal—or they could be called the fumblings of creeping old age. [*Long laughs*] Let's see.

Long: Of the three of you, who was the real promoter of *Jefferson in Paris?*

Ivory: I was.

Long: What attracted you to it?

Ivory: I read an interesting book by Olivier Bernier about life in eighteenth-century cities: life in Naples, in Paris, and in Philadelphia. That's what gave me the idea at first to make a film about Thomas Jefferson in Paris. There was quite a lot about Jefferson's life in Paris in that book, which for some reason I'd never thought very much about, and it intrigued me.

Long: Didn't some of your own interests enter into it, too?

Ivory: Various things. As you know, I've always had this affection for the South. I think of myself as being half southern (on my mother's side), and I've always

JEFFERSON IN PARIS

Thomas Jefferson's years in Paris from 1784 to 1789 as American ambassador, accompanied by his daughters and slaves, on the eve of the French Revolution. With Nick Nolte, Greta Scacchi, Thandie Newton, and Gwyneth Paltrow. 1995. Feature. 35 millimeter; color; 139 minutes.

wanted to do something on a southern theme. In some strange way these elements—Jefferson and life in the South, the eighteenth-century world, and my long-term interest in France and the French all came together.

Long: Your interest in the South goes back to your childhood?

Ivory: To seeing *Gone with the Wind* and, as an adolescent, reading various novels set in the old South. We also made family trips to New Orleans to visit relatives and to eastern Texas to see my grandmother De Loney, who had been born in 1865 and grew up on a haunted plantation.

Long: Tell me about some of your other childhood interests.

Ivory: Another childhood obsession would be dynastic Egypt. I used to amaze my classmates (maybe "enrage" is a better word) by reciting the names of the Pharaohs of the Eighteenth and Nineteenth Dynasties. I didn't always get to the end of my recitation. By the time I'd reached Horemheb or so I was being beaten up.

Long: Who was Horemheb?

Ivory: The first Pharaoh of the Nineteenth Dynasty. He had been a general who seized power, like Pervez Musharraf. Anyway, it wasn't such a feat as all that. There were something like twelve Pharaohs, all named Ramses, one after the other.

Long: Were you often beaten up?

Ivory: I was a good target for teenage terrorists: lanky and skinny, with a reputation for being a snob and a know-it-all. After one bad episode my father put me in a gym program to build me up. To learn to run faster might have been more to the point. So . . . ancient Egypt, the South, France . . . a poor fourth was the "Wild West," where I lived. So really, making *Jefferson in Paris* was a continuation of childhood play. These childish interests were woven together in an adult way. And that's really how *Jefferson in Paris* came about. It really was play . . . as a grown-up.

Long: Don't all films, and novels too, contain an element of child's play?

Ivory: I suppose. I mean, they ought to, but you know it's difficult with films, because they cost so much money. You have to involve so many people, convince so many people.

Long: You've said that developing *Jefferson in Paris* proved to be a long, halting process, with a first script that was begun but never completed.

Ivory: First there was research, and then a script was begun in France by a young American writer named Anthony Chase. He was a published writer off and on, and he wrote a little bit for the *New Yorker.* He had grown up partly in France and loved being there doing research, and was interested in Jefferson

The corps of Swiss Guards accompanies the French royal family on its way to Mass, marching through the Hall of Mirrors at Versailles, in *Jefferson in Paris* (1995).

and in the whole Sally Hemings side of things, as I was. After the research he started on the script, on which I also sporadically worked. But that took a long, long time, and he never really got very far with it, which was probably more my fault than his, as I was busy doing my other films. Also, unrealistically, I suppose I thought of his work as a labor of love and not a professional assignment. Well, a labor of love isn't going to pay a young man's bills.

Long: At some point you must have had your first break, which in time led to the finished Jefferson film.

Ivory: It was when we began our arrangement with TriStar. We had a three-picture deal with them, part of which was that we would develop the *Jefferson in Paris* idea. Ruth by then was interested in it and liked the whole idea of writing a script about Jefferson. A new script was now undertaken by her. That took a couple of years. I think she was still working on it while we were doing *Mr. and Mrs. Bridge*, but I remember it was very close to being finished at that time.

Long: So how did things go with TriStar?

Ivory: We made *Slaves of New York* with TriStar . . . but it didn't work out. It was not a successful film, and as often happens with these kinds of multipicture deals, they weren't so eager to make another movie with us after *Slaves* failed, and they certainly didn't want to do *Jefferson in Paris*. They didn't see it as being commercial in any way. Plus the fact that TriStar was being turned upside down; all the people who liked us were leaving, and Gary Hindler, who had been our main champion at TriStar and was our partner in all of this, got sick and died. We tried to get *Jefferson* financed and offered it to all kinds of people, kept putting it forward. . . . And then a wonderful thing happened.

Long: What was that?

Ivory: Jeffrey Katzenberg went to see *Howards End*. We would never allow *Howards End* to be shown privately to studio executives. They were always asking if they could have a print, but we decided, along with Sony, that anyone who wanted to see it had to go buy a ticket, stand in line, and see it in a proper theater with an audience. That's exactly what Jeffrey Katzenberg did. He went out to Santa Monica where the film was playing, saw it there, and was absolutely bowled over by it. He called us in London the next day and said, "You know, guys, this is a wonderful movie. I was so impressed. I wonder if we maybe could do something together. Do you have something you want to do but haven't been able to get financed? Do you have any script that you can show us?" We said, "Well, as a matter of fact, we *do*. We have this script about Jefferson." And he said he would be interested in seeing it.

Long: I wonder why a script about Jefferson would be of such interest to him . . .

Ivory: What I didn't know at the time was that he and Peter Weir had also been planning a Jefferson film a couple of years before and had even made a trip together to Monticello. Anyway, we sent him the script, and he liked it and said, "Let's make it." He wanted to set up a three-picture deal like TriStar's, with the Jefferson film additional to the deal. In effect there would be four films involved. They were also to have first refusal for anything else we did. We entered into an arrangement with them for *Jefferson in Paris* while we were preparing *Remains of the Day.*

Long: Did Ruth's script undergo any changes . . . any conceptual changes in the course of your making the film?

Ivory: The script we shot is the one she wrote. The only changes occurred when we got to France and began to look into things and found opportunities for developing certain scenes in various kinds of ways and doing more with the French scenes—the public scenes, you might say, as opposed to the domestic ones between Jefferson and his daughters and the Hemingses, brother and sister.

Long: Until recent DNA evidence became available, there was no proof that Jefferson had a sexual relationship with Sally Hemings and fathered her children . . .

Ivory: No proof, but the circumstantial evidence is overwhelming.

Long: The historian Dumas Malone, who spent his life studying Jefferson and wrote an authoritative five-volume biography of him, said that he didn't know whether or not Jefferson had a sexual relationship with Sally Hemings, but that if he *did,* it didn't conform to the Jefferson he knew. Many people said that it didn't seem likely at all, so how did you know . . .

Ivory: As I say, there is all the circumstantial evidence: here was a recently widowed man in his early forties, with normal sexual appetites, who literally owns a beautiful young girl, who also happens to be his dead wife's half sister. Then there is the fact, evident from his journals in which he wrote everything down, that every time he went back to Monticello during his public life, nine months later Sally delivered a child. And then there is the clincher: the fact that at the end of his life, when he was bankrupt and all his slaves were destined to be sold, he arranged, uniquely, to give Sally's children their freedom. That must be one of the most basic kinds of evidence of his affection and concern toward her. He had already allowed their grown son Beverley and daughter Harriet to leave Monticello and disappear—or "pass"—into white society. That daughter's subsequent life, of which nothing at all is known, became the subject of a melodramatic English novel in the 1830s. Beyond this, all you have to do is to read memoirs of plantation life to know how common liaisons such as Jefferson's with Sally Hemings were. And all you have to do is to go down the street in New York or anywhere and see all our light-skinned Afro-American neighbors, and you know there's been an awful lot of . . .

Long: Racial intermixing . . .

Ivory: If you want to call it that. Read any memoir, read Mary Chestnut, or read Fanny Kemble about life on a Georgia plantation. Racial mixing was everywhere. Ours was a two-hundred-year-old story, a story that began in Jefferson's own day when he was running for president, and a disgruntled journalist dredged up material in the Monticello neighborhood and published stuff about Jefferson's "dusky Sally" and his harem of dark-skinned children and so on. Other people at the time also wrote about it, and much later there was the publication of Madison Hemings's reminiscence in an Ohio newspaper in the 1870s. He was Sally's eldest surviving son, and he had a great deal to say, though his account of Sally's life at Monticello of course was dismissed by most twentieth-century scholars.

Long: There was certainly miscegenation in the South, but many people assumed that this couldn't touch Jefferson.

Ivory: Why not? To those of us who were persuaded it had, people like Dumas Malone and all the rest of the modern scholars and biographers . . . to the extent to which they said that it would have been impossible for Jefferson to have had a slave mistress because he was too *fine* a person, had too *fine* a sensibility to have done something like that . . . to that extent these people are racists. What they are expressing is their own antipathy to the idea of having a sexual relationship with a black woman, and to black people generally.

Long: But didn't Jefferson also write that the races should be kept separate?

Ivory: He wrote a lot of things, and he wrote different things at different times. He had a calculus whereby after so many generations of racial mixing a person was no longer black. He wrote all this out, you know, one-half, one-fourth, one-eighth, and so on. There were people on his plantation who were one-eighth black and seven-eighths white, who were born and remained slaves, and this included his own children by Sally, who were only an eighth black. The law in Virginia was: if your mother was a slave, you were too.

Long: How did black Americans react to *Jefferson in Paris?* I imagine they liked

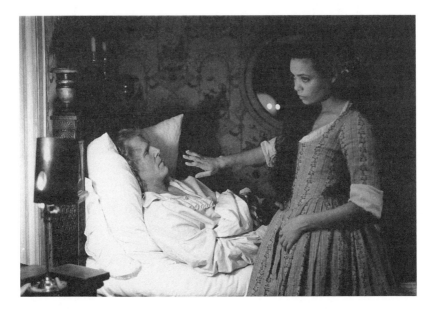

Thomas Jefferson (Nick Nolte) and Sally Hemings (Thandie Newton) during a scene from *Jefferson in Paris* (1995).

it as an affirmation of some long-held, or at least orally transmitted, romantic legend about Jefferson and his slave girl Sally.

Ivory: You would think so, yes. But in fact they mostly disliked the film. And those in a position to publicly write about it, like the *New York Times* writer Brent Staples and Annette Gordon-Reed, who wrote an excellent book about the affair, were dismissive. No black friend of mine ever voluntarily praised the film—at least to me. I had to ask, and the praise was grudging. Sally Hemings, as imagined by Ruth Jhabvala and then played by Thandie Newton, seemed to be the reason. She wasn't "refined" enough; she was too much an untamed, wild thing. As far as I was concerned, Thandie Newton's Sally was an enchanting creature.

Long: I agree. She enlivened the whole film.

Ivory: She's one of my all-time favorite Merchant Ivory heroines. But American blacks (and even some whites) didn't like the way Sally, or her brother

James, or her son Madison, shown as an old man in the film, spoke. They weren't educated enough and used bad grammar, and therefore seemed to embody some racial stereotype—probably because of this. House servants didn't speak like our Sally and James; only field hands did, and so on. And especially the house servants of President Thomas Jefferson could not have spoken like that. We should have shown Sally speaking French, I guess, and doing embroidery and playing the harpsichord. Above all, never saying "Yes, Massa," and "No, Massa."

Long: Did Ruth do a lot of research on how slaves might have spoken?

Ivory: Of course! A lot of their language came out of the WPA oral histories of surviving American ex-slaves made in the 1930s. Our dialogue was as authentic as we could make it; our ideas about it came from all sorts of people, from all over the South: house-servants, field hands, freedmen who were better educated, city dwellers. Not only was there an existing written record transcription of the ex-slaves' memories, but also some actual audiotapes, which we also listened to. A year ago a picture book came out about Sally's descendants through her somewhat shadowy son named Thomas Woodson, as well as Eston Hemings. But there was no mention at all of our *Jefferson in Paris* film, though there was approving coverage in this picture book, if I remember rightly, of the rubbishy American TV miniseries *Sally Hemings: An American Scandal.* Their Sally was better spoken, a perfect little lady, but played by an actress far, far inferior to Thandie Newton, much less charismatic, with much less presence.

Long: Do you have any personal feelings about Jefferson, as a hypocrite or . . .

Ivory: He was a Virginian of his generation, a planter in the South with a slave workforce. He had to make a living and to maintain his plantations. As a young man he was in fact very much against slavery. He said that slavery was an abhorrent thing and should be abolished. He had tried to get that belief into the Declaration of Independence but was overruled. He knew that slavery made a mockery of the words he wrote: " . . . that all men are created equal."

Long: You're speaking of Jefferson as a young man.

Ivory: As he got older, he developed a strong interest in architecture; he was always transforming things at Monticello and was more and more dependent on the slaves working for him. He lived a kind of simple but luxurious life there, and his ideas against slavery weren't expressed as often. By the end he wasn't

expressing them at all. You may call this hypocritical, but what was he supposed to do? The end of his life was tragic: debt-ridden and knowing full well
that slavery was both morally offensive and economically ruinous in the long
run. He foresaw the consequences of slavery to our country, saw it as a gather-
ing cloud that would shadow us down the generations, to paraphrase. Again,
to paraphrase, he said that if God was just, then he—Jefferson—trembled for
his country. By this he meant a country of slaveholders.

Long: Washington freed all of his slaves.

Ivory: But Washington also died a millionaire. Jefferson died practically in-
digent, and his slaves, the house, and all the contents of the house had to be
sold because he left no money. It was all very well for Washington, who was
supposed to have had a million dollars in the bank—and think what a million
dollars would have been worth in 1799!—to free his slaves. Jefferson was a
hundred thousand dollars in debt, and don't forget, horrible as that was, slaves
represented capital. They were to be sold to pay off his creditors.

Long: But what about . . .

Ivory: I think we can't be too judgmental about an old man in his seventies
and eighties, who was broke. There he was on his uneconomical and debt-
ridden plantation. His daughter had twelve children and a mad husband, whom
they locked up in one of those pretty pavilions at Monticello, and he had to
look after all of them, and look after all those unproductive slaves whom he
had to support from birth to death. I'm sure in his heart he had a continual
realization of the bad thing slavery was. His fate would have put it into
sharper focus for him, if anything.

Long: You must have really been wrapped up in the man when you made the
film. What was there about Nick Nolte that made you decide to cast him as
Jefferson? Of course Nolte is tall and lean like Jefferson, and facially there may
be a certain likeness, but what was there beyond that?

Ivory: Well, these were all reasons. There were other actors who were physically possible probably. One of them was Christopher Reeve. I thought Chris
Reeve would also have made a good Jefferson, and in a way he was almost put
on this earth to play the part. But over the years our ideas changed. I don't know
at what point I flailed around with the idea of casting Jeremy Irons in the part.

I think we actually gave him the script before we went to Nick Nolte. I remember I was supposed to meet him in London and ride back with him in a car from his set, while talking with him about the script and about his playing Jefferson. But we never took that ride together, which is probably just as well.

Long: Was there anyone else you ever had in mind?

Ivory: Yes, I went to see a young actor in England named Iain Glen. He looked exactly like Jefferson and was a wonderful actor. He appeared with Nicole Kidman in *The Blue Room* on Broadway in 1998. But he was too young. As I say, he even looked like Jefferson, having the same kind of handsome, bony face and red hair, and was a fabulous actor to boot. But he was only thirty-one, while Jefferson had to be about forty.

Long: Couldn't he have been made up to look a little older?

Ivory: He was too young for that, and also if you're doing a film for a studio, they want a star. You can't make a film like that without a star. And Nolte has another side to him which isn't that apparent from the films he's made. He's somewhat scholarly, well-spoken, even reserved. When we met, it wasn't that hard for me to imagine him as Jefferson.

Long: The film opens with Jefferson writing a letter with an eighteenth-century copying device that is meant to introduce, according to several articles I have read, the idea of Jefferson's dual nature, his contradictions. Is that so?

Ivory: That's a question that guys like you like to ask. [*Long smiles*] You'll find that I'm always innocent of such calculation.

Long: It's surprising that someone who made the film, which is, after all, about Jefferson's inner conflicts and dualities (like head and heart), would fault anyone's questioning the implications of Jefferson's dual method of writing at the opening. The image of the copier has very clear psychological resonance, and critics picked up on it.

Ivory: Writers are very good at seeing what might be, what might have been, in the mind of the director. For me it was simply a wonderful chance in and of itself to show his copying contraption that he had at that time—which, in fact, he *didn't* have at that time. We fudged a bit. Jefferson bought a pantograph, the copying machine we see in the film and which is still at Monticello, somewhat later, in 1806.

The American envoy to France (Nick Nolte), with his copying machine, called a pantograph, in *Jefferson in Paris* (1995).

Long: How did he make copies before that?

Ivory: At the time he was in Paris he had to manage with a letter press, and it was almost a kind of . . . you did that [*makes a cranking motion with his hands*]. The "head and heart" letter is one of those. He didn't sit down to do *this* with one pen while another pen did *that*. He put it in a kind of press, and then they do *that* to it [*twisting motion with two hands*] and a mirror image will come out. The original was sent off to Maria Cosway; the copy today is in the Library of Congress. We just put the pantograph in because I loved it, and I never thought at all about his dual nature. Really, he had something like a quadruple nature.

Long: The riveting image at the opening reminds me a little of *The Bostonians,* which begins with a man playing the organ at the music hall with the camera focused on his feet as they pump away at the pedals frantically. I found myself asking, "What does this mean? What's going on here?"

Ivory: It doesn't mean anything, except what it is. . . . Actually, I'll tell you how that sequence in *The Bostonians* happened. There is a huge organ in the music hall in Troy, New York, where we were shooting, and I noticed how these organs actually worked with the organist's feet dancing all over the foot pedals. We didn't have time then to include that in our footage; we had to do that later in England. But I loved to look at it, you know, with the hands pulling out the stops and the feet doing this frantic dance. I'd never seen anything like that. All film directors are the same, you know . . . it's playing, isn't it?

Long: It's very involving. For some reason it seems to carry you away with the wonderment of what you are seeing. But we were talking about *Jefferson in Paris.* It struck me that in the film, Jefferson is made to seem as if he were the sole American emissary in France. But wasn't Franklin there also, or did he arrive earlier? And what about John Adams, who was also abroad at that time?

Ivory: They weren't there. Who said they were? John Adams was in London. They had been in Paris but not at the time covered in the film. Jefferson went to France in 1784. The Peace of Paris had been signed; Adams went off to become the first American ambassador to England, and Benjamin Franklin went home, having been replaced by Jefferson. While Adams was in London, Jefferson went to see him and to tour English gardens. Later on, when his youngest daughter came with Sally, Jefferson would not go to London to pick them up. He sent the French butler for her. It has been written that Abigail Adams was so sharp-eyed that she would have caught on at once if Jefferson had gone for his daughter, who was accompanied by this beautiful, nubile Sally, of what Jefferson was up to, or was perhaps capable of . . .

Long: There are other historical figures in the film from that period, however. There's Dr. Guillotin, Mesmer, Lafayette . . .

Ivory: Richard Cosway, the painter . . .

Long: Simon Callow pulls out all the stops in playing Cosway as a fop. Could Cosway really have been such a foolish figure?

Ivory: He appeared so to many. But if you read about him, you learn that he was acknowledged to be a superb artist. He was a great collector also. He put together an art collection which was a marvel apparently, full of things

The king and queen of France stop to exchange compliments with the American ambassador and his sixteen-year-old daughter in *Jefferson in Paris* (1995). Louis XVI was played by Michael Lonsdale and Marie Antoinette by Charlotte de Turckheim.

that hadn't been taken seriously before, like Gothic tapestries and medieval pictures. He was a society painter that everybody made fun of, but actually his pictures were very, very good; he was certainly taken seriously by other English artists. They couldn't stand his personality, but they admired his work.

Long: Maria Cosway says to someone in the film that Cosway cannot perform his husbandly duties or something like that. What is she really saying about him?

Ivory: Perhaps he was more interested in men, but that was never proved. However, they managed to have a daughter who lived to the age of six or so, and when she died, the broken-up Cosway kept her body in some sort of special glass sarcophagus in their house in London. Maria Cosway forced him to bury the child finally.

Long: There are all these figures. There's Guillotin, who thinks of himself as a benefactor of mankind through his invention. He demonstrates a little scale model of his decapitation device with a stalk of asparagus at a dinner table to the delight of the other guests, who have no inkling that the guillotine—a big, life-size guillotine—will soon be used on them.

Ivory: Do you want to know where that particular prop came from? It was being put to Mitterrand when he became president of France in the early 1980s that capital punishment should be abolished. Some colleagues had a miniature guillotine made and demonstrated it for Mitterrand; supposedly they put a little sausage under its sharp blade and said, "This is what happens with the guillotine." Mitterrand was so repelled by the spectacle that he immediately abolished capital punishment. We got this prop from someone who knew about it: the actual model that persuaded the French president to do away with the beheading of criminals.

Another historical artifact-prop in the film was the skeleton of a huge moose that Jefferson sent to Buffon, the French naturalist, to refute his claim that animals in the New World were of smaller stature than those in Europe. In order to stage the scene we had to find a moose skeleton, and did find one at the Museum of Natural History, in the Jardin des Plantes in Paris, with a plaque on it that read, "a gift from the United States of America to the people of France." It was apparently the skeleton of the very same moose that Jefferson had sent to Buffon.

Long: Instead of the skeleton you might have been able to use a real moose. Had you thought of that?

Ivory: Yes, a live moose was what we had really wanted. The company got such a moose from Sweden or Norway; he was shipped on a plane after being drugged. When they got him on the set, he was beginning to come to and would walk like this [*imitates the animal's awkward and unsteady gait*]. The more he came to, the wilder he got, until it was impossible to bring him into the house where we were shooting because he would kick everything to bits. We had to give up on that idea. I'd been warned that a moose could be uncontrollable, so we were prepared, with the moose skeleton standing by.

Long: Another of these historical figures, as I mentioned, was Dr. Mesmer, hypnotist and healer, supposedly, who sends women into fits by overexciting their nervous systems. What is that weird music supposed to be when Mesmer is demonstrating his magnetic powers before the French nobles?

Ivory: We know what went on because the sessions were documented by people who had gone to them. Strange music was heard from no one knew where—strange voices, as at a séance, that sort of thing, and we . . .

Long: In the film there is a figure out on the lawn making strange sounds through a megaphone, and one assumes that she is helping to stage-manage Mesmer's performance with the nobles and the fainting ladies.

Ivory: Well, no one knew exactly how the eerie effects were obtained. They're just described, the strange voices . . .

Long: Are the figures like Mesmer and Guillotin in the film because they add some color to your depiction of a certain era in France, or do they have thematic importance, too, as untrustworthy harbingers of a bright new future about to dawn?

Ivory: Both. You know, the enlightened nobles, the sort of radical-chic nobles, are shown at a dinner party where everyone is talking about liberty and freedom and all the rest of it; and they of course were the very ones who would soon be going to the guillotine. There are several scenes of that kind. They are all looking for a better world and a better form of French government, not necessarily without a king but at least with a more enlightened king who would defend the law, which should be for the good of all. That was all part of Jefferson's world. Jefferson was looked up to by the French radical-chic noblemen. Here was this man who had successfully accomplished a revolution in America against the English king. He would have much to tell them, and they could learn from him how to better man's lot in France.

Long: We hear Jefferson speaking at times like a son of the French Enlightenment. When a grain speculator is being hanged in a public square, the camera cuts to Jefferson at home as he writes: "There is nothing to fear from the triumph of the people"; and in a sudden transition from another scene of public violence, Jefferson announces that the people "are naturally good, warped by centuries of tyranny but . . . "

Ivory: Those are his words.

Long: Yes. I saw the film with someone who said, "They've made Jefferson speak like a fool." And I said, "But those were his own words."

Ivory: They *are* his own words. He could not have imagined when he wrote things like how "the tree of liberty has to be manured by a bit of blood from time to time" what the French Revolution was going to turn into. And, in fact, he left just after the fall of the Bastille and was not around to witness the excesses of the Terror.

Long: But he continued to have strong ties with France.

Ivory: He remained an ardent Francophile. This caused him trouble later on when John Adams was president and the alien and sedition laws were passed by Congress, laws that were really against the French "anarchists." He would not publicly damn the French during the excesses of the Revolution, which got him into trouble politically in the United States. It was said about him that he was bloodthirsty and he . . .

Long: That Jefferson could be blinded by his idealism, however, seems to me to be at the heart of the film. As the storm clouds of revolution gather, Jefferson is shown standing by a window of his house, declaring, "I will agree to be stoned as a false prophet if all does not end well in this country." Aren't self-deceiving comments like these relevant to his telling Maria Cosway that his plantation in Virginia is a paradise, where slave owners have affectional "family relationships" with their slaves?

Ivory: We don't know what he told Maria Cosway about the slaves. That's in the script, but we actually don't know.

Long: Apart from everything else, *Jefferson in Paris* is a physically, or visually, beautiful film. Of course there is Versailles, but elsewhere there are many moments of exceptional beauty. Take that scene of the opera-ballet of Antonio Sacchini's *Dardanus.* It's a wonderful spectacle, which includes a tenor who comes down seemingly from the clouds in a kind of basket. What is going on in the opera at this point?

Ivory: It's one of those deus ex machina descents to the stage. Dardanus, the tenor, is singing about "happy days."

Long: Ah, yes.

Patsy Jefferson (Gwyneth Paltrow) and Maria Cosway (Greta Scacchi) meet at Patsy's convent school in *Jefferson in Paris* (1995).

Ivory: It's the actual aria that Jefferson heard at the opera in Paris. Jefferson loved it, and Maria Cosway spoke of it again and again when they were no longer seeing each other, referring to their own earlier "happy days." The sheet music was found among Jefferson's music at Monticello.

Long: What about the ascent of the brilliantly designed, blue-and-gold hot air balloon?

Ivory: Sheer spectacle for its own sake. I can't remember any more if Jefferson actually witnessed it. The first balloon of that kind went up at Versailles in front of a hundred thousand people who had assembled to see it. But I don't think that Jefferson was part of the crowd. Having him there was just stretching things.

Long: Did it have any connection to the belief of the nobles that a new age was about to dawn?

Ivory: I believe these first balloon ascents were in fact described in that way in the newspapers and by philosophers: man could now fly, for better or worse. But in the film it's just a spectacle.

Long: In making *Surviving Picasso*, you and Ismail had quite a to-do with Picasso's companion, Françoise Gilot, and her son Claude Picasso over your right to do the film at all. Two books were involved in the controversy—Gilot's memoir, *Life with Picasso*, published in 1964; and Arianna Stassinopoulos Huffington's best-selling biography *Picasso: Creator and Destroyer*, which was published in 1988. The latter included her interviews with Gilot concerning her years with Picasso and afterward—material that Huffington could now make use of herself without fear of copyright infringement.

Ivory: It was more complicated than that. Before Gilot published her book, bits of it were printed in *Paris Match*, and Picasso contested it, took her to court, and lost his case. He did the same thing when the complete book came out a few years later, and again he lost the case. The French court said that he had no right to privacy because he was a man who had spent his whole life attracting publicity and had forfeited any hope of privacy by the way he lived. The French judge was convinced, it is said, by the argument that Picasso had allowed, even encouraged, the media to photograph him in his bath. Could such a person, then, say his rights to privacy had been invaded? So he lost, and the book came out and had been around for about twenty-five years by the time we got involved. Then, in the late 1970s, Arianna Huffington began to write her own book about Picasso and needed to talk a lot to Françoise Gilot. She needed to ask her questions, particularly about things that weren't covered in Gilot's book—things which happened after the period the book had covered that had to do with Picasso.

Long: Did she come to know Gilot well?

Ivory: She came to know Gilot quite well, and Gilot retold her a great many things that Huffington was able to put into her own book. In doing so, in some kind of way, and I don't know the legalities of this, Gilot lost her own right to privacy, and also in a sense her copyright, because she had given so much of her book's material to Arianna Huffington that somehow she no longer could claim possession of it. I don't know how such things work in the law, but that is what happened. After Arianna Huffington published this book, Warner Brothers optioned the rights to it. They wanted to turn it into a big series on the entire life of Picasso for television.

Long: Was this the idea of anyone in particular?

Ivory: It was David Wolper's idea. David Wolper, who was a producer at Warner Brothers, mainly of documentaries, and a great Picasso admirer and Picasso collector, especially of his sculpture, wanted to do a homage type of series about his hero, Picasso. Wolper was best known for *Roots.* He got Huffington and Gilot together to write a script for Warner Brothers. This is back in the mid-1980s. They worked on the script for a long time and came up with an immense life of the artist that may or may not have been finished, I don't know. Warner Brothers eventually decided that it was too much to attempt to do all that and the project ran out of steam and was abandoned, at least in that form.

Long: But obviously this Picasso project didn't end there for Warner Brothers.

Ivory: No, it didn't. David Wolper still wanted to do something about Picasso and Françoise Gilot, whom he had come to know, but concentrating now on just that part of Huffington's book that covered the Picasso-Gilot years. And at that point Warner Brothers telephoned us. We were just beginning to make *Howards End* when they called us in London and asked if we would be interested in making a film out of this book of Françoise Gilot's. They didn't say out of the Huffington book, which they had rights to, but to Françoise Gilot's book, which they referred to always as a novel, and which they didn't have rights to. By an extraordinary coincidence I had just read Gilot's book. I had bought it when it came out twenty-five years earlier, and it had sat on my bookshelf for a quarter of a century. I never opened it. Then one day, about the time we were preparing *Howards End,* I noticed it and began reading it. I thought it was a marvelous book about Picasso and his work and their life together, and so on . . . but I didn't think about making a movie about it. I read it, put it back, and that was that. Then, not long after, Warner Brothers called out of the blue and said, "Would you like to make a film based on Françoise Gilot's *Life with Picasso?*

Long: One of those eerie coincidences . . .

Ivory: But they didn't realize, in fact, that they didn't have the rights to her book; they only had the rights to the Huffington book. When they asked if we would be interested in doing a film from the Gilot book, I said, "Sure." After a little time we had a meeting with Françoise Gilot in New York. We had lunch with her at the Russian Tea Room, and she was extremely friendly and couldn't have been more pleased that a film was going to be made of this part of her life. She gave us signed books of her own; she had a collection of collages that she had made that had just been published, and she brought it, signed it, and gave it to us. She had also come out recently with a book about the friendship between Picasso and Matisse that she had observed when she was with Picasso. And she gave us a copy of that, which she also signed and dedicated to us.

Long: This all sounds very promising.

Ivory: It was. The lunch was very pleasant, very upbeat, very enthusiastic. But at the end of the lunch she suddenly said, "Unfortunately, I can't really give you the rights to *Life with Picasso* because my children won't allow it. They would be very angry with me if I were to give you the rights to my book." So we said, "OK." We then found out that it was actually the Huffington book that Warner Brothers had the rights to. The Huffington book, however, had somehow absorbed virtually all the contents of the Gilot book. The Gilot book couldn't be quoted directly; a passage of her dialogue, for instance, couldn't be quoted. If Picasso said so and so, you couldn't put that in the screenplay. But you could paraphrase it, as Huffington herself had often done, have him say it in a slightly different way. That's how our script was put together. Portions of it were based on the Huffington book, which was a kind of paraphrase of the Françoise Gilot book. And don't ask me why one's OK to turn into a movie and the other's not. I just don't know. But other parts of the story came from the known record of the artist's life that had not been copyrighted; we had to imagine and construct it in much the way we had done just before with *Jefferson in Paris.*

Long: Somewhere I read that Gilot had cooperated with the making of the film.

Ivory: Gilot? She did not; anything but. There was a silence from her for about a year while Ruth worked on the Picasso script. When the script was finished, we sent a copy of it to Françoise Gilot as a courtesy, wondering what she might say about it. There was a further silence. We never heard from her. Neither did Warner Brothers or Wolper or anybody. Later it came out that the Picassos were unhappy about the movie we were planning to make.

Long: How did you learn that?

Ivory: Gilot gave an interview to the *Times* of London in 1994, while we were making *Jefferson in Paris.* In the interview she said that "those people," meaning us, were going to make this movie, and it was all ridiculous and absurd. The script was just an absurd thing, she said, and we'd have to make the film over her dead body.

Long: What she said in the interview came as a complete surprise?

Ivory: It was a big shock. She turned on us just like that.

Long: Do you know why?

Ivory: I think it was because her family put pressure on her. I think her children must have said, "You can't have anything to do with this film. This is an abomination, and we don't want this film to be made."

Long: Did you ever meet Gilot's children?

Ivory: Claude Picasso only, brother of Paloma. He was in charge of the family business, you might say, the Succession Picasso, as it's called. Ismail and I went to see him in his office in Paris sometime in 1995 to talk about ways of resolving our conflict because, by that time, that's what it was. He kept us waiting for an hour and a half, exactly as his father had kept people waiting (sometimes for much longer); we could glimpse him inside shifting papers, reading the day's mail, talking on the phone. He had an expression like that of a stressed-out child. Finally we were admitted, but the conversation went nowhere, was doomed before it began. Ismail, no less an imperious person— in fact, a more imperious, or even imperial, person—had not liked cooling his heels outside and spoke too aggressively. I asked Picasso whether he knew or not of the encouraging conversation we'd had with his mother in the Russian

Tea Room, and he replied coldly, "Do you suppose that I know what my mother is doing every hour of the day?" Ismail had hoped at this meeting to introduce the subject of big payments conceivably to be made to the Picasso estate for the use of the father's art. But that bait wasn't taken by the son. When I asked him whether he'd read our script—hoping for some indication of whatever it was that had offended the family—he said he hadn't, that no one had given it to him. I didn't believe him—in the same way I didn't believe it when I was told that his mother, Françoise Gilot, living a few blocks away from the Paris theater in New York, where *Surviving Picasso* was having its first run, had never gone to see it.

Long: What exactly did Françoise Gilot do to try to prevent the film's being made?

Ivory: She talked about bringing legal action, but she didn't have a leg to stand on. She tried to sue Warner Brothers for invasion of privacy, but the same thing happened to her as had happened to Picasso. By publishing all of this in the first place in her own book, and then retelling it for the Huffington book, and adding further unpleasant details of her life with Picasso, she had forfeited any rights to privacy. Gilot couldn't sue on those grounds. If we had directly quoted her book in the screenplay, she could have sued for copyright infringement. But Warner Brothers' lawyers made very, very sure that we never did that.

Long: Could the Picasso family sue on any other grounds?

Ivory: The only thing they could now do was to forbid the use of any of Picasso's art in the film. We could never show a single work of art that Picasso had made, or anything that he had written. It didn't matter who owned the art because the copyright—and the right of reproduction—was still controlled by the Picasso estate and would be for decades. Nothing could be reproduced without the estate's permission. That's the curse from beyond the grave that many modern artists as well as writers have flung at filmmakers.

Long: But you were obviously expecting trouble from the Picasso estate because, from what I have read, you shot the film very quietly in England and the south of France.

Ivory: When we were shooting the movie in France, we called it "Film 19"

instead of *Surviving Picasso* because we didn't want some misinformed local po-
lice force to come crashing down and maybe confiscate the film or make trouble. But nothing like this happened. If we had actually copied some of Picasso's
work, they could have shut us down. And we never did that. Not once. We made
up some look-alike Picasso art and also collected paintings and prints from
the forties and fifties that resembled Picasso, were very much in his style or
under his influence. This art was never a copy of anything of his.

Long: It had features that made you think of Picasso . . .

Ivory: It was very nice . . . all of it. The Picasso-like paintings done by the
West Coast artist Vern Witham back in the early fifties had a lot of style and
panache. We dotted those around the set. They were in no way pastiches, any
more than, say, a Juan Gris is a pastiche of Picasso. They were products of
the time.

Long: But this "false" art was ridiculed by reviewers.

Ivory: It was ridiculed, definitely. Though not by everyone. Adam Gopnik
wrote in the *New Yorker* somewhat mischievously that if the experts were being honest, they'd have to admit that it was better than the stuff Picasso was
making then—that is, in the fifties. Sort of a backhanded compliment.

Long: In his book about the making of *The Proprietor,* Ismail tells of some
legerdemain that was involved in scenes you shot in the Place de la Concorde
in Paris.

Ivory: That's right. We needed to do two big scenes in the streets before the
Parisians came back from their summer vacations; we shot the scenes in August, when Paris was relatively empty. The first scene was the one where the
occupying Germans were in the Place de la Concorde marching up and down
and playing German martial music; the other involved the arrival of the Allied
army in Paris in August of 1944. Both scenes were done in one day. How we
actually did them both in one day I don't know, but we did. And we did them
well. But we didn't put on the clapper board that this was *Surviving Picasso.* We
put on it that it was *The Proprietor,* which also had episodes that dealt with the
Nazi occupation of Paris, mostly of a dreamy, flashback sort. It's said that
people staying at the Crillon Hotel looked out of their window to see swastikas
and goose-stepping Germans and panicked.

Long: If you had received permission to use Picasso's images, would you have used them more extensively than the substitutes you used?

Ivory: We wouldn't have used them very much more than what you saw in the film. The rights would have been prohibitive. You saw the episodes with Matisse . . .

Long: Right . . .

Ivory: They're *real* Matisses. I mean real in the sense that they were exact copies of actual Matisse works. We had an arrangement with the Matisse estate and were able to photograph whatever we wanted. These pieces were scattered all about Matisse's studio, and it could have been the same kind of thing with the Picassos. When you see Picasso at work in his studio in the film, you have a sense of unfinished paintings here and there, and it didn't really look a lot different from the old photographs you see of his real studio. You had glimpses of things. I don't think you would have seen much more than what we actually showed. He often turned his canvases to the walls. The main difference would have been in the scenes where he is shown painting and drawing. Then it would have been better to use actual copies. That's where the difference would have been.

Long: The controversy surrounding *Surviving Picasso* was increased by the fact that John Richardson, the Picasso biographer, wrote a savage review of your movie in the *New York Review of Books.*

Ivory: Absolutely. Of course he has a vested interest in doing so. He's someone whose whole life and name has been formed by Picasso. His whole raison d'être at this point, as an old man, is being able to write about Picasso and to come out with a monumental life of the artist. We spoke to him several times, and were we to have beguiled him into helping us in some way, he would for sure have run afoul of the Picasso family. They might have then said, as punishment, "You can't show a single one of Picasso's paintings in your next book." He had already written the first installment and was now working on the second. He didn't dare get on the wrong side of them.

Long: Wasn't there anyone in Picasso's circle, or anyone writing about him, who tried to support the film—tried to make things easier for you when the artist's estate came down on you?

Ivory: With the exception of the author James Lord, not one of them came to our defense before the film was made or after it was finished and released. They seemed to be vying with each other in conspicuously distancing themselves, if you can say that. But James Lord was fearless. He gave me a lot of information, particularly about Picasso's studio and apartment on the rue des Grands Augustins in Paris—how it was laid out, or rather, what exact use each room was put to by Picasso and Françoise Gilot. Lord also told me a lot about Dora Maar's apartment and her house at Menerbes.

Long: Why was James Lord so supportive, do you think?

Ivory: Apart from being a nice guy, Lord is the only one of Picasso's surviving friends who is not somehow in thrall to the Picasso estate—to its granting of reproduction rights to illustrate books and articles, that sort of thing. John Richardson and the others all knew that they would have been particularly vulnerable to the wrath of Claude Picasso if the news got around that they were making any encouraging noises in our direction. But, as I say, James Lord didn't give a damn. He liked us and looked forward to seeing what we'd do.

Long: But you say that you did meet with John Richardson earlier on, and he apparently had a friendly interest in your projected film at that time.

Ivory: At first, in the earlier stages of the discussion of the film, he was in fact friendly. He said all sorts of things that indicated his interest in the project. For instance, he told us about recently going to see Dora Maar and about what she was like. At one point we all went out to the Brooklyn Academy of Music . . . wait, not "we all," which makes it sound as if he was with us. Ruth and I went out to the Brooklyn Academy of Music to see *Richard III,* and while we were there we ran into John Richardson. All of us came out of the theater at about the same time; it was snowing, and since we had a car, we offered him a lift back into town. While we were driving back, he talked a lot about Dora Maar and how shrewd and sharp she was, and what an interesting woman she was. Of those women who were involved with Picasso early on, she seemed to him to have the most brains—things of that kind.

Long: Had you met John Richardson at some point earlier in New York?

Ivory: No. I had met him years before, really a long time ago, when I was in

Dora Maar (Julianne Moore), an earlier mistress of Picasso, plays with a sharp knife on the terrace of the Café de Flore in *Surviving Picasso* (1996).

my twenties. I was in the south of France and on my army leave. I was with an army friend of mine and another friend I'd known from college. We met up and took a trip around Provence. As it happened, I had seen an article about the villa there, near Uzes, owned by Douglas Cooper, the art collector and an authority on modern painting, particularly Picasso. He was a personal friend of Picasso's as well. We were driving along a road when I saw this grand villa, which I recognized from the article in *L'Oeil* I had read as being Douglas Cooper's. We thought, "What the hell, let's stop and see if we can go in."

Long: This is getting interesting. What did you do next?

Ivory: We went up to the gate, and I rang a bell, then a few minutes later a concierge type came down. I had some sort of card in my wallet, not really a calling card but something I had written my name on, and I gave it to the Frenchwoman to take up to the villa. The next thing that happened was that the young John Richardson came down—slim, handsome in a thin-faced way, amusing, pleasant, not the sort of forbidding-looking, black leather–jacketed person he's since become. When he saw us he said, "Come in, I'll show you around." He then took us up to the house. It was in the middle of the afternoon, a very bright, sunny, rather hot day, and Douglas Cooper was having a party at his swimming pool. You could hear all the splashing going on in the pool and the tinkling of glasses and all that sort of thing.

Long: Don't tell me he asked you to join his party.

Ivory: We weren't asked to join the party, but we were taken all around the house by John Richardson—the entire house and all the bedrooms, all over the place, and that alone was fascinating. The art collection was stupendous. We hoped that we might, after all, still be asked to join the party, but we never were. I think had Cooper caught sight of my two traveling companions, he might very well have asked us to join him by his pool. After seeing everything, we thanked Richardson and drove off. That first meeting with him was in 1955, and coming back with him to Manhattan from the Brooklyn Academy of Music must have been in 1994, nearly forty years later. He didn't remember anything of my having met him at Douglas Cooper's villa in the 1950s, of course, and I didn't enlighten him.

Long: John Richardson had reviewed Françoise Gilot's book when it first appeared, again for the *New York Review of Books*.

Ivory: And hated it.

Long: He said that it was a "wretched" book, a disparagement of Picasso, and a tissue of distortions and prejudices.

Ivory: He said also that the book was horribly indiscreet.

Long: Yet when he attacked your film, he claimed that you had vulgarized Gilot's estimable book.

Ivory: By that time he had obviously come round to thinking that her book was useful to him, and he had become a sort of friend of Gilot's.

Long: Speaking of Gilot again, I've wondered about your casting choices for the part of Françoise Gilot in the film. I came across a clipping that said Emma Thompson was to star opposite Anthony Hopkins in *Surviving Picasso*.

Ivory: No. She was never under consideration. I never thought of her for that film. She was not, I felt, the right type for it somehow.

Pablo Picasso (Anthony Hopkins) and his muse and lover, Françoise Gilot (Natascha McElhone), in the Brasserie Lipp, Paris, in *Surviving Picasso* (1996).

Long: I wouldn't think so. At any rate, I understand that you and Ismail happened to spot Natascha McElhone . . .

Ivory: I did.

Long: You spotted her performing Shakespeare in London.

Ivory: My casting agent, Celestia Fox, told me about her, so I went to see her in a production of yet another *Richard III,* this time in Regent's Park. She was playing Lady Anne and did a very good job. . . .

Long: Did you ever think of anyone other than Anthony Hopkins for the part of Picasso?

Ivory: Well, earlier I gave a little thought to the possibility of two of those great Italian-American male stars, who might be able to convey some sense of Picasso's tremendous allure and vitality. Robert De Niro was one, the other was Al Pacino. De Niro said at once that he wasn't interested, but we were encouraged immediately by Pacino. I met with him on several occasions and talked about the project. He liked the script and said he was interested in working with us and that kind of thing. But neither of them were really old enough, and probably they couldn't physically have transformed themselves into Picasso. It might have been that De Niro could have made himself resemble Picasso, but he would perhaps have lacked the sharp-witted, foxy qualities that the part required, and the sly humor, which could be savage. Picasso was the master of the calculated insult.

Long: There would have been a lot of energy there.

Ivory: For sure! Which Picasso had—and De Niro has . . . so there was that, and the sexual magnetism, which can't ever be faked. And the sense of arrested adolescence. After a while Al Pacino decided that he didn't really want to do our film. He was also involved with *his* own *Richard III* production. Obsessed by it, in fact. See how that play of Shakespeare's has figured in *Surviving Picasso!*

Long: You mean his film *Looking for Richard* . . . it was intriguing.

Ivory: Yes . . . so he already had his hands full. When he withdrew—it wasn't that he was ever really set to do it, but he did encourage us—we went to Anthony Hopkins.

Long: Speaking of Anthony Hopkins, I've wondered if you didn't perhaps have some difficulty with him while you were making *Surviving Picasso.* A suggestion of it comes up in an interview he gave in the March 1996 issue of *Vogue;* he didn't reveal the name of the director involved, but *Surviving Picasso* had just been completed when he gave the interview, and I wondered if he wasn't referring to you.

Ivory: If he was referring to me, then he was being extremely ungrateful, because after all I had just given him two of his biggest hits, one after the other. To attack me personally, as it appears he did if I *am* the director he was talking about, would be a very churlish thing for him to have done. But I don't know if the person he was talking about *is* me, in fact.

Long: Did anything happen between the two of you while you were making *Surviving Picasso?*

Ivory: There was something. I'll tell you what happened. We were doing a scene in London at Pinewood Studios. It was quite a dramatic scene in which Françoise Gilot tells Picasso that she's going to leave him for a while. He of course assumes that she's found another man, and they have an argument. It's horribly difficult for her, the things she's saying. During the scene I felt that

Natascha really showed her depth as an actress. It was a very emotional kind
of thing she was doing, and it was just right, it was excellent. When the scene
was over, I said, unwisely as it turned out, "Natascha, that was just wonderful, you were really great." Anthony Hopkins heard me tell her that, and as it
happened I had said nothing to him about his performance in that same scene.
He had also been great, both of them were. When is he not? But up to that
time Natascha had not had such a scene to do in the film, something so emotional. So I, you know, just spontaneously praised her.

Long: It was this that sparked an incident?

Ivory: A little time passed. We finished the scene and did some more work.
Then it was time to go home, and he cornered me in the vestibule just off our
stage at Pinewood and began yelling, "God dammit, you know I act my guts
out for you, and you never tell me that you're pleased with *my* performance.
You never say you like anything. And yet the first time she does something you
like, you tell her how wonderful it is. Don't you think I'd like to hear those
same words?" Of course I should have praised him more often, but the un-
fairness of it was that what I had said was meant for a young actress who was
coming into her own, and who had just delivered her first big scene and done
it well.

Long: What happened then?

Ivory: That he would blow up at me for praising Natascha seemed outrageous.
I said, "How dare you!" and such things, and we separated. He went to his dressing room, got out of costume, and took a shower or whatever; and I went to my
office, which was nearby, and for a while at least was shaking with anger. Then
we both came out of our rooms at the same moment, and I went up to him. I
didn't want to end the day with him in anger, so I went up to apologize, to tell
him in a sense that it was OK, we all get like this. But he launched into his own
apology before I could say anything. He said that he was so sorry, he didn't mean
to say such things. When the devil gets in him, there is just no holding him
back, and so on and so on. He was abject in his apology. I thanked him, and he
said that nothing like that would ever happen again, and it never did.

Long: And after that it was all smooth sailing?

Ivory: Well, there was an episode with him when he saw the first cut of the film. I never show a rough cut to actors, ever, because they always start moaning about the things that have been cut out. But in this case I had to show it to him because he needed to post-synch, to dub, a lot of his lines for accent. He had devised an accent that he liked and wanted to make sure it was uniform throughout the film. The only way to do that would be to show him the cut film before he did his dubbing. So I agreed. We had to show it on a video screen, which is always a terrible thing, but when you edit a film by a digital process you have no alternative at that stage. We ran it for him, and he sort of harrumphed and snapped a bit and then wrote us a long letter saying that the editor, Andy Marcus, had ruined his film; that it was all wrong, and that many important things crucial to his character were missing. He said that if what had been cut wasn't restored, we couldn't properly tell the story, and on and on. He said that we needed to totally reedit the film, and he ended the letter by saying that he wasn't really sure that when the film came out he would want to do the publicity for it.

Long: Was he serious?

Ivory: That's always the last recourse kind of threat that actors have; they sometimes come up with this form of blackmail, and often you think, "Well, good, I'm glad you aren't going to do the publicity because I don't want to see you again." So he made this kind of old empty threat and also the implied threat that he would not come to do the post-synch until we had recut the film along the lines that he thought ought to be. But we let him calm down, let some time pass. I knew that he would be stewing away and feeling guilty and all this kind of thing. After about a month I wrote to him and said that I was surprised at his letter and that I didn't agree with it and hoped he would not do anything that would be bad for the film and so forth. When it came time to do the post-synch he was there and did it very well and seemed to enjoy himself. He enjoys himself when he works. If he didn't work, he'd go crazy. When he's working, he's happy. It's the only time I think he *is* happy.

Long: He's in picture after picture.

Ivory: He has to be constantly working. That's why those threats to leave the industry and give up acting and all that kind of thing that he constantly makes are just hollow; you know that this is a man whose demons are so strong that the only way he can keep them under control is to work all the time. If he didn't have that work, he would probably become very unhappy.

Long: Can Anthony Hopkins be enjoyable, even delightful, to work with?

Ivory: Sure. Yeah, often. He's a lot of fun.

Long: Is he witty?

Ivory: Very, very.

Long: Lively?

Ivory: Sure. Usually, at least in our films, he's always been in a good mood. Except a bit on *Picasso,* and I think the main reason for any of his bad moods on *Picasso* is that he was unsure of himself. He didn't know whether he was giving a good performance (as we know, *I* wouldn't tell him if it was). I think he felt uneasy . . . with Stevens in *The Remains of the Day* he knew the man, he knew the character, he knew everything about him. The same with Wilcox in *Howards End.* He knew that kind of man, all his life he's known this kind of Englishman. Apparently with Oliver Stone when he had to play Nixon, he was in a terrible state all the time. Again, it could be that he was uneasy playing that part and didn't feel that he was quite right for it, though he understood Nixon well enough, I'm sure, to play the part. Nixon was always the butt of mimics—his twitches and speech patterns and body language.

Long: I thought Hopkins was awfully good in that movie.

Ivory: I did too. I liked him very much. But if he feels insecure, then he's going to lash out. That's what actors do; if they feel insecure, they beat you over the head all the time.

Long: You used a video monitor on the *Picasso* set. Do you use a video monitor a lot?

Ivory: Sure. Who doesn't? I understand that actors get fed up seeing the director peering into a TV monitor all the time, and not actually watching them as they deliver the goods. And during emotional scenes I do try to stand just next to the camera so they'll feel I'm *there* and attentive to what they're doing. It may help them; I'm not sure being there helps me. After all, the little screen blocks out everything else that might intrude on the sidelines of one's vision, so the effect is more concentrated. Actually, I now wonder how we once got along without a video monitor, especially in our kind of filming, where there is very little in the way of formal rehearsals. If, like Satyajit Ray, you're also the camera operator and can look through the lens during the take, you have a good idea of how the shot is turning out, where it's right, where it goes wrong, how the timing is. Otherwise you must wait until you see the rushes. That may be too late. So, from my point of view, the video monitor is one of the greatest aids to a director to have come along in years and years. As I said, I don't know how we managed without it all this time.

Long: Was it helpful when you were shooting scenes with Anthony Hopkins?

Ivory: Not always. Hopkins got mad at me on the day, a long and frustrating one, when we were shooting at the Matisse chapel in Vence, near Nice. On that day where and how we placed the lights dominated everything, and there were many delays. That night after the wrap, Tony complained in a note he sent me at our hotel that it was very irritating to see me with my head stuck in the video monitor all the time. I don't know what else I could have done on that tense day; there was no room for me to huddle up close to the two actors— the other was Natascha McElhone—who, let it be said, weren't at their most red-hot in their brief scene. My fault? Probably. Who would have supposed that on a brilliant sunny day in the south of France it would be necessary to double, triple the amount of light coming through the famous stained glass windows so that we could get on film the color saturation that makes them so famous? The actors were pushed and pulled this way and that until they got cranky. I have to say it was Matisse's art I was more interested in on that day, not theirs. When I looked into the monitor I was thinking—and most likely saying too loudly to the cameraman, Tony Pierce-Roberts—"Is that the bluest you can get? Why is the yellow so pale? Try putting his head against the green, where those colored lights will be reflected on it," and so on.

Long: Was the scene with Matisse in *Surviving Picasso* taken from real life? Picasso pays a visit to Matisse, and Matisse gives him a ceremonial headdress as a present.

Ivory: That was a real incident that happened, and that *was* the headdress.

Long: The actual headdress that Matisse gave to Picasso?

Ivory: We had it exactly copied.

Long: What is that scene all about?

Ivory: It's amusing to read about that incident in Françoise Gilot's book about the two painters. Picasso thought that the gift was a veiled insult, an ugly thing. It wasn't really a present at all, he thought, but a form of insult. But coming from Matisse he had to accept it.

Long: Joss Ackland, who plays Matisse, was superb.

Ivory: Yes, he was.

Long: In that scene you pay attention to Matisse more than Picasso.

Ivory: It had to be shot that way. In Matisse's scene you couldn't put the camera on Picasso, who is meant to be in something of a sulk there. In real life at that moment Picasso thought that Matisse was flirting with Françoise, and he thought that Françoise was being a little fool and was flirting back. This is what he was actually thinking the whole time he was sitting there, according to Gilot's book, the book she wrote about Picasso and Matisse. She tells about this—and how after they left, Picasso complained not only about the gift of this ugly aboriginal mask from Oceania but also about her behavior and Matisse's behavior. This "old man" playing up to this young girl.

Long: I wondered if the brilliantly colored designs that accompany the end credits of the film are variations on themes in Picasso's art. As a matter of fact, most of your films have their own ingenious visual designs with the credits. Are these designs yours, or are they entirely the work of your production designer?

Ivory: The Picasso-like figures that keep turning in circles were thought up by Bruno Pasquier-Desvignes, who also created the look-alike sculptures you see in the film. The production designer usually has nothing to do with titles. You think the thing up according to the needs of the edited film. A lot of filmmakers, and I sometimes do this too, plan in advance for the titles. It's a fine thing to do, but often you end up throwing all that away and doing something else. So I've almost entirely given that up now. I rarely go to the trouble of shooting actual title backgrounds because the finished film, that is to say, the edited film, gives you a new, or better, idea of how it should be presented; before you've made the film, you can't know what that better idea is.

Long: Cyrus Jhabvala once told me that you have a really deep, a really informed, knowledge of the fine arts; but that if someone were to comment on it, you might just pooh-pooh the whole thing.

Ivory: Why would I pooh-pooh it?

Long: Your films always make one think that you *are* unusually well informed about the fine arts.

Ivory: But why would I pooh-pooh the notion that I was?

Long: I don't know why Cyrus Jhabvala had that idea. Certainly *Surviving Picasso* is all about art and those who make it. There is also a lot of darkness in the film, since Picasso is portrayed as a kind of monster. Yet it's not a morose or depressing film.

Ivory: Any more than Picasso's pictures are. Picasso's art can be monstrous, depressing sometimes, tragic, ugly, and so forth; but we are attracted to it because there is something about it that is also intensely enjoyable and likable, and we accept it for the most part. And, of course, his art changed from period to period, so there is tremendous variety of mood in it.

Long: There is an entertaining worldliness in the film as well as a soberness. It's very different from a film like *Pollock,* a documentary-like picture about the life of Jackson Pollock, which starred Ed Harris in a powerful performance that should have won an Academy Award. The variation of mood and the lighter spirit of *Surviving Picasso* are all the more conspicuous when compared to the unrelenting somberness of *Pollock.*

Ivory: Picasso was anything but a gloomy man, or had anything but a gloomy life. His women were gloomy; he made them gloomy. No doubt they did an awful lot of moping around, but his own life was very colorful and exuberant, and that is expressed in his art. He was a showman and very much a public person, extroverted, always a performer, performing for the world. Jackson Pollock really wasn't like that.

Long: Did you see *Pollock?*

Ivory: Yes, and I liked it. I couldn't help but think how lucky Ed Harris was to have been able to show Pollock's paintings. But you can't couple Picasso and Pollock; they are not similar in their temperament at all. There was a whole tragic side to Pollock's life, his demons really did consume him. Picasso didn't have demons, or if he did . . . if he felt his demons, he turned them against the people who were closest to him and made them miserable instead. But he himself seems not to have been miserable. In fact, you feel he was basically light-hearted most of the time.

Long: Was he a misogynist?

Ivory: That's a good question. Who knows? I don't know. Maybe.

Long: Was it difficult to arrange to shoot in Picasso's wartime studio in the rue des Grands Augustins, as I believe you were able to do?

Ivory: It seemed at first that that would be impossible, and in fact the closest we got to the famous studio where Picasso painted *Guernica* was the courtyard below, on the street. The building itself, now as then, is owned by the administration of the Paris *hussiers.* When a Frenchman defaults on a loan or debt—doesn't make his payment, or ends up on the wrong side of a lawsuit—the *hussiers* seize the car and sometimes storm the apartments of intransigent debtors. Every weekday morning Picasso's old courtyard is filled with the motorbikes of the debt collectors, who have assembled to get their day's orders. When we applied to shoot there—the actual studios and living quarters of Picasso and Françoise Gilot have become offices—I was summoned to meet the chief *hussier,* who looked me over. He had never seen any of my films and perhaps had never seen any of Picasso's paintings either. "Who was Picasso?" the head *hussier* demanded. "He was no painter. Now, Velázquez, Rembrandt, *they* were painters. Why not make a film about them?" I must have hung my head a bit and looked disappointed, but perhaps he had already decided to let us shoot in his courtyard. He would agree to our request, he then told me, not because he thought anything of Picasso, who was nothing, but because I was an American. He could never forget that in the Second World War America had helped drive the Germans out of Paris and out of France. For that one reason, he told me, we could shoot at 15, rue des Grands Augustins. And we did, though the interiors had to be constructed at Pinewood Studios outside London. These matched so perfectly that we were able to shoot out of our studio windows on to the upper floor of Picasso's house (also constructed) and then from the real courtyard in Paris looking up. This wonderful set built by Luciana Arrighi convinced me (so late in my career) of the ease and freedom of shooting in a studio.

Long: Do you have any reservations about *Surviving Picasso,* apart from the fact that the artist's estate wouldn't allow you to use his art?

The official cast and crew photograph of *Surviving Picasso* (1996) taken in Pinewood Studios outside London in 1995. Behind and above are the upper stories of the rue des Grands Augustins set.

Ivory: Several. It should have been in French, but that would have been an utter impossibility then with a big American film company like Warner Brothers, which financed it. But it should have been in that language—and it eventually was, in the dubbed version of the film. Dubbing it into French was part of the delivery requirement, and we had wonderful actors to do it. The French version of the film, I think, holds together better. It's just right. You shouldn't have a whole bunch of English and American actors putting on accents, trying to be French or Spanish people. It gave a basic falseness to it that I regret, but there was nothing I could do about that.

Long: What else would you have done differently?

Ivory: What I could also have done differently would have been to break up the narrative line more; the script allowed that, in fact. I might have been able to find a narrative style that in its visual appearance and pacing reflected Picasso's own broken, many-faceted, simultaneous viewpoints or way of perceiving things. I might have used more opticals in the scenes of the artist's studio, of the kind where he and Françoise are "painting" with flashlights, which was so effective on the screen.

Long: That was great, and I wondered how you did it.

Ivory: The double face the audience saw was produced digitally and exactly matched the "outline" the two flashlights made. We later, in the editing room, traced it all out on the glass screen of a Steenbeck frame by frame, like an amateur artist connecting the dots in a picture. Then that line was digitally superimposed over the two actors lunging about. The result was more truly "Picasso-esque" than anything else in the film.

Long: I notice in these later films that you create very striking set pieces. There's the stunning opera-ballet scene in *Jefferson in Paris;* there's a wild performance of *Salome* at the Paris Opera in *A Soldier's Daughter Never Cries;* there's an elaborate costume ball performed at the London house in *The Golden Bowl;* and in *Surviving Picasso* there's the performance of a ballet by Diaghilev's company in 1920s Paris. There's also a little circus scene in *Picasso* in which acrobats perform and a line of little dogs walk on their hind legs pushing a cart.

Ivory: I've always had such set pieces. They've been in every one of my films, practically. They're worth doing, first of all, for their own sake. They're fun to do and fun for the audience. Structurally, they're usually catchall scenes so that a lot of plot stuff can go on in the background or in the foreground. Such scenes are not there just to be visually attractive or whatever, because a dramatic scene is usually unfolding in their midst. You can bring a lot of different characters on stage who may have all kinds of confrontations or discussions. The story goes forward within this colorful event.

Long: Do reviewers ever comment on these set pieces?

Ivory: Sometimes the more masochistic critics will object to these scenes. The *New Yorker,* for instance, objected to the costume ball in *The Golden Bowl,* called it padding. But if they'd really recalled the novel, or bothered to glance through it before writing the review, they would have found that scene there

Drawing with light: Picasso and Françoise Gilot in his studio on the rue des Grands Augustins, Paris, in *Surviving Picasso* (1996).

almost word for word. I made it into a costume ball; it had been a white-tie diplomatic reception in the novel. Costume balls were all the rage in grand London houses in Edwardian times. It was a good idea, no?

Long: Scenes of that sort certainly perk up an audience.

Ivory: They're not there to "liven up" the story as such or to add interest that the story may lack. I don't see why they can't be enjoyed for what they are. The opera scene in *Jefferson in Paris* is beautiful in itself. The music was wonderful and probably hadn't been performed since Jefferson's day. The whole atmosphere we created was probably something that nobody had ever seen in a movie—that kind of confused circus atmosphere of the eighteenth-century Parisian theater. That was a new thing. If people don't get it or are put off by it, well, I'm sorry, they can go out and have a cigarette. [*Long laughs*]

Long: I liked Kaylie Jones's novel *A Soldier's Daughter Never Cries* very much.

Before I opened the book, I wondered if she was being published because she was James Jones's daughter, but as soon as I began to read her novel, I could see that she had a fine talent of her own. What was there about her novel that made you want to make a movie from it?

Ivory: There were two things about it that appealed to me. One was that it was about a transplanted American family in Paris with young children, which in many ways was like some very close friends of mine who had been living in

Paris with their four kids. Reading the novel brought back those years. Another thing was the whole situation with Francis, which attracted me. He was a very interesting character, and I saw something of myself in him. I was a precocious type like that when I was his age, or younger.

Long: You've told me that "like Francis, both as a small boy and later as a teenager, I lived a life of constant self-dramatization . . . a fact most people meeting me now might not imagine."

Ivory: Yes, that's right.

Long: Can you enlarge on that?

Ivory: Well, I did self-dramatize a lot.

Long: What form might that take?

Ivory: All sorts of things. . . . I remember a time when I was a teenager growing up in Oregon and my father unfairly punished my younger sister for something he believed she had done. I knew that it was unfair. Maybe I had done it, and she had been punished for it. I don't know. She went up to bed crying, and he went up to his bed feeling that he had done the right thing. [*Long laughs*] He left me alone in the kitchen, where I took a bottle of black liquid shoe polish from a cupboard and, with all my strength, smashed the bottle against the floor. When it hit the floor, it made a loud noise like a bomb exploding, or a shot.

Long: I suppose this aroused your father.

Ivory: The next thing I knew my father was thundering down the stairs. As he came into the room, he saw me standing there with the broken bottle and black liquid shoe polish spattered all over the floor. He knew that I had created this mess. He didn't know *why* I had done it, but he knew I *had* done it. He spanked me, turning my tall and lanky self over his knee. It was the last time in my life I was spanked: I was too shocked to laugh. [*Long laughs*] The whole episode was a kind of self-dramatization and didn't have that much to do with any outraged sense of justice or my sister's tears, I think. I was quite capable of all sorts of things like that. The reasons behind these episodes would no doubt be transparent to a psychiatrist.

Long: So at this early age you were a kind of household "performer."

Ivory: In a way, my father may actually have contributed to my sense of myself as a performer.

Long: How so?

Ivory: He would observe me at Sunday Mass from his pew while I carried out my duties as an altar boy, and if he thought I had been sloppy and imprecise in my movements in front of the altar (and in front of the congregation), he told me so later. These must have been a little like the notes a director gives his actors. In time I improved my performance until he was satisfied. His criticism extended to my Latin responses to the priest's Latin prayers; my gabbled-out words (that I didn't know the meaning of) became crisp and exact: "AD DEUM QUI LAETIFICAT JUVENTUTEM MEAM," for instance. I got so good at this that when I was thirteen and we moved temporarily to Palm Springs, where I offered my services to the parish church, the priest, hearing my clipped Latin diction during Mass, asked me afterward if I would tutor the other boys.

Long: Which you did? But does anybody know now what good Latin diction should sound like?

Ivory: Probably not, but the priest in Palm Springs could at least make out my words—which, as I said, I didn't really know the meaning of, nor could I enlighten my pupils. All this has now been swept away at Catholic masses— as has the teaching of Latin in most American high schools. Gone, too, I imagine, are all the Latin clubs and their nerdy, bespectacled "A"-student members.

Long: What other things did your father instruct you in when you were growing up?

Ivory: He drilled me relentlessly on my multiplication tables—not knowing them perfectly was to him another form of sloppiness. He taught me to ride, to shoot a gun. Most of all, the big lesson I learned from him was that, like the hungry crew of a sawmill, a film crew needs to be fed well, and on time. I remembered our cookhouses, with their three kinds of roast meat and all the different cakes and pies.

Long: You not only directed but also co-wrote *A Soldier's Daughter Never Cries.* You wrote it with Ruth, but the copy of the screenplay I read gave the name of your collaborator as Erin Uday. Who is that?

Ivory: It's actually Ruth. That's a pseudonym she used. It doesn't say "Erin Uday" on the screen. It says "Ruth Jhabvala." She had a pseudonym made up because there was always the possibility in our contract with the people who developed *A Soldier's Daughter* that the movie might in fact turn up on TV. Ruth wanted an out; if it turned up on TV in a different form from the way she had written it, or was perhaps directed by other people, she wanted to make sure that her name would not be on it. When her contract was originally drawn up, it gave her the right to use a pseudonym, which was Erin Uday, a name made up from the names of her eldest grandchildren, Erin and Uday. When we actually had finished the film and it was about to come out, she agreed to put her name on it. If she hadn't done that, it wouldn't have been good commercially for the film.

Long: Do *you* have a pseudonym?

Ivory: Yes. Julian Branch, a name made up by George Trow for the song-writer/monk in *Savages* played by Louis Stadlen. Luckily I've never had to use it, except on a few occasions when I wanted to leave mysterious messages on the telephone.

Long: Leelee Sobieski, young and at the time practically unknown, was an inspired choice for Channe Willis, the fictional stand-in for Kaylie Jones. An unspoiled quality, a wholesome innocence shines in her face. I was intrigued to learn that she's the daughter of an American writer and a French painter. That she should have a parent (a mother in this case) who is an American writer and have herself lived in Paris as a child gives her some sort of personal connection to the role she plays in the film. Of course it's just a coincidence.

Bill Willis (Kris Kristofferson) and his daughter Channe (Leelee Sobieski) in the Brasserie de l'Ile Saint Louis, a favorite of author James Jones, on whom the part of Willis is largely based, in *A Soldier's Daughter Never Cries* (1998).

Ivory: Yes, her father is a painter. I've been in his studio. I don't know about her mother. I've never seen anything she's written, or perhaps it would be more fair to say published. I'm really rather ignorant about Leelee's parents, I have to admit.

Long: You cast Kris Kristofferson as Bill Willis, a well-known American novelist. Was there anyone else that you considered for the role?

Ivory: That was a part with a long history. Originally it was to have been played by Nick Nolte. When we met him at the premiere of the Jefferson film, he said, "Now, if there is anything else that you guys are coming up with, I want to know about it. Please tell me if you think I'm right for anything." Well, the next thing we were doing was *Surviving Picasso*, but after that we were planning to do *A Soldier's Daughter.* We told him about it, in fact, as soon as we had a script. We sent it to him, and he said yes, he wanted to do it.

Long: But he didn't actually do it.

Ivory: No, instead he went off to the South Pacific to make *The Thin Red Line.*

Long: A nice coincidence, a James Jones novel . . .

Ivory: At first he was only going to stay a month there or something of the sort. There wasn't any reason why he couldn't have been in that film *and* our film, even though the other film was very delayed in starting. But it was getting a little iffy. He stayed and stayed and stayed, and we were never able to reach him . . . we never even heard from him. We learned that he would be staying in the South Pacific much longer than he had expected. We heard this from third parties. And so we thought, "Well, we've lost him, he's not going to come back and do this film, so we will have to get someone else." And this started a process of trying to interest other people in doing the part.

Long: Who was the first actor you thought of for the part after you decided that Nick Nolte was not available?

Ivory: The first person I thought of was Willem Dafoe, who physically resembled James Jones facially and in his form and—superficially—personality. He was a very good James Jones type. But he declined—or so we thought. Only recently, in conversation with Dafoe at a party, I learned that his agent had never given him the script. Those people can sometimes be appallingly irresponsible or treacherous! Then we went through a list of people who didn't look like James Jones at all but who could have been very good—at least five or six others.

Long: How did Kris Kristofferson enter into this?

Ivory: While the casting process was going on, Kris Kristofferson, knowing that the film was about to be made, read the script, which *his* agent had given him, and contacted our office in New York. He wanted it known that he was interested in playing the Bill Willis role. For some reason at first we didn't pay much attention to this, and then suddenly we woke up. When I met him, I realized that I had just been very unaware and unimaginative as far as he was concerned, because he seemed perfect, better than anybody. There was nobody who could have played that role as he did, I think.

Long: He has a very unusual background. He was a Golden Gloves boxer but also a Rhodes scholar at Oxford. He was an army officer, a pilot, and a Ranger, yet he was also a country singer and composer of best-selling songs like "Help Me Make It through the Night." There's a lot of life written in his face. He's a man's man but also has a quality of gentleness. This was true of James Jones himself.

Ivory: That's it. And he has a down-home way of speaking. James Jones was from Indiana, and Kris Kristofferson's down-home way of delivering his lines had a western, or southwestern, twang to it.

Long: He's originally from Texas.

Ivory: He doesn't have a very broad Texas accent, but he does have a quality of the wide-open spaces in his speech, and that was, I thought, essential. His speech reminded me of a close friend of mine, someone I grew up with. They used the same kind of expressions, the cuss words they came out with and all that was almost exactly the same. They actually ended up being in a scene together because this friend of mine (his name is Bruce Anawalt) came to Wilmington, in North Carolina, where we were on location, and was one of the poker players in the American section of the film. I loved seeing the two of them sitting there at the table face-to-face. They didn't realize it, but all the while they talked and joked, I was consciously comparing Kristofferson to my friend Bruce. It was a pleasure to listen in.

Long: I was struck by your handling of children and adolescents in the film. You have a completely natural touch with them, and this is the more surprising since children have not played much of a role in your earlier films. The scene-stealer among the small children is, I think, the little French boy who tries to seduce Channe in his tree house. He has a rather beautiful face, together with an unsettlingly precocious awareness of sex. The scene between them with the snails slithering across their skin is as sexually suggestive almost as an adult encounter. Where and how did you ever find such a striking and lascivious little boy?

Ivory: He didn't think he was lascivious, of course [*Long laughs*], and he didn't really have that quality. . . . He played it, but I don't know if that was really his nature. The whole business of the snails pushed it all a bit more,

In the tree house: the ten-year-old Frédéric Da as the sexually precocious Stephane, with his pet snail in *A Soldier's Daughter Never Cries*
(1998).

heightened it all. That snail episode, I'm sure, comes out of Kaylie's past life.
Something like that must have happened to her, and that's why it's in the book
and why it's in the film. I would not have thought of that. I might have thought
of other kinds of childishly sexual things, but I would not have thought of snails
crawling around on my bare skin. [*Long laughs*] That idea pushed it into another kind of area, but I didn't think the little boy was conscious of it, really.
The children were at first nervous about doing that scene, but it wasn't truly
because of the sexual nature of it, or the snails. It was because the little boy
had to kiss the little girl, and that was so disgusting to both of them [*Long laughs*]
that the little girl cried. His name, by the way, was Frédéric Da, and hers was
Louisa Conlon.

Long: Was it difficult to direct the children in this scene?

Ivory: We had a run-through of Frédéric kissing Louisa at rehearsal, where
she announced that she couldn't bear to do it. She was afraid that her friends

would see her on screen being kissed, and he was equally afraid of being seen by *his* friends kissing a girl. But eventually they got used to the idea, and by the time we had to shoot it, they were fine.

Long: How did their parents feel about the scene in the tree house, by the way?

Ivory: Here was this scene in a tree house, a sort of simulated sex scene with a little boy aged ten and a little girl aged eight and some snails, in which the little boy also exposes himself to the little girl, and all of that. You would think that the parents would be standing down underneath looking at their wrist-watches and wondering what the hell is going on, or maybe insisting on being up in the tree house also.

Long: The parents weren't nervous about it?

Ivory: Not at all. Knowing absolutely what was taking place on that day, they brought the kids to the tree house and then left and just assumed they'd be fine. And they were. As I say, the children were not in any way embarrassed by the sexual side of this. It was the whole issue of actually having to kiss someone that was so repugnant to them. I think *we* were more upset than the kids. The continuity girl and the cameraman and I were all nervous. Nervous and apprehensive. What was going to happen? Were they suddenly both going to burst into tears and run away? Were they going to rebel and say, "We won't do these things"? Were they going to start crying for mama? [*Long laughs*] But nothing at all. I mean, they were like hardened professionals.

Long: Someone who really stands out in the film is Anthony Roth Costanza, who plays Francis Fortescue, the opera-loving—and self-dramatizing—boy who quickly becomes Channe's best friend. Where could you ever have found an adolescent boy so perfect for the role? Only one thing puzzles me about him, as it must have puzzled others in the audience. He sings a passage from Mozart in the classroom, but surely what we are hearing is someone else's voice.

Ivory: Surely you are not.

Long: Someone with a trained operatic voice . . .

Ivory: It is *his* trained operatic voice. No one else is singing that aria for him. That's a straight performance done to the camera.

Long: Where did you find him?

Ivory: Through an agency in New York that specializes in kids.

Long: Was he going to school?

Ivory: He was going to the High School for the Performing Arts here in New York. He was fifteen.

Long: Fifteen and precocious.

Ivory: I didn't know that he was a singer. He had given me a very good reading of the lines—better than anybody else. He just got it. Quite a few kids came and read who didn't get it. In the script he was supposed to play the violin, not sing Mozart. In any case, at the end of the audition session he slipped me a little cassette and said, "You might want to listen to this." I didn't think about it; I took it and put it aside. But after a day or two I listened to it while I was driving up to Claverack; I put it in the cassette player and was amazed. There were three or four arias on that cassette, operatic arias; and I thought: "This is terrific, and how much more interesting it would be to have him sing the 'Voi che Sapete' aria from *The Marriage of Figaro*—and sing it very, very well— than to play the violin badly, as Kaylie had written in the novel." So I decided to change the script and let him sing instead.

Long: What was the reaction of people in the audience to his singing?

Ivory: They loved it.

Long: Did they really understand that *he* was singing the aria?

Ivory: I think a lot of people assumed it was all dubbed . . .

Long: That's what I meant.

Ivory: He sang, even though his voice had already changed, with a soprano voice, and was a consummate young performer and singer. He had the most delicate kind of skills and musicianship of a very special sort, and the most wonderful taste. Many people assumed that this was a much older voice, and probably a woman's; but, in fact, although his speaking voice is much deeper, his singing voice was a soprano—and still is.

Long: What is he doing now?

Ivory: He's now at Princeton in the music school; he's beginning to do big parts in operas. He sang the part of Cherubino from *The Marriage of Figaro* out at the Santa Barbara opera the year before last. It's one of the rare times that Cherubino has ever been sung by a young man; it is now almost invariably sung by a woman. At Princeton he's singing countertenor parts in Monteverdi operas and things of that kind.

Long: Speaking of opera, the avant-garde production of *Salome* in the film is very striking, with its bright colors, leopard-skin couches, and red plastic inflated furniture—a setting in which Salome injects herself with drugs and makes love to the decapitated head of John the Baptist. One reviewer called the opera sequence the best, wildest thing in the film. Who thought up this production, and who designed it?

Ivory: The designer was the art director of the film, Jacques Bufnoir. But the mad idea for the scene was that of my assistant, Andy Litvack, who has since become a director himself (he did *Merci, Dr. Rey* with us, containing a demented scene from *Turandot,* with Dianne Wiest in foot-long red fingernails singing—or lip-synching—the princess). The opera sequence in my film is certainly one of my favorite moments. While I was off in the bar in another part of the Paris opera house directing Leelee Sobieski and Anthony Roth Costanzo, Andy was down in the main auditorium of the Palais Garnier, as the old Paris opera is called, with *Salome*—having a good time.

Long: In addition to Channe and Francis Fortescue, there's Billy, the little French boy who was named Benoît originally and who was adopted by the Willises. When the family comes to America to live, Billy has a particularly difficult time adjusting. Why is he so disengaged, so withdrawn? Why is he so unwilling to read the diary his French mother kept during the time just before he was born?

Ivory: Well, I think he just didn't want to know any of that. There are adopted children who turn their backs on all of that, and he was one of those. Not all adopted children go rushing to the Internet to find their real parents, you know.

Long: When he's out of school, Billy just watches television and eats potato chips . . .

Ivory: He has a sort of couch-potato life of a slobbish boy of sixteen. Everybody passes through that. That stage of his life was what we also showed in the film. He'd been this slightly withdrawn—"withdrawn" is not the right word—he was someone who as a little boy was very self-contained, very much his own person, and those qualities continued on into his adult life. He was never an excessively outgoing kind of boy. He's discreet and reticent in the same way that Francis is overblown and flamboyant. In fact, he remains French.

Long: There are some nice scenes set at the French school in Paris that both Channe and Francis attend. In particular there is a strange, comic moment when the headmistress comes into the classroom as stiff and proper as ever, and as she moves forward she seems to glide into the classroom as if she were on a conveyor belt. The audience I saw it with seemed puzzled for a second and then began to burst out laughing. What is this all about?

Ivory: It is the re-creation of scary moments when I myself was a child, going to a parochial school in Oregon. The mother superior, who was named Sister Philomena, used to pay periodic visits to the classroom. She was very stern, gliding almost motionlessly to the front of the room, in a terrible silence, her eyes glinting behind rimless eyeglasses. We were always in awe. When I grew up and began to go to the opera and first saw *The Magic Flute*, the Queen of the Night reminded me of Sister Philomena. So that was what I wished to set up in the scene you describe. Recently I saw Cocteau's *Beauty and the Beast* again, and there is a moment in it when Beauty similarly glides along a corridor in Beast's palace. Was I remembering that, too?

Long: Janet Maslin's review in the *New York Times*, while not unfriendly, noted that the film suffered from "autobiographical sprawl" and had "no real narrative shapeliness." How would you respond to that?

Ivory: I thought it was unusually shapely—almost formally so. The story was in three parts: "Billy," which covered the adoption of the younger brother and his relationship with his new family; "Francis," which was centered on Channe's years of early puberty and her intimate friend, Francis Fortescue; and "Daddy," which was about the family's life in America and the father's death. This arrangement was not the conventional one of "coming-of-age" films.

Long: What would you say is the single overarching thematic idea of *A Soldier's Daughter?* It's about the relationship of the father and daughter, but that is the subject matter rather than the thematic idea. Is the idea the forming of a bond among the different members of the family that survives even the loss of the all-important father?

Ivory: We had to come away at the end with that kind of positive idea or the audience would feel let down. The novel is not quite like that, however. Channe and Billy grow very close, but Channe becomes ever more distant from her self-indulgent mother. Our audience had to be left to imagine the two children growing up, perhaps starting families of their own, yet remaining close. A true brother and sister, with all of Channe's old hostilities toward Billy cast off for good. That is the "overarching" theme of the novel, I think, and the film reinforces it.

Long: Your latest picture, *Le Divorce,* which I liked a lot, is not exactly like any other film that you have made. The pace of the film is swifter than usual for you, and the spirit of the film is very, very French—animated, lighthearted, lively. *Quartet* was set in Paris, too, but its mood was entirely different.

Ivory: Well, *Quartet* told the sad story of the downfall of a beautiful young girl who was also animated, lighthearted, lively, but it was a gloomy tale. The two Santa Barbara girls at the center of *Le Divorce,* though they also had troubled love lives, weren't lost or doomed souls, and of course they had money. Diane Johnson set out to write a sort of high-spirited comedy, but Jean Rhys was describing, or using, her tortured life with Ford Madox Ford and his wife in a very different Paris seventy years earlier.

Long: I felt so much empathy with the French mind that I had the feeling at times that I was watching a film by a French director. Is this an effect that you were, in fact, aiming for?

Ivory: Not exactly. I admire French movies very much and always have; I feel complimented. But I know those kinds of French people—the Persands—or I think I do. Diane Johnson got them right, despite the fact that she doesn't really know French all that well (neither do I,

LE DIVORCE

Two American sisters from Santa Barbara love and suffer in Paris. The elder's French husband deserts her; the younger sister then starts an affair with the husband's rich uncle, while everyone squabbles over a Georges de La Tour painting that both sides claim. With Kate Hudson, Naomi Watts, Leslie Caron, Thierry Lhermitte, and Glenn Close. 2003. Feature. 35 millimeter; color; 117 minutes.

as I've said). This is really the first film I've made in France in which the French characters have leading roles and not supporting ones. I cast them very carefully; that took a long time.

Long: In making the film, were you influenced, do you think, by any particular French directors, such as, say, Eric Rohmer?

Ivory: No, not at all. At home French directors work, you can say, from the inside out; I can only work, as a foreigner, and with my very imprecise French, from the outside in—as I had to in England, and as I did in India, even working in English. French actors speaking sharp French dialogue help to make *Le Divorce* seem Gallic or whatever. It would be nice to think the film has the light touch of certain French comedies, but maybe that also comes from me to some extent and from Diane Johnson's book, as well as from Ruth—what do you think?

Long: I don't rule it out . . . You postponed the opening of the film from spring until late summer of 2003. Was there a problem with your distributor, or could you possibly have felt that with French-American relations strained over the invasion of Iraq, and with some Americans boycotting French products, spring would not be a good time to bring out the movie?

Ivory: Again, not at all. There were no such considerations, or if there were, I never heard about them. The film wasn't actually completed—negative cut, prints graded and all that—until the third week in April. It takes several months to prepare a film for its release, you know; the magazine press has to see it, theaters have to be booked—all that. Iraq and *Le Divorce* coinciding was an accident. The distributor, Fox Searchlight, releases twelve films a year, and it was our turn; *28 Days Later* preceded us, and *Thirteen* came after.

Long: While you were preparing the film, did you do any research into present-day French-American relations or read any books on the subject, such as Adam Gopnik's recent book *Paris to the Moon,* which makes perceptive observations on comparative differences in American and French customs, rituals, and behavior?

Ivory: I read *Paris to the Moon* and liked it and, actually because of it, set a scene in one of the locations Gopnik wrote about at length—the little carousel in the Jardin du Luxembourg. There were other books: I reread William Maxwell's *The Chateau,* a sixties novel (a noble book) that really focuses very sharply on the French in their relations with Americans and each other. I read that recent little book, *The Flaneur,* of Edmund White, which is perhaps a kind of distillation by a longtime American resident in Paris of much of what Gopnik saw.

Long: New York reviewers of *Le Divorce* complained that you hadn't done justice to Paris. I wondered what they were looking for.

Ivory: Yes, that was odd, and I was reminded of the Indian reviews of our very first film, *The Householder,* in 1964. We read in the Indian newspapers that we had failed to present "our India" well. So, again with *Le Divorce,* we have not presented "our" Paris well, either. But just what exactly is the true Paris of A. O. Scott of the *Times,* or of Peter Rainer of *New York* magazine? Whatever could it be? What could it be?

Long: How was it that you happened to discover Diane Johnson's novel? Was it recommended by someone?

Ivory: The *Paris Herald Tribune* recommended it in a review that I read while I was in Paris, getting ready to make *A Soldier's Daughter Never Cries.* I bought the book there and read it and then got in touch with Diane Johnson through her agent. It turned out she was in Paris also, so we had lunch. As it happened, *Le Divorce* had been optioned by a film company in California called Radar Films, which was trying, without much success, to get it off the ground. So— as I have done in other cases—I decided to sort of wait it out. *The Remains of the Day* was also like that.

Long: The screenplay was co-written by you and Ruth. Judging by the result, I wonder if it wasn't a labor of love. Was it?

Ivory: Well, not really for Ruth so much; she was involved with writing her novel *My Nine Lives* then; I had to sort of carry the ball. I wrote the first draft of the screenplay in Trinidad while Ismail was shooting *The Mystic Masseur.* Paris seemed a very long way off in those days. Writing the script brought it closer— so in that way it was something of a "labor of love." Or, anyway, love for Paris. Ruth doesn't have that love for Paris; if anything, she's skeptical about the French, like many Europeans. You know, Americans are much more addictive where France is concerned, and have always been. It's a surprising, and maybe an irritating, trait to the French. I think they are surprised by our uncritical love of them or dismayed.

Long: In the screenplay an important late scene takes place at Disney World in Paris (called U.S.A. Dream in the script), but in the film it is set at the Eiffel Tower. Why the change? Visually, of course, it adds further richness to the film.

Ivory: We were refused when we tried to get permission to shoot at Euro Disney. It came from the top man himself, Michael Eisner, who said shooting there wouldn't do them any good. But he said he loved our films! There actually *was* an attempted hostage taking there about then; some guys held up an American Express office in the park and took two Germans prisoner.

Long: Speaking of that suspenseful Eiffel Tower scene, isn't there a Hitchcockian reference in it? You know, the deranged Tellman in pursuit of the Walkers to the uppermost platform, with Dick Robbins's nerve-racking music surging.

Ivory: Yes, almost by accident, you could say. I wasn't really thinking "Hitchcock" as we shot. But maybe—or probably—Dick Robbins was, when he scored that scene. I'm sort of slow sometimes; it was only at the music recording after all the editing that I thought, "Oh, this is like Hitchcock! Gee!"

Long: I also wonder if there isn't a reference to the French film *The Red Balloon,* when the Hermès purse, or "Kelly bag," is thrown from the top of the Eiffel Tower, sailing every which way on the wind over the rooftops of Paris as background accordion music is heard that is evocative of all that is unpredictable and magical about Paris?

Ivory: Yeah, I guess. It's nice to compare our flying Hermès bag—symbol of sexual pleasure and marital infidelity—flying over the rooftops of Paris with a gun inside it, to *The Red Balloon.*

Long: Was it very hard working up in the Eiffel Tower? I notice the weather seems constantly to be changing.

Ivory: The worst thing about working in the Eiffel Tower was that the crew and equipment could only be up on the observation deck where most of the action took place from six thirty until nine thirty in the morning, when the public was let in. I don't know how we managed, frankly, but somehow we did. To make matters worse, Kate Hudson suddenly discovered she had an extreme fear of heights, saying mad things like we should "build a set somewhere." And she wasn't the only one. One of my assistants wouldn't even set foot in the elevator and was spotted hiding in the bushes. Luckily, Kate didn't go as far as that.

Long: The story of *Le Divorce* concerns an American girl, Isabel Walker, from California, who goes to France and becomes embroiled in all sorts of inter-

Le Divorce: James Ivory, Matthew Modine, and a problematic prop gun at the top of the Eiffel Tower (2003).

national marital complications. I don't want to bear down too heavily on this, but don't you suppose that Diane Johnson was suggesting, in a playful way, that her Isabel is a more liberated, end-of-the-twentieth-century descendant of James's Isabel Archer in *The Portrait of a Lady*—another American girl who went to Europe in what turns out to be a voyage of self-discovery? Fortunately, Johnson's heroine comes through the experience better than Isabel Archer.

Ivory: I've heard and read these comparisons to *The Portrait of a Lady* being made, but we know—certainly *you* know—that such implied comparisons shouldn't be taken very seriously, if at all.

Long: The film is also about two families, the Parisian Persands and the American Walkers from Santa Barbara and the tensions in their relationships when the Persand son, Charles-Henri, suddenly deserts Isabel's sister Roxy for another woman. Interestingly, the families are also alike in some ways, belonging to the upper-middle class and being suspicious of the others as "foreigners." Does the way they both want to take possession of the painting of Saint Ursula by Georges de La Tour remind you a bit of *Hullabaloo Over Georgie and Bonnie's Pictures?*

Ivory: Only in the sense that the more hardheaded members of the Walker family begin to think about their heirloom in a new way, like Bonnie did of the Tasveer miniatures, with dollar signs in their eyes. It very quickly falls out that, apart from Roxy's interest in the picture as some sort of reminder of home and her childhood, the Saint Ursula is identically interesting to *both* families as a source of cash.

Long: Is the painting we see of Saint Ursula, protector of young girls, really the work of La Tour, or have you had an artist paint it as if it were a La Tour? I'm not sure of this.

Ivory: No. La Tour never had any interest in Saint Ursula, as far as anybody knows, though her morbid stubbornness and self-denial ought to have attracted that French painter. We made up Saint Ursula, composition and all, making sure all the iconography was appropriate and so forth. It's a very good job, I think, very convincing. Better than our Picasso look-alikes. You know, people speak of some other career I might have had. Why not as a forger of old masters? Very applicable, in all sorts of ways. [*Long smiles in agreement*]

Long: Le Divorce is a beautiful film visually. How would you describe the look of the picture that your cinematographer, Pierre Lhomme, has given it?

Ivory: It's similar to the look he brought to *Jefferson in Paris,* everything a kind of harmony of form and color and light that is French: a little bit formal, yet a little bit sensuous; everything somehow self-contained, poised, like all good French art; maybe like the French themselves, at their best.

Long: It seems to me that there is a "luscious" quality to the look of the film— from the close-up of the produce in the market at the opening to the clothes, including the scarves, that the Frenchwomen wear, and the stunningly elegant entrées served in the restaurants. All very French, very piquant. The series of lunches at stylish restaurants with views overlooking Paris makes me wonder if they may not be a new version of the signature Merchant Ivory dinner scene.

Ivory: We usually go in for formal banquets, and we all know how much fun *those* can be. Lunch at a three-star Paris restaurant is certainly more appealing.

Long: Dick Robbins's musical score also creates the mood of Paris in the film. There is a delicate love theme that underscores Isabel's time with Edgar Cosset, and there are snatches of ballads that might have been sung by Yves Montand or Edith Piaf in some French music hall. What are we hearing principally?

Ivory: Well, we're hearing Serge Gainsbourg sometimes—or his wife, Jane Birkin. He was the master of all that is sophisticated and witty in modern French songs. The music hall resemblance is maybe only apt for the opening song over the titles by Patrick Bruel and Johnny Halliday: "Qu'est-ce qu'on attend pour être heureux." Edith Piaf goes too far back to be contemporary, I think; it might be sort of caricaturish to hear her in this film. We used her in that way in *A Soldier's Daughter*, when the kids imitate her.

Long: The opening credits, with their caricatures of French types in pursuit of love, elegant dining, and champagne (some of which come from the jacket of Johnson's novel) move across the screen briskly and with a sense of joie de vivre, as if to foretell the nature of the film about to begin. Was the idea of using the book jacket drawings yours?

Ivory: Yes, I liked the artist's work very much. Her name is Nina Berkson, and she's Canadian, living in Montreal.

Long: The scenes in the film seem to flow into one another, without any abruptness. There is one, for example, when Isabel and Edgar Cosset attend a concert of classical music. Before long the singer's voice carries us into another scene where people are peering at the Saint Ursula painting, but we cannot see how or where the transition was made. Is this your doing, or was the transition made by the film's editor?

Ivory: If you look at the script again, you'll see that the concert is followed by the scene where the appraisers come to Roxy's apartment. The music—of Marc-Antoine Charpentier—flows over into the scene where the Louvre expert is examining and rejecting the Saint Ursula painting as a La Tour. But both scenes were shot in a sort of half-light, with silhouetted figures, and that is why there seems to be no break in continuity.

Long: The film's editor, John David Allen, is new to me. You have had a series of earlier editors, notably Humphrey Dixon, Katherine Wenning, and Andrew Marcus. Can you tell me something about them and their contribution to your movies?

Ivory: Two of them—Humphrey Dixon, who is English, and Andy Marcus, who is American—started out as assistants. Humphrey goes way back to *The Guru,* and Andy Marcus to *Maurice,* on which he was the assistant editor. Kathy Wenning joined us when we had to let the original editor of *The Bostonians* go suddenly. She was a New York editor with a lot of experience. And it's also been my luck to have worked with Noëlle Boisson, the French editor, on *A Soldier's Daughter Never Cries.* She's a legend in France. My current editor, John Allen—who I fear I'm going to lose because he's about to direct his own film—started out as Ismail's editor when he made *Cotton Mary* and *his* editor on that film got sick and had to be replaced. You know, you're locked up for months and months with your editor, so you've really got to get on well with him—or her. And on *Le Divorce* I had to entrust John Allen with more than the editing. When we decided almost overnight to shoot in the Eiffel Tower and not at Euro Disney, we had to come up very quickly with a plan for the hostage-taking scene; it was John who devised a storyboard we could work from. I was busy shooting other scenes, so he left the editing to concentrate full-time on that. I don't know what we would have done without him short of shutting down—and that's an impossibility because of the expense involved. But all my editors have been very influential. And, you know, they see what you've done—what you've shot—in the most minute detail. There's that English saying that no man can be a hero to his valet. Well, no director can be a hero to his editor.

Long: Kate Hudson plays Isabel, Roxy's sister (or rather half sister), and is ideal for the part; she and Naomi Watts even look alike. What made you choose her for the part?

Ivory: She was actually our first choice but was in one of those periods of "not reading anything"—as her agent put it—when we began casting. Months and months later she was persuaded somehow to read the script. I'd liked her very much in *Almost Famous.* There was something infectious about her, so full of life, and the camera obviously loves her.

Long: An actress I would not have thought of for the role of Suzanne de Per-

Isabel (Kate Hudson) in bed with her boyfriend (Romain Duris) in *Le Divorce* (2003).

sand, the matriarch of the French family, was Leslie Caron, yet she was perfect for the part. People remember her from the 1950s—in *An American in Paris*, for instance—and here she is, as if she had aged overnight, as a woman in her seventies. I thought she was wonderful, with a tension you could feel behind her composure and discretion. Could you talk about her a bit?

Ivory: Casting Leslie was Ismail's doing, actually. When he suggested her, it seemed like a very good idea to me; I'd always wanted to work with her. She's obviously a very good actress. She is the type I was looking for, to perfection. Very chic and French, but speaking beautiful, nuanced English, yet with the suggestion of a tough personality, Then, I thought it would be fun to include this French actress who is so connected with a sort of legendary Paris—the Hollywood Paris of Vincente Minnelli and Gene Kelly of over fifty years ago.

Long: In the novel, Mme. Persand's brother Edgar is in his late sixties or is even seventy, a rather advanced age for an affair with a young girl. In the movie you have taken his age down to fifty-five and, in the person of Thierry Lhermitte, made him handsome and charming. What can you tell me about Thierry Lhermitte?

The matriarch of the Persand clan, played by Leslie Caron, informs the family of the badly timed affair between her brother Edgar and Isabel Walker in *Le Divorce* (2003).

Ivory: He's a huge French star who made his name in comedies that are virtually a part of the popular culture in France, comedies that sometimes in tone are the equivalent of *Saturday Night Live* on American TV or *Monty Python* in England. He's an absolute prince of a man, the consummate gentleman. We could never find a seventy-year-old French actor who was as handsome, charming, vital, and—a big, big factor—who spoke good English. In a way, it was too bad that we couldn't find a charming septuagenarian—some virile old man with white fur on his back, as Diane Johnson put it. That relationship with a twenty-year-old was one of the biggest jokes in the book, and would have been in the film. But Edgar didn't just have to be masterful in the bedroom; his command of English had to be equally masterful.

Long: Your younger French actors are attractive, too, and each of them is distinct from the others—Romain Duris, Isabel's unlikely suitor, with jet black hair like a nest of writhing snakes; Jean-Marc Barr, who is a strong presence as Roxy's lawyer—and admirer; and Melvil Poupaud, Roxy's husband,

Charles-Henri. With his good looks, dark, flashing eyes, and gentle manner, he is easy to like even if, curiously, he slips away rather easily into oblivion after being dispatched by the crazy Tellman. Were these actors all new to you?

Ivory: Yes. I'd never met any of them, except for Jean-Marc Barr, when we began to cast the film. I'm grateful to all of them for accepting their relatively small parts, because their profile in France is that of stars on the ascent. We mustn't forget the elegant Samuel Labarthe, either, who played the unpleasant and somewhat foolish older brother, Antoine. He's a very good actor. Many French people asked me as we went along, "Oh, how are your French film actors behaving?" It's assumed that they'll be temperamental, not know their lines, and so on. That must be their reputation in France—I mean, of French actors generally. But mine were all perfectly professional, had prepared very well, at times showing up some of the veteran American actors, who had to sort of wing it where their lines were concerned.

Long: And there is Stephen Fry (the finest Oscar Wilde ever put on the screen) as Piers Janely, Christie's art expert. When he appears in that scene in which he has lunch with the Walkers and informs them that their painting is, in his opinion, a La Tour, he takes over the film. In this respect he reminds me a bit of Joss Ackland in his scene as Matisse in *Surviving Picasso.* They both have charisma, some deeply personal quality that demands attention.

Ivory: Both are consummate English artist-performers—or were; Joss Ackland has died. Fry is also a director, a novelist, a superbly witty MC at all sorts of British functions. That's where we found him, doing a sort of Billy Crystal equivalent at the BAFTA ceremonies last year.

Long: Not long before you made *Le Divorce,* you made *A Soldier's Daughter Never Cries,* the first half of which is set in Paris. Apart from their involving some Americans in Paris, do the two films have anything in common?

Ivory: I think so. Both arose out of a desire—almost a necessity—to work in France again after *Jefferson in Paris* and *Surviving Picasso.* Paris is such a congenial place to make a film, and I mean that in the sense of one's working conditions. It's in the atmosphere of the set itself, where everybody connected with the project feels involved, committed, and part of a tradition of French craftsmanship. The métier is filmmaking, but the spirit shown on a set is equivalent, I feel, to what must have been that of the great ateliers of any of the crafts at which the French have traditionally excelled: furniture making and haute couture and haute cuisine, as well as carving the saints and angels for the fronts of Notre Dame and Chartres in the Middle Ages. I was most struck by this during the making of the flying red crocodile purse sequence: the fanatical French pursuit of perfection. I know that's an absurd comparison—our Kelly bag and the saints and angels on the front of Chartres, but you get my point about French craftsmanship, which extends to the beautiful props and sets in their movies, plus trick movie photography, which they invented one hundred years ago.

Long: Although humor runs through the film, so, too, does a sense of irrationality. When the Walkers come to visit the Persand family, the elder brother, Antoine, tells them of the "beauty" of the French deer hunt, in which the stag is pursued by hounds until it can no longer move and is then torn to pieces by them. The one really repellent character in the work, a figure in the grip of the irrational, is Matthew Modine's Tellman, who thinks of his wife, Magda, as a "puppy" that has been stolen from him—a thought that drives him to murder. So *Le Divorce* isn't all laughs.

Ivory: No, far from it. It's a sort of schizophrenic comedy maybe, with two murders, a very messy divorce, and a suicide attempt. But these were never allowed to get in the way of the fun and frivolity of the novel as far as Diane Johnson was concerned. The people maybe the most puzzled by this odd mixture of comedy, sex, and what conventionally should have been depressing were the financiers, Fox Searchlight. They kept trying to get me to cut down Matthew Modine and his weird wife. They would have been happier, I think, without the Eiffel Tower. Well, who knows? So far the film's mixture of the sinister and the lighthearted seems to be going down well with a lot of people.

Long: Isabel's relationship with the much older Uncle Edgar may be a bit daft, but it is surprisingly engaging; and Edgar Cosset is something more than the French social type of the aging roué strolling the boulevards. He is rather complex in his rigid right-wing politics and his romanticism and devotion to the pleasures of the moment. His relationship to Isabel is at the center of the film, is what impels it, but there is also another focus of interest—the growing together of the two sisters in the course of their experience in Paris. There are really two forms of attachment in the picture, romantic and sisterly, and I am not sure where the primary emphasis lies. Are you?

Ivory: I think we come away feeling that the sisterly ties are the long-lasting ones, always the strongest, and that the Edgars (and Charles-Henris) of this world are ephemeral.

Long: How did French critics like *Le Divorce?*

Ivory: It was hardly their favorite Merchant Ivory movie. You know, it wasn't a *masterpiece.* They didn't get it—my sort of frivolous, sort of decorative, take on the French—or want to get it. But no less a publication than *Le Monde,* in— how to put this?—its restrained review, praised the film's social observation of the French upper classes "caricatured to perfection with the help of Leslie Caron and Nathalie Richard." This backhanded compliment pleased me no end, since that would be the hardest thing for a foreigner to pull off. *Le Monde* might have mentioned the Persand men, too. Thierry Lhermitte, who is a consummate mimic, said that he had based his Oncle Edgar on the French foreign minister, Dominique de Villepin—the flamboyant diplomat who gave the Bush administration such a hard time over Iraq.

Long: And your French friends who aren't film critics, were they more encouraging?

Ivory: Yes, actually—and I don't think they were just being polite. A woman I know who works for the publisher Gallimard in Paris called the film the perfect modern French fable: the spoiled, self-absorbed Charles-Henri, unshaven son of the jeunesse dorée, marries an American girl to spite his family. When he dumps her, he then takes up with an even more impossible Russian. His reward is that he gets shot dead.

Long: You have quite a lineup of talented and well-known American performers in the film, including Sam Waterston and Stockard Channing as the sisters' Santa Barbara parents, and of course Glenn Close. But what can you tell me about the very funny young actor who plays Roger, the girls' let's-get-down-to-business brother. Who is he?

Ivory: His name is Thomas Lennon. He comes from television. He's appeared in *The State* on MTV and in *Reno 911!*—which he writes—on the Comedy Central channel. I was attracted to him because he reminds me a lot of myself when I was that age—even a bit in looks, bright-eyed and close-cropped, as well as in the deadpan delivery of his lines. The scene where the immensely experienced and worldly Piers Janely from Christie's is being interrogated by Roger is like looking back at myself at twenty-five. The mixture of diffidence and woodpecker-like drilling for nuggets of information when facing a confident and well-informed older person reminds me of my poker-faced self then, as well as in the deadpan delivery I affected at such critical moments. It was a kind of humor, a sort of style that came out of the smart-alecky antics of high school and college.

When I was a teenager in Oregon in the early 1940s, there was an actress-singer named Virginia O'Brien who was featured in MGM musicals. She was slim, dark-haired, pretty, with very pale skin. She would do a little turn, always singing a song, standing motionless, with an expressionless face and singing in expressionless tones. I can still hear her. "In a little Spanish town 'twas on a night like *this.*" I remember her in *The Harvey Girls* with Judy Garland and in several other MGM musicals like *The Ziegfeld Follies* and *Lady Be Good.* She was an early minimalist, I guess, and it seemed amazing that she could have had such a vogue appearing in raucous, high-energy MGM musicals. She was the opposite of all that. I always waited for her to come on; it was probably the high point in the movie for me. Does anyone else remember her these days, or recall her fondly? Does she now have a cult following?

Long: I looked her up once. According to the Internet Movie Database, her Hollywood nickname was Miss Red Hot Frozen Face. [*Ivory laughs*]

Ivory: Then, when I was about sixteen, very skinny and white like her (and too pretty for a boy), I developed a little comedy routine of my own called "Solid Ivory." This I exhibited at the Friday high school assemblies in the Klamath Union High School auditorium (usually held before a big football game). And, similarly, the audience would wait for me to appear at the side of the stage as a sort of frivolous interruption of the proceedings, then glide across and disappear. Dressed in a baggy sweater and holding a large, bright pink paper mum in my hand, I crossed in front of my teachers and schoolmates with a completely deadpan face to much laughter. From time to time I would turn my head like a robot and stare out at them. "Solid Ivory" became a feature of these assemblies for a couple of years, like Virginia O'Brien's MGM solos. I never altered my routine; all I had to do was walk across, keeping a straight face. There was something of the alien from outer space, and also something perhaps a bit androgynous, in this act. In my last appearance I seemed to glide in a determined sort of way toward the band, or maybe it was the football players—so that they scattered. This was "Solid Ivory"'s swan song; perhaps I felt I'd gone too far, or—more likely—that I was becoming too "sophisticated" and even too grand, in the high school social scene, to do such a silly thing anymore. In that year I also gave up acting in school plays. The roar of applause for "Solid Ivory" was the last that I was to hear coming specifically my way until, decades later, I would stand up to bow at film festivals, to acknowledge the applause of my audience, but on these occasions smiling—though no doubt, if the ovation was a long one, my expression became as fixed as Virginia O'Brien's had been.

INDEX

PHOTOGRAPHY CREDITS

Numbers refer to pages; Merchant Ivory Productions is abbreviated MIP.

9 Tara Pada Banerjee; 11 James Ivory; 55 Van Bucher; 60 ©MIP/BBC; 71, 74 Subrata Mitra © MIP; 80 Mitter Bedi; 81 James Ivory; 82 Subrata Mitra © MIP; 86, 89, 91 Douglass Webb © MIP/Twentieth Century Fox; 93 Studio Nataraj; 94 © MIP, courtesy of National Film Archive/Stills Library; 104 © MIP; 108, 112, 115 Mary Ellen Mark © MIP; 111 Christopher Cormack © MIP; 119, 122, 124 © MIP; 127, 130, 131 Morgan Renard © MIP; 138 © MIP; 144, 147, 149 Christopher Cormack © MIP; 152 © MIP/WNET, New York; 154, 158 © MIP; 164, 165, 168, 170 Karan Kapoor © MIP; 181 Joel Warren © MIP/TriStar Pictures; 187, 189, 192 Mikki Ansin © MIP/Cineplex Odeon; 203, 205 Sarah Quill © MIP; 209, 215 John Gardey © MIP; 221, 223, 225 Derrick Santini © MIP; 228, 229, 231, 232 Derrick Santini © MIP/Columbia Pictures; 248 Erica Lennard © MIP; 251 Arnaud Borrel © MIP; 257, 259, 261 Juan Quirno © MIP; 265, 275 Seth Rubin © MIP; 269, 273, 279 Arnaud Borrel © MIP; 288 James Ivory © MIP/Warner Bros.; 290 Marina Faust © MIP/Warner Bros.; 299, 301 Seth Rubin © MIP/Warner Bros.; 305, 308 Seth Rubin © MIP; 317, 321, 322 Arnaud Borrel © MIP/Fox Searchlight Pictures.

DESIGNER: NOLA BURGER

TEXT: 12.5/15/5 VENDETTA LIGHT

DISPLAY: AKZIDENZ REGULAR

COMPOSITOR: INTEGRATED COMPOSITION SYSTEMS

PRINTER AND BINDER: MAPLE-VAIL MANUFACTURING GROUP